Unit 4

Troubleshooting Components

D1159370

The HVACR Training Authority

TABLE OF CONTENTS

INTRODUCTION

Congratulations on your decision to further your education and career by participating in an RSES training course!

This book belongs to you. It is your primary learning tool, and should serve you well as a source of reference in the future. Feel free to write in your book, and make notes as needed in the page margins. Note that the information contained in RSES training courses reflects "standard" trade practices in the U.S. Some infomation may not be in compliance with regulatory codes in your area. Be aware that *local codes always take precedence*.

RSES comprehensive training courses cover all aspects of the HVACR service industry, beginning with basic theory and extending to complex troubleshooting. Training courses can be conducted by local Chapters, corporate training facilities, or through self-study. RSES training course series include refrigeration and air conditioning, electricity, controls, heating, heat pump, and the RSES Technical Institute Training Manuals.

Continuing education units (CEUs) are issued only to those students who participate in an instructor-led course. Some courses have been recognized by North American Technician Excellence (NATE). Technicians who successfully complete one or more of these instructor-led courses may receive credit toward renewing their NATE certification.

In addition to its renowned training course manuals, RSES offers a selection of CD-ROMs, DVDs, and other materials intended to assist technicians enhance their skills and knowledge of the HVACR industry. Membership in RSES offers a wide variety of benefits. For membership information and to find out more about RSES, please visit the RSES Web site at www.rses.org.

OBJECTIVES

Lesson 1
Test Equipment (Part 1)
- Describe the basic operation of the d'Arsonval meter movement.
- Explain the difference between analog and digital measuring instruments.
- Distinguish between voltmeters, ammeters, ohmmeters, and multimeters, and describe the operational principles of each.
- Explain how the *sensitivity* of a voltmeter is calculated.
- Describe how various electrical meters are used to measure resistance, voltage, and current, and to check for continuity.
- Demonstrate how clamp-on ammeters are used.
- Describe the basic operation of a Wheatstone bridge, and explain how it can be configured to act as a resistance bridge or a capacitance bridge.

Lesson 2
Test Equipment (Part 2)
- Explain the operation of a wattmeter.
- Demonstrate how to read a watt-hour meter.
- Describe how to determine the power factor of a circuit by using a power factor meter.
- Describe how a varmeter can be used in correcting power factor problems.
- Explain the purpose and use of various instrument transformers.
- Explain the operation of megohmmeter.
- Explain the purpose and use of various recording instruments.
- Describe how a compressor analyzer can be used in troubleshooting.

Lesson 3
Resistors
- Observe the proper safety precautions when taking ohmmeter readings.
- Select the best *range* for a particular resistance measurement.
- "Zero adjust" an analog ohmmeter.
- Determine the resistance values of various types of resistors.
- Use an ohmmeter to test resistors, potentiometers, rheostats, bleeder resistors, thermistors, PTC start-assist devices, and diodes.

Lesson 4
Capacitors
- Observe the proper safety precautions when taking capacitance readings.
- Explain the differences between start and run capacitors.
- Discharge a capacitor safely.
- Describe the four main problems or conditions that identify a faulty capacitor.
- Describe the operation of the various types of instruments used for testing capacitors.

Lesson 5
Relays, Contactors, and Starters
- List common causes of relay failure.
- Describe the physical indications that identify defective relays and contactors.
- Explain how to test pilot-duty relays and line-duty relays.
- Explain how to test contactors and starters.
- Explain how to test potential relays and current relays.
- Explain how to test time-delay relays.

Lesson 6
Transformers
- Describe the conditions that cause transformers to fail.
- Describe the physical indications that identify defective transformers.
- Explain the differences between residential and commercial transformers.
- Determine the current-carrying capacity of a control transformer.
- Explain how to test different types of transformers.
- Deflne *open circuit voltage* (OCV).
- Test continuity between the primary and secondary windings of a transformers.

Lesson 7
Thermostats
- Describe the basic construction and operation of a bimetal mechanical thermostat.
- Explain the concept of *anticipation*.
- Describe some of the physical indications that identify defective thermostats.
- Test a mechanical thermostat with a voltmeter and/or ohmmeter.
- Set an adjustable anticipator.
- Calibrate a mechanical thermostat.
- Explain the differences between residential and commercial thermostats.
- Identify common problems that affect electronic thermostats, and explain basic troubleshooting techniques.

Lesson 8
Motors
- List the basic types of motors used in the HVAC/R industry.
- Describe some of the visual indications that identify defective motors.
- Explain the difference between fractional-horsepower motors and integral-horsepower motors.
- Determine the speed and rotation of a motor.
- Use appropriate test instruments to troubleshoot various types of motors and their associated starting circuits.
- Describe some of the causes of overheating in electric motors.
- Explain what causes *single phasing* in a three-phase motor.
- Calculate voltage and current imbalances in three-phase motors.
- Explain how variable-speed motors differ from ac induction motors.
- Describe basic motor replacement procedures.
- Read a motor nameplate.
- Use NEMA data to determine motor frame sizes and dimensions.

Lesson 9
Hermetic Compressors
- Explain the differences among open, semi-hermetic, and hermetic compressors.
- Describe the various starting methods used for single-phase hermetic compressors.
- Explain the function and operation of overload protection devices use in hermetic compressors.
- Check a single-phase hermetic compressor for proper resistance, voltage, and current readings.
- Identify the terminals of a single-phase hermetic compressor, even if they are unmarked.
- Check a three-phase hermetic compressor for proper resistance, voltage, and current readings.
- Calculate voltage and current imbalances in three-phase hermetic compressors.

Lesson 10
Semi-Hermetic Compressors
- Explain the differences between hermetic and semi-hermetic compressors.
- Describe the various starting methods used for single-phase semi-hermetic compressors.
- Check a single-phase semi-hermetic compressor for proper resistance, voltage, and current readings.
- Identify the terminals of a single-phase semi-hermetic compressor, even if they are unmarked.
- Check a three-phase semi-hermetic compressor for proper resistance, voltage, and current readings.
- Calculate voltage and current imbalances in three-phase semi-hermetic compressors.
- Explain what causes *single phasing* in three-phase semi-hermetic compressors.
- Explain the function and operation of overload protection devices use in semi-hermetic compressors.

Lesson 11
Electronic Compontents
- Explain how to test diodes, both with an analog meter and a digital meter.
- Explain how to test NPN and PNP transistors.
- Explain how to test silicon-controlled rectifiers (SCRs).
- Explain how to test triacs.
- Describe the effects that electrostatic discharge (ESD) can have on electronic components.
- List the precautions that you should take to prevent ESD damage when servicing electronic components.
- Demonstrate logical troubleshooting procedures when diagnosing printed circuit (PC) boards.

Lesson 12
Wiring Systems
- Describe the different types of wiring systems used in the HVAC/R industry.
- Test single-phase residential power circuits for voltage drop, voltage imbalance, and current imbalance.
- Test three-phase commercial power circuits for voltage drop, voltage imbalance, and current imbalance.
- Define *ampacity*, and explain how wire sizes are selected for given applications.
- Troubleshoot low-voltage control circuits.
- Troubleshoot high-voltage ac control circuits.
- Troubleshoot direct digital control (DDC) circuits.
- Describe some of the basic problems encountered in all wiring systems.

Test Equipment (Part 1)

METER PRINCIPLES

Good, reliable test instruments are among the most valuable tools that any service technician can have. As you become more familiar with the various types of electrical measuring instruments, they will become an extension of your senses. It is very important to know how to use test equipment properly, and how to keep it in dependable working condition. This Lesson will discuss the operating principles of some of the test instruments that you will use in equipment troubleshooting.

All meters need some form of indicating device. A *galvanometer* is a basic indicating device used in instruments that measure current and voltage. The galvanometer, which responds to very small amounts of current or voltage, operates on the principle of magnetic attraction and repulsion.

Galvanometers are used in laboratory environments to measure extremely low currents, such as those in bridge circuits. In modified form, the galvanometer has one of the highest sensitivities of all of the various types of meters in use today. However, the galvanometer generally is not small enough or rugged enough for industrial use. Instead, a more compact, portable, and rugged type of meter movement, known as the *permanent-magnet moving-coil meter movement*, is used.

Most analog electrical measuring instruments, especially those designed for servicing dc equipment, use a stationary permanent-magnet moving-coil meter movement. (*Analog* instruments produce a continuously variable reading or output. *Digital* instruments will be discussed later in this Lesson.) This type of meter movement is commonly called the *d'Arsonval movement*, named for the French scientist who invented it.

The basic d'Arsonval movement consists of a stationary permanent magnet and a movable coil. When a current flows through the coil, the resulting magnetic field reacts with the magnetic field of the permanent magnet and causes the coil to rotate. The greater the amount of current through the coil, the stronger the magnetic field produced—and, therefore, the greater the angle of rotation of the coil. A pointer is fastened to the rotating coil so that it turns when the coil turns. The end of the pointer moves across a graduated scale in proportion to the amount of current flow.

In a galvanometer, the movable coil is suspended by means of flat metal ribbons, usually made of phosphor bronze. These ribbons provide the conducting path for the current between the circuit under test and the movable coil. They also provide the return force for the coil. In the d'Arsonval meter movement shown in Figure 1-1, the coil is restrained by two springs mounted on either end of the coil. The springs return the coil to its starting position and carry the current to the coil. If the current in the coil is reversed, the direction of motion of the coil and pointer is also reversed.

Figure 1-2 shows the principle of the d'Arsonval movement more clearly. In the drawing, only one turn of wire is shown. However, in an actual meter movement, many turns of fine wire are used, with each turn adding more effective length to the coil. As stated previously, the deflecting (moving) force on the coil is proportional to the current flowing through the coil. This deflecting force causes the coil to rotate against the restraining force of the springs. When the deflecting force and the restraining force are equal,

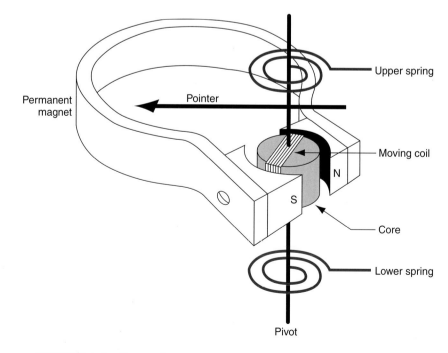

FIGURE 1-1. *Parts of a permanent-magnet moving-coil instrument*

the coil and the pointer stop moving. The pointer indicates (on the scale of the instrument) the amount of current in the coil, as shown in Figure 1-2.

VOLTMETERS

A *voltmeter* is an instrument used for measuring potential difference. The meter movement of a voltmeter operates because of the current flow through the meter, but the scale is marked in volts. The addition of a series resistance is what allows the meter to be calibrated in terms of voltage. Resistors (high-resistance paths) added in series with this type of meter movement are called *multipliers*.

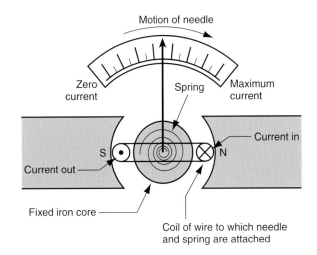

FIGURE 1-2. *d'Arsonval meter movement*

Look at Figure 1-3 on the next page. The drawing on the left shows a representation of the face of a voltmeter with a graduated scale ranging from 0 to 0.1 V. For the purpose of instruction, assume that the meter has a 1-mA movement—that is, it will take a current of 1 mA to deflect the needle to full-scale. If the internal resistance of the meter is known, then the proper voltage-dropping series resistance can be calculated for use in enabling different full-scale voltage readings.

Before reviewing a sample calculation, it might be helpful to refer to the drawing on the right in Figure 1-3, which shows a circuit schematic of the same meter. R_{meter} is the internal resistance of the meter, and R_{series} is a resistor placed in series with R_{meter}. If the meter's internal resistance is 100 Ω, then by applying Ohm's Law you can determine that it will take 0.1 V to deflect the needle to full-scale:

$$E = I \times R_{meter}, \text{ or } 0.001 \text{ A} \times 100 \text{ Ω} = 0.1 \text{ V}$$

To make the meter indicate 10 V at full-scale, $R_{meter} + R_{series}$ must equal 10,000 Ω, or the series resistor must equal 9,900 Ω. In this case, each scale division would represent 1.0 V:

$$E = I \times (R_{meter} + R_{series}), \text{ or } 0.001 \text{ A} \times (100 \text{ Ω} + 9,900 \text{ Ω}) = 10 \text{ V}$$

To make the meter indicate 100 V at full-scale, $R_{meter} + R_{series}$ must equal 100,000 Ω, or the series resistor must equal 99,900 Ω. In this case, each scale division would represent 10 V:

$$E = I \times (R_{meter} + R_{series}), \text{ or } 0.001 \text{ A} \times (100 \text{ Ω} + 99,900 \text{ Ω}) = 100 \text{ V}$$

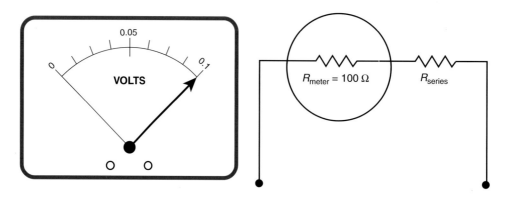

FIGURE 1-3. *Voltmeter operation*

Voltmeter sensitivity

Voltmeters are placed in parallel with (or "across") the circuit that is under test. It is important that the meter does not draw significant current from the circuit, or erroneous readings will occur. This is especially important when reading lower voltages.

The *sensitivity* of a voltmeter is given in ohms per volt. This is derived by adding the resistance of the meter and the series resistance, and dividing the sum by the full-scale reading in volts:

$$\text{sensitivity} = \frac{R_{\text{meter}} + R_{\text{series}}}{E}$$

This is the same as saying that the sensitivity is equal to the *reciprocal* of the full-scale deflection current. For example, the voltmeter described in the preceding paragraphs has a sensitivity of 1,000 Ω per volt:

$$\text{sensitivity} = \frac{100\ \Omega\ +\ 9{,}900\ \Omega}{10\ V} = 1{,}000\ \Omega \text{ per volt}$$

This is not a very sensitive meter movement, because it may draw too much current from the circuit under test. In this case, it would draw 1 mA at 10 V. More sensitive meters will be discussed later in this Lesson.

Vacuum-tube voltmeters

Before the development of integrated circuits, both vacuum tubes and transistors were used to make meters more accurate. *Vacuum-tube voltmeters* (VTVMs) usually required 115 V ac, so a line cord and power outlet were necessary.

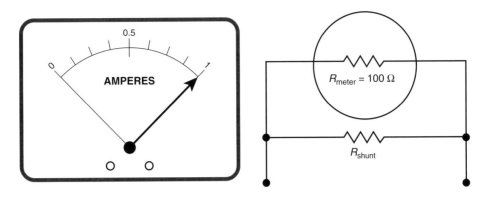

FIGURE 1-4. *Ammeter operation*

Because of their high input sensitivities—often as high as 11 MΩ per volt—these instruments were very reliable and precise. By contrast, the more modern meters discussed in this Lesson have sensitivities ranging from 1 to 20,000 Ω per volt.

AMMETERS

An *ammeter* is a meter used for measuring current. By adding low-resistance paths called *shunts* (that is, resistors in parallel with the meter movement) to the basic meter shown in Figure 1-3, the same instrument can be made to respond proportionally to different ranges of current. When configured in this way, the meter functions as an ammeter. The range of the meter's scale can be adjusted. The current to be measured is determined by selecting the appropriate shunt resistance.

Recall that this meter has a full-scale deflection of 1 mA (0.001 A). Assume that you want to make the meter read 1 A, as shown in the drawing on the left in Figure 1-4. A parallel resistor, R_{shunt}, must *shunt* 0.999 A around the movement. Refer to the circuit diagram shown in the drawing on the right in Figure 1-4 while studying the following sample calculations. The voltage drops across R_{meter} (the meter coil's resistance) and R_{shunt} are equal because they are in parallel with each other. For this example, then:

$$E = I_{shunt} \times R_{shunt} = I_{meter} \times R_{meter}, \text{ so}$$

$$R_{shunt} = \frac{I_{meter} \times R_{meter}}{I_{shunt}} = \frac{0.001 \text{ A} \times 100 \text{ }\Omega}{0.999 \text{ A}} = 0.1001 \text{ }\Omega$$

The meter will now read 1.0 A, or any division less, when placed in series with the circuit under test.

OHMMETERS

An *ohmmeter* is a meter used for measuring resistance, and for checking the continuity of electric circuits. Figure 1-5 depicts a very basic ohmmeter circuit. As you can see, the ohmmeter is very similar to the ammeter, but with the following added features:

- a source of dc potential (a battery)

- one or more resistors (one of which is variable).

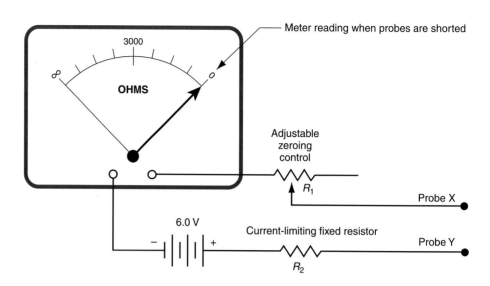

FIGURE 1-5. *Ohmmeter operation*

Recall that the meter movement previously discussed requires a 1-mA current for full-scale deflection. If the battery in the circuit supplies an EMF of 6.0 V, then by applying Ohm's Law you know that a resistance of 6,000 Ω is needed to limit the current to 1 mA when the probes touch each other (are shorted):

$$R = \frac{E}{I} = \frac{6.0 \text{ V}}{0.001 \text{ A}} = 6,000 \ \Omega$$

Notice that the zero point on the ohmmeter is located at the extreme right side of the scale. Thus, the zero resistance indication occurs when the needle is at full-scale deflection. This reading occurs when the probes are in contact with each other, or are placed across a length of conducting material of zero resistance (actually a short circuit condition). Note also that there is a zero adjustment control (R_1) in the circuit, as well as a current-limiting resistor (R_2). As an example, assume that R_1 is adjusted to 500 Ω, and that R_2 is a fixed 5,500-Ω resistor. These two resistances in series provide the total 6,000 Ω of current-limiting resistance necessary to maintain a full-scale deflection at 1 mA.

The midpoint on the scale can be determined by placing a separate 6,000-Ω resistance between the probe contacts in order to double the total resistance in series to 12,000 Ω. This would limit the current to 0.5 mA and result in half-scale deflection. (The midscale position then would be marked 6,000 Ω). Other calibration points on the scale can be determined in the same way. When there is infinite resistance between the probe contacts (such as when there is only air between them), the meter will show no deflection.

If the terminal voltage of the battery were to weaken slightly, the adjustable resistance, R_1, could be changed to a lesser resistance to allow sufficient current increase to bring the needle back to full-scale deflection. This is called *zeroing* the meter. Once the meter is zeroed, the meter can be used to measure an unknown resistance. (*Caution:* Be sure to de-energize the circuit first—that is, turn it off or open it.)

MULTIMETERS

During troubleshooting, you will often be required to measure voltage, current, and resistance. Rather than using three or more separate meters for these measurements, you can use a *multimeter*, which is a combination of voltmeter, ammeter, and ohmmeter. A good multimeter (analog or digital) is probably the most versatile meter that a service technician can carry for troubleshooting electrical problems.

The meters discussed so far in this Lesson measure only dc voltages and currents. However, meters can be converted to measure ac voltages and currents simply by adding a diode or rectifier circuit. They can be switched back and forth from ac to dc with the aid of a simple switch circuit. This makes the multimeter even more versatile. In general, the current-measuring function of the multimeter is not as important as its ability to measure voltage and resistance. Most of the multimeters that meet the current and resistance measurement requirements for HVACR work can also measure ac and dc currents over different scales ranging from 0 to 10 A.

WAVETEK CORPORATION

Analog multimeters

Because a multimeter contains circuitry that allows it to be used as a voltmeter, an ammeter, or an ohmmeter, it is often called a *volt-ohm-milliammeter* (VOM). A typical analog VOM is shown in Figure 1-6. Analog meters are best for observing changes and peak or dip indications when making adjustments. The accuracy of an analog meter is based on the percentage of the meter's full-scale reading that the error range represents (typically in the range of ±1.0 to ±5.0%). Electrical protection is normally provided, but analog meters can be easily damaged as a result of improper testing procedures. VOMs are used in all phases of service work, including installation, preventive maintenance, and troubleshooting.

Digital multimeters

A digital meter indicates readings by means of a numeric display rather than a moving meter needle. The *digital multimeter* (DMM) is an extremely accurate

FIGURE 1-6. *Typical analog VOM*

hand-held device. It may be a *self-ranging* instrument—that is, it can be set on one scale and read the voltage, resistance, or current over a wide range. A typical DMM is shown in Figure 1-7.

DMMs are direct-reading, high-resolution instruments that give accurate readings without the need for scale interpretation. Accuracy is generally in the range of ±0.1 to ±0.5%. Because they have no moving parts, DMMs are less likely to lose their calibration than analog multimeters.

USING METERS

Small analog multimeters (VOMs) or digital multimeters (DMMs) are used for field service work. The technician must identify the proper scale to use when making measurements and, when working with analog instruments, must be able to interpret the pointer location to obtain the reading. Scale divisions may limit resolution.

The multimeter feature most needed for field servicing HVACR equipment is the capability to measure ac voltage accurately over several scales, ranging from 0 to 1,000 V. Generally, the multimeter should also measure dc voltages over several ranges, but the 0 to 50-V dc range is the most important for servicing low-voltage dc control circuits. The full-scale accuracy for the readings should be about ±0.5 to ±2% or better (less). The multimeter should be capable of measuring resistance over several scales, ranging from 0 Ω to 30 MΩ.

The multimeter is used to measure high-level ac voltages in power and load circuits, and low-level ac voltages in control circuits. When used as a troubleshooting tool, the multimeter is frequently used to measure voltage and make continuity checks on system and component wiring. Accurate resistance measurement is also important, since the meter is used to check motor windings, relay coils, and motor starter/contactor coils for resistance values and for short, open, or grounded circuits. Another common use of the multimeter is to check the start and run capacitors of motors for a shorted condition. (Digital multimeters are normally used to measure low-level ac and dc currents in the microampere range. This feature is useful for servicing the flame-sensing system on heating equipment.) *Note:* Know the capabilities and limitations of your multimeter before attempting any measurements. Read and follow the manufacturer's instructions.

Measuring resistance

Multimeters can measure the resistance (in ohms) of almost any part of a circuit. Resistance values for HVACR components can vary greatly, from a few ohms to

FIGURE 1-7. *Typical DMM*

several million ohms. Most multimeters can measure below 1 Ω, and some can measure as high as 300 MΩ. Always make sure that the equipment power is turned off and that all capacitors in the circuit are discharged before making resistance measurements. If you do not, damage to the meter can result. Some multimeters include high-voltage protection (500 V or more) in the resistance mode in case of accidental contact with voltages. The level of protection varies greatly from model to model.

Resistance measurements may be made to determine the resistance of a load (relay, contactor or starter coils, motor windings). Resistance measurements are also used to check electronic components, such as diodes and resistors. Make resistance measurements as follows:

1. Turn off the power to the equipment or circuit.

2. Select the resistance range using the function/range switch. If you are using an analog meter (see Figure 1-8), and if the value of the resistance to be measured can be estimated within reasonable limits, select the lowest range that will accurately read that value. If you cannot estimate the resistance to be measured, set the range switch to the highest scale, then work your way downward to a lower range. Always select a range on the ohmmeter that will give approximately half-scale deflection when the resistance is inserted between the probes. Exercise caution when using high resistance ranges to check electronic circuits—the battery voltage in the meter may damage the circuit.

3. Plug the test probes into the meter jacks. Usually the black probe is connected to the common (COM) or minus (–) jack, and the red probe to the plus (+) or V-Ω jack. If you are using an analog meter, always zero the meter before making the first measurement (and whenever you change range scales). To zero the meter, touch the tips of the test probes together, then use the zero adjust knob (see Figure 1-8) to set the pointer to zero.

4. Before measuring resistance, make sure that the component being measured is electrically isolated. You can do this by disconnecting at least one lead of the component from the circuit. This is important in order to get an accurate resistance reading. Otherwise, the meter will read the combined resistance of *all* the components that are connected in parallel with the component to be measured.

5. Connect the test probe tips across the component or portion of the circuit that you want to measure.

SIMPSON ELECTRIC COMPANY

FIGURE 1-8. *Analog ohmmeter*

6. View the reading on the digital readout or analog scale. If you are using a digital meter, be sure to note the unit of measurement—ohms, kilohms (kΩ), or megohms (MΩ)—shown for the reading.

If you are using an analog meter, you can determine the resistance value by multiplying the scale reading by the number (R × 1) next to the function/range switch. In Figure 1-9A, for example, the reading ("10") is multiplied by the selector setting (R × 1), yielding a resistance of 10 Ω. In Figure 1-9B, the reading is the same ("10"), but because the R × 100 setting is selected, the resistance is 1,000 Ω. At the R × 1000 setting, the resistance would be 10 kΩ, as shown in Figure 1-9C.

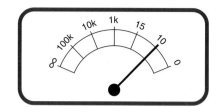
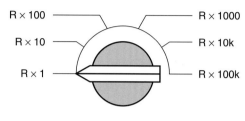

A. 10 × 1 = 10 Ω

Checking continuity

A *continuity* test is a yes/no resistance test for finding open and closed circuits. An *open* circuit is one in which the flow of current is interrupted by a broken wire, defective switch, or other means. A *closed* circuit is one in which there is a complete, uninterrupted (*continuous*) path for current flow. An ohmmeter (which contains its own batteries) is excellent for checking continuity. An open circuit is indicated by a very high or infinite resistance, and a closed circuit by a very low or zero resistance.

A good fuse, for example, offers very little resistance. Therefore, when you use an analog meter to measure a good fuse, the pointer will move all the way to the right (0 Ω). Figure 1-10 represents a continuity test on a good fuse. If the fuse is open, however, it has no path for current flow, so the pointer remains at the far left, displaying infinite resistance. Figure 1-11 represents a continuity test on a blown fuse.

A *short* circuit is one in which two conductors touch each other directly or through another conducting element. For example, two conductors with frayed insulation may touch and cause a short. You can use an ohmmeter to detect a short between two conductors by measuring the resistance between them. (Be sure that the electric power has been disconnected.) A low resistance reading indicates a short.

A digital meter indicates infinite resistance by displaying "OL," flashing digits, or a similar message indicating that the resistance

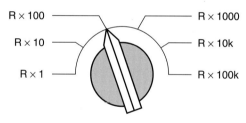
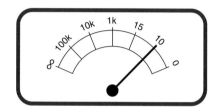

B. 10 × 100 = 1,000 Ω

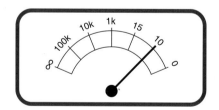
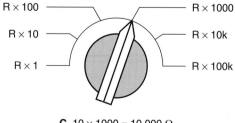

C. 10 × 1000 = 10,000 Ω

FIGURE 1-9. *Reading resistances*

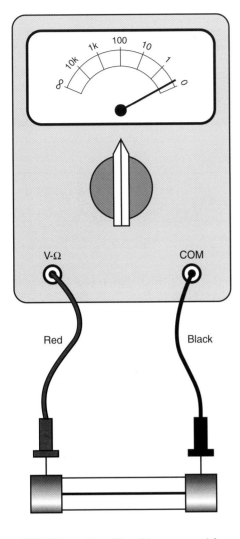

FIGURE 1-10. *Checking a good fuse*

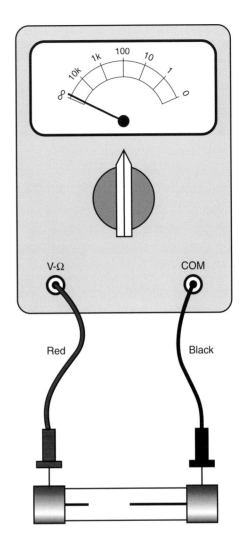

FIGURE 1-11. *Checking a bad fuse*

is greater than the digital meter can measure. Some DMMs may beep to indicate that continuity has been detected. The digital readout also will show 0 Ω. The level of resistance required to trigger the digital beeper varies from model to model. The audible beep feature is helpful because it allows you to make continuity checks without having to look at the meter reading.

Measuring voltage

Voltage measurements are usually made to determine source voltage, voltage drop, and/or voltage imbalance. Voltage tests must be made with the power applied—therefore, the prescribed safety precautions *must* be followed to prevent injury to personnel and damage to the equipment. A primary rule of safety is that *the voltmeter must always be connected in parallel with (across) the circuit being tested.* Make voltage measurements as follows:

1. Use the function/range switch to select ac or dc volts. (Some meters may have a different plug for the test leads to measure ac voltage.) Always select a range higher than the highest anticipated reading. For example, if you expect to measure 24 V ac, select the 300-V ac range on the meter. Take a reading at the higher range, then carefully lower the range step by step until a suitable reading is obtained. This provides a more accurate result. Select a range in which the meter pointer is as close as possible to the middle of the scale. Figure 1-12 shows how a meter would read if it were measuring 5 V. The selector switch is set on the 10-V scale, and the needle is reading 5 V, or midway up the scale.

2. Plug the test probes into the meter jacks. Usually the black probe is connected to the common (COM) or minus (–) jack, and the red probe to the plus (+) or V-Ω jack.

3. Connect the test probe tips to the circuit in parallel with the load or power source. Measurement is easier and safer if an alligator clip is used on one of the leads. *Be sure to shut off power to the equipment before attaching the alligator leads.* If you are using an analog meter to measure dc voltage, you must observe correct polarity (+/–). Connect the red test probe to the positive side of the circuit, and the black test probe to the negative side or circuit ground. If you reverse the connections, the meter movement will go off the scale in the opposite direction and damage to the meter may result. If you are using a digital meter with "auto" polarity, the reading will display a minus sign to indicate negative polarity.

4. View the reading on the digital meter readout. Be sure to note the unit of measurement being indicated. If you are using an analog meter, read the voltage value indicated by the pointer on the ac or dc voltage scale. Make sure to use the scale that matches the selector switch voltage setting.

CLAMP-ON AMMETERS

The "clamp-on" ammeter is the instrument most frequently used for making quick, convenient ac current measurements. It is a hand-held tool, and may have either an analog pointer or a digital readout. The clamp-on ammeter has a trigger-operated jaw at the top. Figure 1-13 shows a typical clamp-on ammeter.

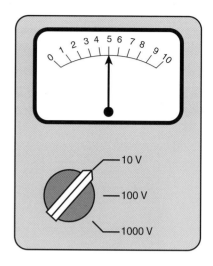

FIGURE 1-12. *Measuring voltage*

FLUKE CORPORATION

FIGURE 1-13. *Typical clamp-on ammeter*

The clamp-on ammeter is a unique member of the ammeter family. Like other ammeters, it measures the current in a conductor and displays the value of the current on a graduated scale or readout. Unlike other ammeters, though, the clamp-on instrument eliminates the need for breaking the circuit under test or shutting down the equipment. In fact, it does not require any physical contact at all between meter and circuit. Instead, the jaws are clamped around the conductor in which a current measurement is to be made. This is illustrated in Figure 1-14.

Clamp-on ammeters are time-savers. They are safe and convenient to use, and are ideally suited for applications in which it is impossible or impractical to open the circuit being measured. Both ac and dc clamp-on ammeters are available. *Note*: The clamp-on ammeter's jaws must be placed around only one wire in a circuit at a time.

Operation

In operation, the trigger of the clamp-on meter is pressed to open and then released to close the jaws around the conductor in which current is to be measured. The value of the current is indicated on the analog scale or digital readout.

The whole operation of the clamp-on ammeter is based on the "transformer effect" of the jaws and the conductor that they encircle. The conductor, or wire, acts as the primary of the transformer. The jaws act as the iron core and transfer the magnetic fields to the secondary winding inside the ammeter. The voltage derived at the secondary is then converted to a direct current, which activates the meter movement. A basic diagram of this operation is shown in Figure 1-15 on the next page.

FIGURE 1-14. *Checking the current draw of an electric motor with a clamp-on meter*

BRIDGE CIRCUITS

A wide variety of ac *bridge circuits* may be used for the precision measurement of resistance, capacitance, and inductance. These bridge circuits are composed of capacitors, inductors, and resistors in various combinations. They operate on the principle of the *Wheatstone bridge*, which is perhaps the most widely used of all the electronic measuring circuits.

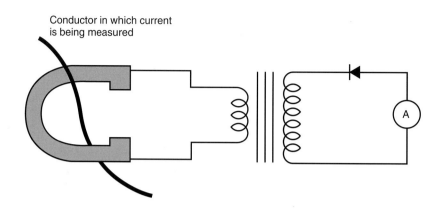

Conductor in which current is being measured

In order to understand the operation of the bridge circuit, consider the results of connecting multiple resistors in series. A *series* circuit is characterized by the fact that it has only one path for current to follow. Therefore, all current must flow from its starting point to its ending point, as illustrated below:

FIGURE 1-15. *Clamp-on ammeter operation*

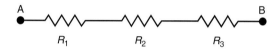

Three important facts apply to series circuits. Keep these in mind when analyzing the operation of a bridge circuit:

- The current flow is the same at any point in the circuit.

- The sum of the voltage drops across all the components in the circuit equals the applied voltage.

- The total resistance is equal to the sum of the individual resistances.

Resistance bridge

Figure 1-16 shows a Wheatstone bridge being used to measure resistance—that is, it is functioning as a *resistance bridge*. Note that series resistive branch ABC of the circuit is in parallel with series resistive branch ADC. Both branches are connected across the same fixed dc voltage source (V). If $R_1 = R_2$ and $R_3 = R_x$ (R_x represents the unknown value), then the voltage (potential) at point B, when measured with respect to point A, must be exactly equal to the voltage at point D, also with respect to point A (because one-half of the source voltage would appear across each resistor).

Since the voltage at point B is equal to that at point D, no current flows between these points, and the meter would indicate a zero reading. This zero potential is called the *null* or *null balance* point, since the bridge is said to be properly "balanced" when no difference in potential exists across terminals B and D. Therefore:

$$V_{AB} = V_{AD} \text{ and } V_{BC} = V_{DC}$$

When resistances R_1, R_2, and R_3 are known and the voltmeter connected between points B and D shows zero potential (is adjusted to the null balance point), the bridge circuit can be used to measure the unknown resistance R_x. The meter as used in this example may also be called a *null detector*. Use the following equation to solve for R_x:

$$R_x = \frac{R_1 \times R_3}{R_2}$$

The derivation of this equation, as explained below, is consistent with the three rules for resistive series circuits referred to on the previous page. Let the current in branch ABC be I_1, and let the current in branch ADC be I_2. Using Ohm's Law, you can calculate the voltage drops across R_1 and R_x, respectively, as follows:

$$V_{AB} = I_1 \times R_1$$

$$V_{AD} = I_2 \times R_x$$

Since $V_{AB} = V_{AD}$, then:

$$I_1 \times R_1 = I_2 \times R_x, \text{ and}$$

$$\frac{I_1}{I_2} = \frac{R_x}{R_1}$$

Similarly, since VBC = VDC, then:

$$I_1 \times R_2 = I_2 \times R_3, \text{ and}$$

$$\frac{I_1}{I_2} = \frac{R_3}{R_2}$$

Note that:

$$\frac{R_x}{R_1} = \frac{I_1}{I_2} \text{ and } \frac{R_3}{R_2} = \frac{I_1}{I_2}$$

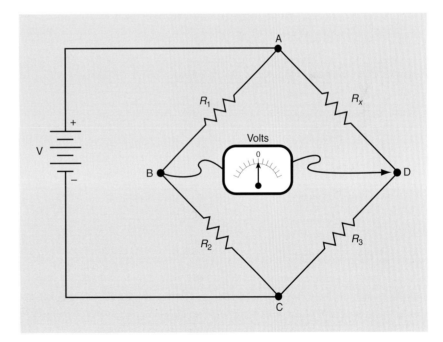

FIGURE 1-16. *Resistance bridge circuit*

15

Therefore:

$$\frac{R_x}{R_1} = \frac{R_3}{R_2}$$

And, finally:

$$R_x = \frac{R_1 \times R_3}{R_2}$$

Sample calculation 1. Determine R_x when the other three resistances are:

$R_1 = 10\ \Omega$
$R_2 = 20\ \Omega$
$R_3 = 30\ \Omega$

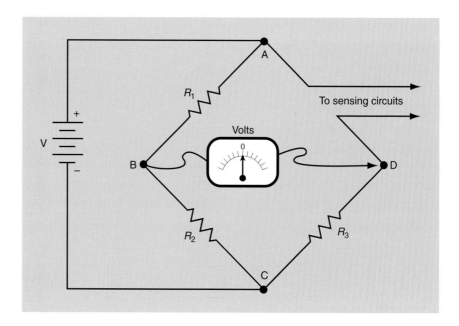

FIGURE 1-17. *Resistance bridge circuit with remote sensor*

Substitution of the known data in the equation yields:

$$R_x = \frac{10\ \Omega \times 30\ \Omega}{20\ \Omega} = 15\ \Omega$$

Sample calculation 2. Determine R_x when the other three resistances are:

$R_1 = 10\ \Omega$
$R_2 = 20\ \Omega$
$R_3 = 10\ \Omega$

Substitution of the known data in the equation yields:

$$R_x = \frac{10\ \Omega \times 10\ \Omega}{20\ \Omega} = 5\ \Omega$$

Operationally, the principle of the balanced bridge circuit is used for many applications—control circuits and test equipment are among the most prominent ones. In practical applications, when used as a piece of test equipment, R_x in Figure 1-16 is a variable resistance, actually replaceable by an electronic sensing circuit that measures voltage or current. A simplified example of such a circuit is illustrated in Figure 1-17.

This circuit is used as a *comparator*. The null detector, between points B and D, indicates a signal difference between some sensing element and a standard reference (i.e., control setpoint). When they are equal, there is a balanced condition, which usually results in the comparator having no output signal (or zero output). The null detector most often used in conjunction with the resistance bridge is an electronic circuit called a *differential amplifier*, or *operational amplifier* (op amp). A typical schematic of such a circuit is shown in Figure 1-18.

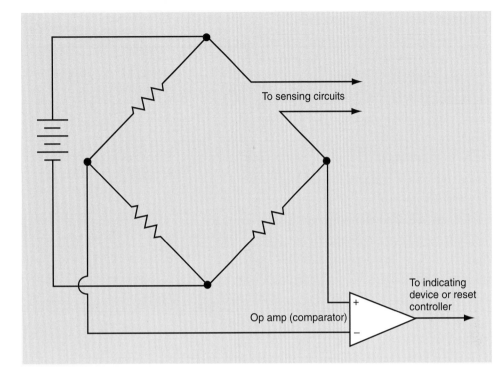

FIGURE 1-18. *Op amp circuit*

When the Wheatstone bridge is used as a control device, the variable-resistance element is either a resistance temperature detector or a thermistor, both of which vary in resistance with a change in temperature. The indicating device can also be a reset controller.

CAPACITANCE METERS

Capacitance measurements are usually taken with a *capacitance meter*. When a Wheatstone bridge is modified to function as a *capacitance bridge*, an ac source of a precise frequency replaces the battery. In Figure 1-19, the unknown capacitor is C_x. The indicating device displays balance or imbalance as the variable capacitor is adjusted.

Remember that current varies inversely with resistance, and directly with capacitance. Be aware, too, that capacitance tolerances vary more widely than resistance tolerances. Capacitance

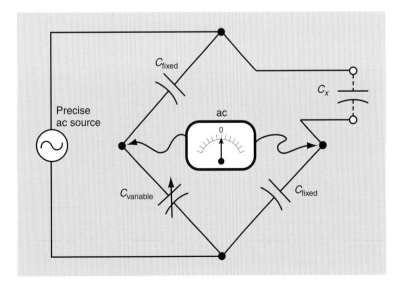

FIGURE 1-19. *Capacitance bridge circuit*

tolerances depend on the type of capacitor, the value of capacitance, and the voltage rating. The actual measurement of capacitance is very simple—however, you still must make the important decision of whether to reject or to continue to use the capacitor after it has been tested.

Early versions of capacitance bridges used vacuum tubes. Although their accuracy was more than adequate, they were not rugged enough for field service work. Advances in solid-state electronics have led to new instruments that will read and display the value of a capacitor directly on an LCD readout. They are very durable, and more accurate than their tube-type predecessors. Figure 1-20 shows a typical digital capacitance meter. It is very rugged and very accurate. The capacitor is placed across the connectors on the front of the meter, and the value is read directly on the LCD readout.

FIGURE 1-20. *Digital capacitance meter*

1. Describe the basic operation of the d'Arsonval meter movement.

2. What modification is made to a d'Arsonval meter movement to enable the meter to measure voltage?

3. The *sensitivity* of a voltmeter is measured in _____.

4. An ammeter can be made to respond proportionally to different ranges of current by adding _____ in parallel with the meter movement.

5. A full-scale needle deflection on an ohmmeter indicates _____ resistance between the leads.

6. What is the purpose of an ohmmeter's zeroing control?

7. A multimeter is a combination of what other meters?

8. An analog multimeter is also called a(n) _____.

9. What are some of the advantages of digital multimeters?

10. What precautions must you take before making resistance measurements?

11. If the resistance to be measured is unknown, you should select the meter's _____ range scale.

12. A multimeter's black test probe usually is connected to the _____ jack, and the red probe to the _____ jack.

13. If an ohmmeter scale reading is 15 when the selector switch is at the R × 10k setting, what is the value of the measured resistance?

14. Using a resistance test to find open and closed circuits is called checking _____.

15. When you use an analog ohmmeter to test a fuse, what reading on the scale indicates that the fuse is good?

16. A voltmeter must always be connected in _____ with the circuit being tested.

17. What is the most important characteristic of the clamp-on meter?

18. The sum of the voltage drops across all the components in a series circuit equals the _____.

19. When the potential between two points in a circuit is equal, how much current can flow between the two points?

20. When you use a Wheatstone bridge to measure resistance, what is the value of R_x if $R_1 = 200\ \Omega$, $R_2 = 300\ \Omega$, and $R_3 = 150\ \Omega$?

Test Equipment (Part 2)

WATTMETERS

Electric power is measured with a *wattmeter*. A wattmeter is an *electrodynamometer*-type instrument. It varies from the galvanometer-type instruments studied in the previous Lesson in that two fixed coils are used to produce the magnetic field, instead of a permanent magnet. As shown in Figure 2-1 on the next page, a wattmeter consists of such a pair of fixed coils, known as *current* coils, and a movable coil, known as the *voltage* or *potential* coil. The fixed current coils are wound with a few turns of a relatively large conductor. The movable potential coil is wound with many turns of fine wire. It is mounted on a shaft that is supported on jeweled bearings so that it can turn inside the fixed coils. The movable coil carries a needle, or pointer, which moves over a suitably graduated scale. Flat coil springs hold the needle at the zero position in the absence of a signal.

The stationary current coils of the wattmeter are connected in series with the circuit (load), and the movable potential coil is connected across the line. When line current flows through the current coil of a wattmeter, a magnetic field is set up around the coil. The strength of this field is proportional to and in phase with the line current. The potential coil of the wattmeter generally has a high-resistance resistor connected in series with it. The purpose for this connection is to make the potential coil circuit as purely resistive as possible. As a result, current in the potential coil circuit is practically in phase with the line voltage.

The actuating force of a wattmeter is a result of the interaction of the magnetic fields of its current and potential coils. The force acting on the movable coil at any given moment (the force that tends to turn it) is proportional to the product of the instantaneous values of line current and voltage.

The wattmeter consists of two circuits (the current and the potential), either of which may be damaged if too much current is passed through them. This fact must be especially emphasized, because the reading on the wattmeter will *not* tell you whether or not the coils are being overheated. If an ammeter or voltmeter is overloaded, the pointer will advance *beyond* the upper limit of its scale. In the wattmeter, both the current and potential circuits may be carrying enough of an overload to cause wire insulation to burn, even though the pointer may be only part way up the scale. This is because the position of the pointer depends on the power factor of the circuit, as well as on the voltage and current. Therefore, a circuit with a

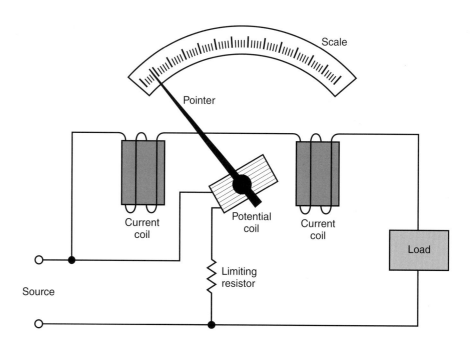

FIGURE 2-1. *Simplified electrodynamometer wattmeter circuit*

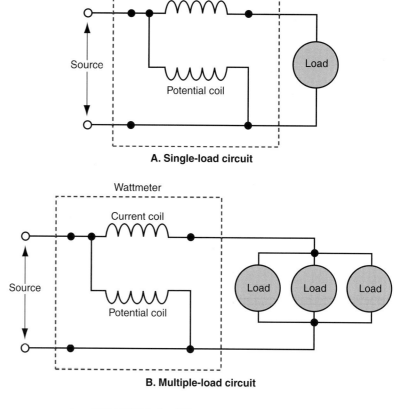

FIGURE 2-2. *Wattmeter connections*

low power factor will produce a very low reading on the wattmeter, even when the current and potential circuits are loaded to the maximum safe limit.

The safe rating is generally indicated on the face of the instrument. A wattmeter is always distinctly rated, not in watts, but in volts and amperes. Figure 2-2 shows the proper way to connect an analog wattmeter. The phase differences in a three-phase circuit make it necessary for three wattmeter circuits to be used. This is depicted in Figure 2-3. Wattmeters are primarily used for servicing small or domestic appliances. Most large equipment does not require the use of a wattmeter to determine power consumption. Figure 2-4 on the next page shows a more recent wattmeter. This type of clamp-on digital model reads true power, not apparent power, and can be used with single, split-phase, and three-phase power sources.

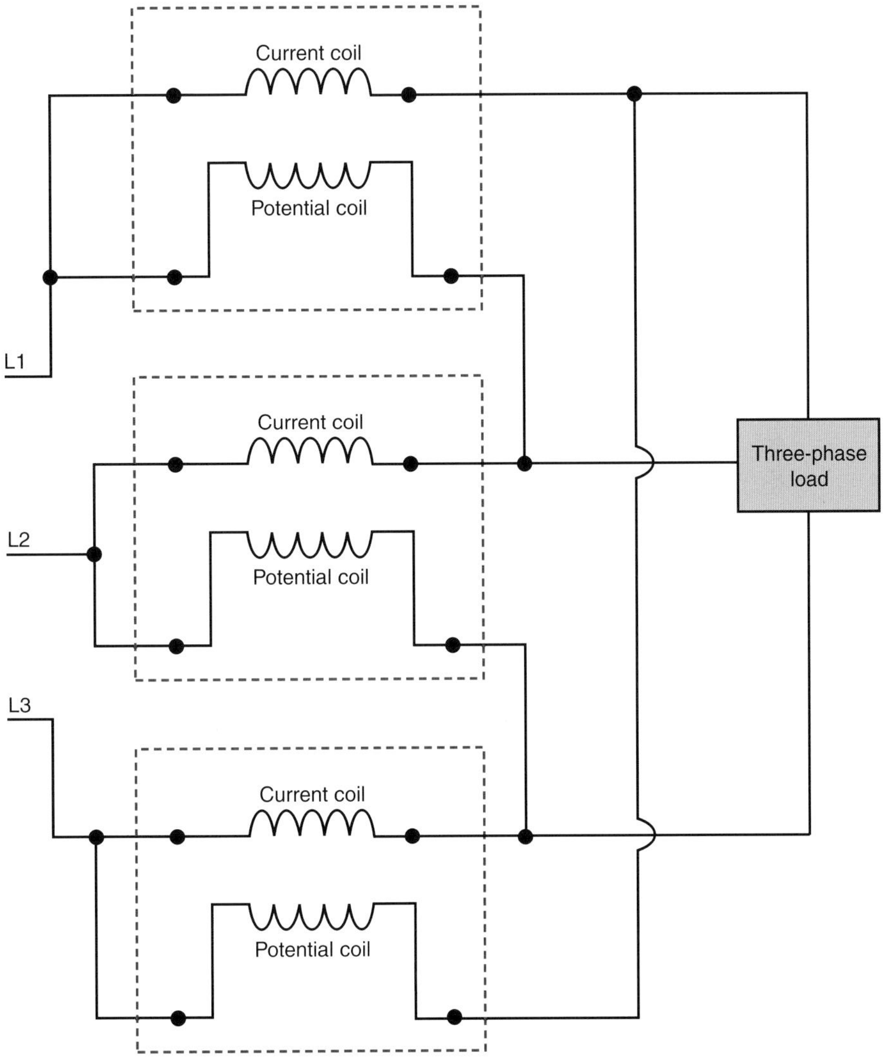

WATT-HOUR METERS

The *watt-hour meter* is not really considered a piece of test equipment. It cannot be carried around on your tool belt. However, knowing its purpose and function can be very helpful to you as a service technician. The watt-hour meter is an instrument used for measuring energy. Since energy is the product of power and time, the watt-hour meter must take into consideration both of these factors. In principle, the watt-hour meter is a small motor whose instantaneous speed is proportional to the *power* passing through it. The number of revolutions of the motor in a given period of time is proportional to the total *energy*, or watt-hours, consumed during that time.

FIGURE 2-3. *Wattmeter connections in a three-phase circuit*

A simplified sketch of an *induction* watt-hour meter, commonly used to measure ac power, is shown in Figure 2-5. The induction watt-hour meter includes a simple induction motor consisting of an aluminum disk, moving magnetic field, drag magnets, current and potential coils, integrating dials, and associated gears.

The potential coil connected across the load is composed of many turns of relatively fine wire. It is wound on one leg of the laminated magnetic circuit. Because of its many turns, the potential coil has both high impedance and high inductance. Therefore, the current passing through it lags the applied voltage by nearly 90°. The two current coils connected in series with the load are composed of a few turns of heavy wire. They are wound on two legs of the laminated magnetic circuit. Because there are fewer turns, the current coils have low inductance and low impedance.

The rotating aluminum disk is the moving member that causes the gears to turn and the dials to indicate the amount of energy passed through the meter. The rotation of the disk is caused by the resultant force between the magnetic fields of the current and potential coils, and the magnetic fields set up by eddy currents within the disk. The speed of rotation (the number of revolutions during a given period of time) is proportional to the true power (energy times time) supplied through the line to the load.

A small copper shading disk (not shown in Figure 2-5) is placed under a portion of the potential pole face. It is used to develop a torque to counteract static friction. The disk has the effect of a shading pole, providing a light load adjustment for the meter.

The two drag magnets supply the counter torque against which the aluminum disk acts when it turns. The drag is increased—that is, the speed of motor is reduced—by moving the magnets toward the edge of the disk. Conversely, the drag is decreased (and the speed is increased) by moving the magnets toward the center of the

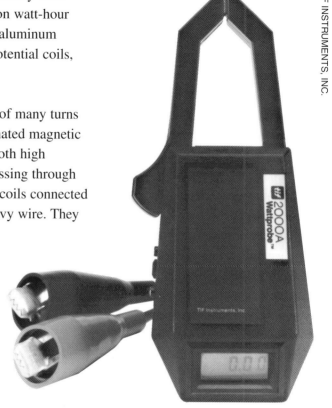

TIF INSTRUMENTS, INC.

FIGURE 2-4. *Clamp-on digital wattmeter*

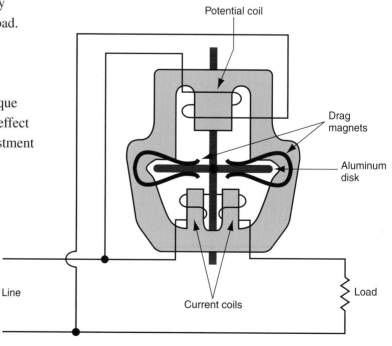

FIGURE 2-5. *Induction watt-hour meter*

disk. Adjustment of the drag magnets should be done only by an authorized instrument and meter calibration company.

Reading a watt-hour meter

You may find it helpful to know how to read the dials of a watt-hour meter. The meter face shown in Figure 2-6 is a four-dial type. To understand how it works, start at the right and work your way left. Each scale division on the dial at the far right represents one *kilowatt-hour* (1 kWh) of energy. (One kilowatt-hour equals 1,000 watt-hours.) A complete revolution of the hand on this dial causes the hand on the next dial (second from the right) to move one division, indicating a change of 10 kWh, or 10,000 watt-hours. In turn, a complete revolution of the hand on this second dial causes the hand on the third dial to move one division, thus registering a change of 100 kWh, or 100,000 watt-hours. And finally, a complete revolution of the hand on the third dial causes the hand on the last dial (at the far left) to move one division, representing a change of 1,000 kWh, or 1,000,000 watt-hours.

Accordingly, you must read the meter from left to right, always remembering to read the dial hands as indicating the figure just *passed*, not the one being approached. Thus, the reading for the meter shown in Figure 2-6 is 3,261 kWh. (Three zeros must be added to the total reading to convert the reading to watt-hours).

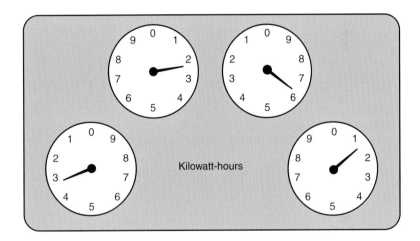

FIGURE 2-6. *Reading a watt-hour meter*

POWER FACTOR METERS

The test instruments discussed in the next several sections are not normally carried aboard a service truck. They are introduced here to demonstrate the availability of these special instruments through specialty testing organizations.

Power factors

The *power factor* of a circuit is equal to the cosine of the phase angle between the current through the circuit and the applied voltage. It also is expressed as the ratio of true power to apparent power. A pure resistance has a power factor of one, or *unity* (that is, the current and the voltage are in phase, and the true power and the apparent power are the same). A pure inductance has a power factor of zero (the current lags the voltage by 90°). A pure capacitance also has a power factor of zero (the current leads the voltage by 90°).

If you are unfamiliar with trigonometry, you can determine the power factor of a circuit by using readings from a wattmeter, a voltmeter, and an ammeter. The power factor is calculated by dividing the wattmeter reading (actual power) by the product of the voltmeter and ammeter readings (apparent power). However, since this procedure is somewhat inconvenient, instruments have been developed that continuously and directly indicate the power factor. Such an instrument is called a *power factor meter*. It also tells you whether the current is leading or lagging the voltage.

Opposed-coil power factor meters

One type of power factor meter is shown schematically in Figure 2-7. The instrument consists of movable potential coils A and B, fixed at right angles to each other, and stationary current coil C. (Coils A, B, and C are shown in cross section.) Coils A and B can pivot about a common axis. The assembly, together with the attached pointer, is free to move

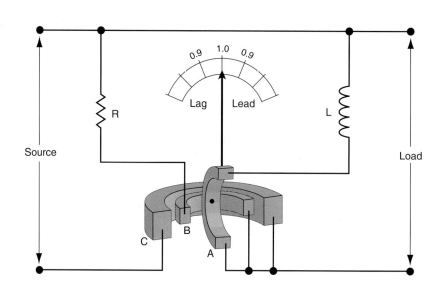

FIGURE 2-7. *Opposed-coil power factor meter*

through an angle of approximately 90°. Coil A is wired in series with inductor L, and the combination is connected across the line. Coil B is wired in series with non-inductive resistor R, and this combination also is connected across the line.

Circuit continuity to the coils is provided by three spiral springs (not shown in Figure 2-7) that exert a small restraining force on the movable coils. When no current flows through the coils, the pointer may come to rest at any position on the dial. Coil C (not drawn to scale) is connected in series with the line. In many switchboard designs, the coils are energized by instrument transformers. In such installations, the currents are proportional to line values but not equal to them.

When the current through coil B is in phase with the line voltage, the current in coil A lags the line voltage by 90°. When the line current is in phase with the line voltage, the currents in B and C are in phase with each other, and a torque is exerted between them that aligns their axes so that the pointer indicates a unity power factor. This condition is shown in Figure 2-7. The average torque between A and C is zero, because these currents are 90° out of phase when the line power factor is unity.

When the current in coil C lags the line voltage, the current in coil A and the current in coil B both will be out of phase with the current in C. If the current in coil C lags the line voltage by 45°, for example, then the current in A will lag the current in C by 45°, and the current in B will lead the current in C by 45°. Therefore, the changing magnetic flux around coil C, which is in phase with its current, will react with the resultant changing magnetic flux around coils A and B. Consequently, the pointer will be moved to an intermediate position (45°), indicating a power factor between zero and unity. In most power factor meters, a lagging line current causes the pointer to move to the left of the center position (marked "1" on the scale), and a leading line current causes the pointer to move to the right of the center position.

VARMETERS

The *reactive* power of a circuit is the power returned to the source by the reactive components of the circuit. It is power incapable of producing work. The unit of reactive power—as opposed to real power in watts—is the *volt-ampere reactive*, or *var*. A *varmeter* is used to measure reactive power, in either vars, kilovars, or megavars. This is especially useful to know when the power factor of an inductive circuit is below 70%, so that corrective capacitors can be added.

A standard wattmeter can be used for measuring vars by applying a voltage to the circuit which is 90° out of phase with the voltage that would normally be used for measuring watts. The phase-shifting required for measuring vars in a single-phase circuit is accomplished by connecting a combination of resistors and capacitors in series with the potential coil of the meter. For three-phase var measurements, a phase-shifting transformer can be used to shift the phase of the voltages applied to each of the elements of the meter.

The connections of a two-element varmeter and its auxiliary phase-shifting autotransformers are shown in Figure 2-8 on the next page. By looking at the transformer circuit, you can see that the voltages across $E_{4\text{-}5}$ and $E_{6\text{-}7}$ lag the voltages across $E_{1\text{-}2}$ and $E_{2\text{-}3}$, respectively, by 90°.

Varmeter scales are usually configured so that the zero is at the center, with the left end of the scale marked "IN" and the right end of the scale marked "OUT." When the meter reads "vars OUT," it indicates that magnetizing vars are flowing from the supply to the load. This happens when a generator is supplying an inductive load—an induction motor, for example. By contrast, a "vars IN" reading indicates that the load is capacitive in nature, and that the load is causing magnetizing vars to flow back to the supply. Applied changes in capacitor values can correct power factor problems.

INSTRUMENT TRANSFORMERS

Many HVACR technicians work in industry. They must service equipment in large mechanical rooms, such as those found in hospitals, main power plants, etc. This portion of the Lesson will explain to some degree how test instruments are designed to help in diagnosing service problems and recording the operational performance of the equipment in such environments.

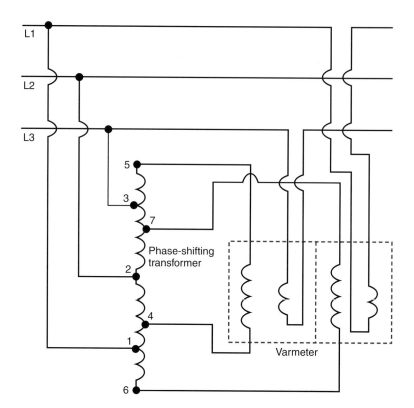

FIGURE 2-8. *Varmeter connections*

Electrical measurements at high voltages

It is not usually practical to connect instruments and meters directly to high-voltage circuits. Unless the high-voltage circuit is grounded properly, a dangerously high potential-to-ground voltage may exist at the instrument or switchboard. Furthermore, because of the electrostatic forces that act on the indicating elements, instruments can become inaccurate when connected directly to high voltages. However, *instrument transformers* have been designed to eliminate this problem.

When instrument transformers are used, the instruments themselves may be entirely insulated from the high-voltage circuit and yet accurately indicate the current, voltage, and power in the circuit. Low-voltage instruments that have standard current and voltage ranges may be used for all high-voltage circuits, regardless of the voltage and current ratings of the circuits, if instrument transformers are utilized.

Potential transformers

Potential transformers do not differ materially from the constant-potential power transformers discussed in an earlier Unit of study. Their power ratings are smaller, however, and they are designed for minimum ratio and phase angle error. At a power factor of unity, the impedance drop through the transformer, from no load to rated load, should not be greater than 1%. For taking measurements below 5,000 V, dry-type potential transformers normally are used. Between 5,000 and 13,800 V, either dry-type or oil-immersed potential transformers may be used. Oil-immersed potential transformers are used above 13,800 V.

Since only instruments, meters, and occasionally indicator lights ordinarily are connected to the secondaries of potential transformers, their ratings range from 40 to 500 W. For primary voltages of 34,500 V and higher, the secondaries are rated at 115 V. For primary voltages of less than 34,500 V, the secondaries are rated at 120 V. For example, a 14,400-V potential transformer would have a turns ratio of 120:1, as shown below:

$$\frac{14,400 \text{ V}}{120 \text{ V}} = \frac{120}{1}$$

The ratio of turns may vary about 1% from this value to allow for the transformer impedance drop under load. Figure 2-9 shows a simple connection for measuring voltage in a 14,400-V circuit by means of a potential transformer. The secondary should always be grounded at one point to eliminate static electricity from the instrument, and to ensure the safety of the operator.

Current transformers

In order to avoid connecting instruments directly into high-voltage lines, *current* transformers are used. In addition to protecting instruments from high voltages, current transformers step down the line current to a known ratio. This permits the use of an ammeter with a lower-range than would be required if the instrument were connected directly into the primary line.

The current (or *series*) transformer has a primary winding, usually of a few turns, wound on a core and connected in series with the line. Figure 2-10 on the next page shows a simple connection for measuring current in a 14,400-V circuit

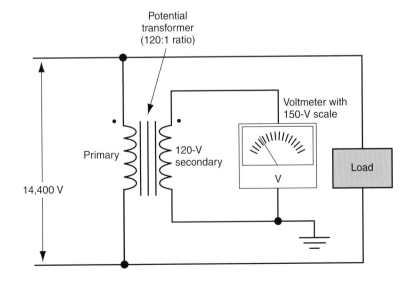

FIGURE 2-9. *Potential transformer*

by means of a current transformer. The secondary windings of practically all current transformers are rated at 5 A, regardless of the primary current rating. Thus, a 2,000-A current transformer has a turns ratio of 400:1, and a 50-A transformer has a turns ratio of 10:1.

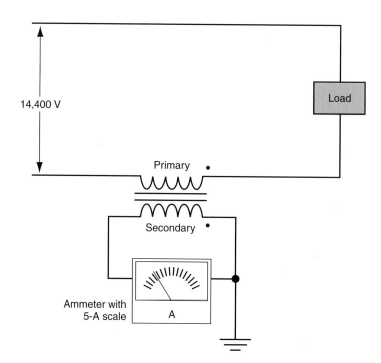

FIGURE 2-10. *Current transformer*

The insulation between the primary and the secondary of a current transformer must be sufficient to withstand full circuit voltage. The current transformer differs from the ordinary constant-potential transformer in that its primary current is determined entirely by the load on the system, and not by its own secondary load.

If its secondary becomes open-circuited, a high voltage will exist across the secondary, because the large ratio of secondary to primary turns causes the transformer to act as a step-up transformer. Also, since the effects of the counter-ampere turns of the secondary no longer exist, the flux in the core will depend on the total primary ampere turns acting alone. This causes a large increase in the flux, producing excessive core loss and heating, as well as a dangerously high voltage across the secondary terminals. Therefore, *the secondary of a current transformer should not be open-circuited under any circumstances.*

Figure 2-11 shows a method for connecting a complete instrument load, through instrument transformers, to a high-voltage line. The instrument transformer load includes an ammeter (A), a voltmeter (V), a wattmeter (W), and a watt-hour meter (WH).

Polarity markings

Instruments, meters, and relays must be connected so that the correct phase relations exist between their potential and current circuits. When you use instrument transformers, it is important to know the relation of the instantaneous polarities of the secondary terminals to those of the primary terminals. It has become standard to designate or mark the primary terminals and the secondary terminals that have the same instantaneous polarity. In wiring diagrams, primary and secondary terminals that have the same instantaneous polarity are marked with a dot (•), as shown in Figures 2-9, 2-10, and 2-11.

MEGOHMMETERS

The insulation that covers the wires in motor and coil windings, and the insulating materials used for isolating terminals, starter and relay contact points, and so on, are subject to severe stress, even under ideal operating conditions. Deteriorating elements gradually lower the resistance of the insulation and increase the potential of grounds and shorts, often resulting in a burned-out motor, contactor, magnetic starter, and/or wiring. Keeping electrical equipment clean is of primary importance for extended service life. Periodic testing with a *megohmmeter* is the best means of detecting faults and potential trouble areas.

The megohmmeter, or "megger," is an instrument that measures very large values of resistance. It is used primarily to check for insulation breakdown in conductors. The older style of megohmmeter consisted mainly of a hand-driven dc generator, which supplied the high voltage for making the measurement, and a direct-reading ohmmeter, which indicated the value of the resistance being measured. A simplified diagram of the electrical connections of the instrument is shown in Figure 2-12 on the next page. Permanent magnets provide the magnetic fields for both the generator and the ohmmeter.

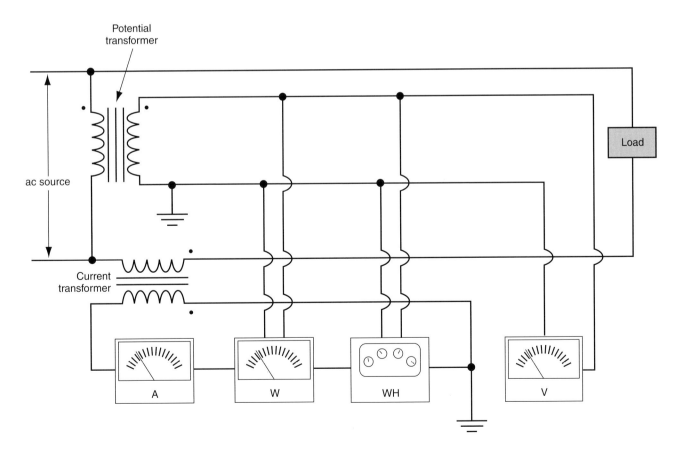

FIGURE 2-11. *Connecting multiple instruments*

The moving element of the ohmmeter consists of two coils, O_1 and O_2, which are mounted rigidly to a pivoted central shaft. They are free to rotate over a stationary C-shaped iron core. The coils are connected to the circuit by means of flexible leads that exert no restoring force on the moving element. Hence, the moving element may take any position over the scale when the generator is not in operation. Coil O_2 is connected in series with the resistance R_x across the generator terminals, while coil O_1 is connected in series with the resistance R_1 between one generator terminal, marked T_1, and the other test terminal, marked T_2.

When current passes from the generator through coil O_2, the coil tends to set itself at right angles to the field of the permanent magnet. With the test terminals T_1 and T_2 open (corresponding to infinite resistance), no current flows in coil O_1. Coil O_2 thus governs the motion of the rotating element, causing it to move to its extreme counterclockwise position. The point on the scale indicated by the pointer under this condition is marked with the symbol ∞ (infinite resistance).

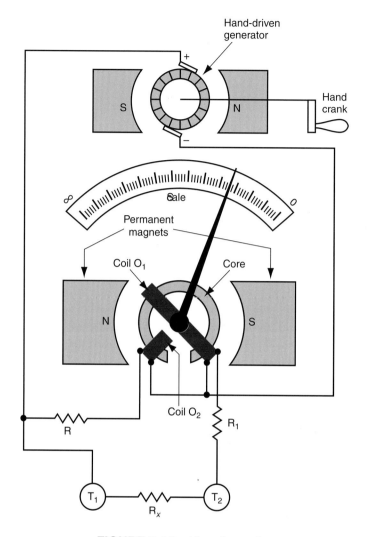

FIGURE 2-12. *Megohmmeter*

Coil O_1 is wound to produce a clockwise torque on the moving element. With the test terminals T_1 and T_2 short-circuited (corresponding to zero resistance), the current flowing through coil O_1 is large enough to produce sufficient torque to overcome the counterclockwise torque of coil B. This moves the pointer to its extreme clockwise position on the scale, indicating zero external resistance. The resistance R_1 protects coil O_1 from the flow of excessive current when the test terminals are short-circuited.

When an unknown value of resistance is connected between the test terminals, the opposing torque of the coils balance each other so that the pointer comes to rest at some intermediate point on the scale. The scale is calibrated so that the pointer indicates directly the value of the resistance being measured.

Generators rated at 500, 1,000, or 2,500 V are used in megger testers. The higher voltages are used in instruments with higher resistance ranges. Variations in generator voltage in a given instrument do not appreciably affect the readings.

With the advent of electronics, a more versatile megohmmeter has been devised. It does not have to be cranked to deliver the required voltage for testing insulation. Today's hand-held meggers, like the one shown in Figure 2-13, allow the service technician to use a convenient single unit for performing general electrical maintenance measurements of wiring, motors, generators, circuit breakers, transformers, and related equipment. Many modern electronic megohmmeters are "three-in-one" models. The three common uses of this type of megohmmeter are:

- Megohm ranges are used for measuring very high insulation resistance. The megohm range provides a direct reading, in millions of ohms (megohms), of the resistance that any electrical insulation offers to the passage of current. It is common practice to measure this resistance with a test potential of 500 V, although lower and higher voltages are also frequently used.

- Low ohm ranges are used for measuring circuit or winding resistance of motors and transformers. This portion of the ohmmeter is powered directly by the batteries in the device.

- Normal voltmeter ranges are used for measuring the voltages (usually ac) of connected lines or other circuits. The ac voltage ranges have a typical accuracy of ±3% of full-scale when standard 60-Hz voltages are in use.

Operation

The relatively high test voltage (500 V in most models) is produced by a battery-powered transistorized oscillator power supply. Figure 2-14 on the next page shows a simplified schematic of how a typical megohmmeter works. The 3 V supplied by two heavy-duty dry cells (some models use more cells) is converted to ac in the oscillator circuit, stepped up to a higher voltage in the power transformer, and then rectified and filtered to produce the direct voltage appearing across the measuring terminals. When the insulation resistance R_x has been measured and the switch is released, resistor R_2 (which has a relatively low value compared to the resistance of the insulation being measured) is connected across the test terminals to discharge any remaining charge stored in the item under test.

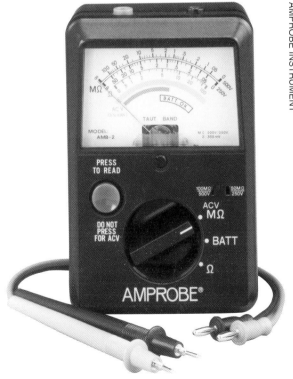

FIGURE 2-13. *Analog megohmmeter*

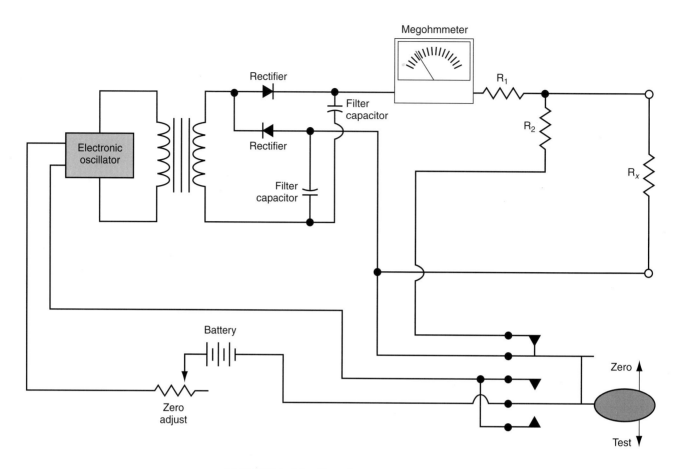

FIGURE 2-14. *Megohmmeter operation*

RECORDING INSTRUMENTS

Although indicating instruments such as ammeters and voltmeters are extremely useful for a wide variety of applications, they have a basic limitation—the information that they provide must be read and interpreted "on the spot." This poses no problem if all that is needed is the value of the current or voltage at the particular time the measurement is made. But if the main interest is, say, the *variation* of current in a circuit over a period of time, then an indicating ammeter would be of limited use, since it would require constant monitoring in order to observe and record the magnitude and duration of the changes as they occur.

As an example, consider a case in which a power source voltage is suspected of varying intermittently. This suspicion could be verified by measuring the voltage continuously over a given period of time, perhaps as much as 24 hr. Obviously, to do this with a standard voltmeter would be impractical, since the cost would be exceptionally high. What is needed is an instrument that, when connected to the circuit, will not only measure the voltage, but will also provide a permanent record that shows how the voltage varies with time. Such an instrument could be left unattended to monitor the circuit for relatively long periods of time. The permanent record produced could then be analyzed later, at a convenient time and place.

Advantages of recorders

Some of the more important advantages to be gained by using a voltage or current recorder are:

- The instrument provides a permanent, continuous record of the operation over an extended period of time.

- The instrument is a time-saver, since the service engineer can be profitably engaged in servicing other customers' equipment while the recorder is in use.

- The chart shows the start and stop points of the equipment, and thus the length of the defrost "ON" and "OFF" times.

Instruments with these capabilities are called *chart recorders*. Basically, there are two types—those that measure and record voltage, and those that measure and record current. Some units are for measuring ac only, and others for dc only. Similarly, some recorders are best-suited for measuring large values of voltage or current, while others are designed chiefly for measuring small values. There are also recorders that can be used to make both voltage *and* current measurements.

Voltage and current are not the only quantities that can be measured and displayed by a recorder. There are recording wattmeters, power factor recorders, temperature recorders, pressure recorders, and humidity recorders, to mention a few. In fact, any physical quantity that can be converted into an electrical signal by means of a transducer can be measured and displayed by some suitable recorder. A *transducer* is a device used for converting a signal of one kind into a corresponding signal of another kind.

All electrical chart recorders provide a paper chart on which a visible trace of the variations in the quantity being measured is produced. In one type of chart recorder, the chart paper takes the form of a long, continuous roll that unrolls as the recording progresses. This type of instrument is called a *strip-chart recorder*.

Another type of chart recorder uses a flat, round chart that rotates as recording progresses. The length of the trace, with respect to time, is thus limited to one revolution of the chart. This type of instrument, called a *round-chart recorder*, normally has the low end of the scale toward the center of the chart and the high end toward the outside. Thus, for a given length of time, a recording of a variable at the low end of the recorder's capability will be more compressed than the record made at the high end. Round-chart recorders are used for applications in which it is more convenient to keep daily or individual records, rather than the long, continuous record produced by the strip-chart recorder. The round-chart recorder also has the advantage of making the entire chart visible at all times.

There are two additional subdivisions of chart recorders—namely, galvanometric recorders and potentiometric recorders. One way in which these two types differ is in the method used to measure the input quantity. *Potentiometric* (null balance) recorders measure by comparing the input signal with an internal value maintained as a standard. When these two signals are equal and opposite, no current will flow in the null balance detector. *Galvanometric* recorders, on the other hand, use a d'Arsonval meter movement (or some other, similar type of meter movement) as the primary measuring mechanism. Galvanometric recorders are more commonly used in service and maintenance work than potentiometric recorders.

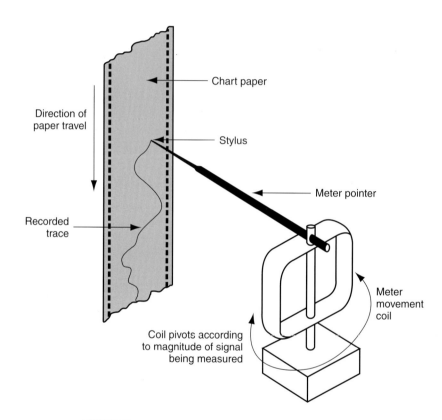

FIGURE 2-15. *Galvanometric strip-chart recorder*

Galvanometric chart recorder operation

Essentially, a galvanometric strip-chart recorder consists of an indicating meter and a roll of chart paper that is made to move past the tip of the meter pointer. As shown in Figure 2-15, a stylus at the end of the pointer is in constant contact with the chart paper, thus producing a visible trace. The pointer pivots in proportion to the magnitude of the input signal being measured. The recorded trace is produced across the width of the chart paper, but since the paper is moving, a two-dimensional trace is produced along its length.

As you can see in Figure 2-15, the trace produced by a strip-chart recorder shows how the measured quantity varies over a period of time. The vertical dimension of the trace shows changes in the magnitude of what is being measured (voltage, current, etc.), and the horizontal dimension represents time. In order to make the record easier to read, the chart paper is marked in the appropriate units (e.g., volts or amperes).

The meter portion of a recording instrument is basically identical to that of indicating instrument. The only major difference in strip-chart recorders is the inclusion of the writing stylus at the tip of the pointer.

Some recorders include a calibrated scale as part of the meter's face plate. This allows the instrument to be used either as a recorder or as a standard indicating meter. When the chart paper is removed, the scale is clearly visible and the instrument can be used as a direct-reading meter.

Producing the trace

The type of trace and the way it is produced on the moving chart paper depends on the type of recorder. Many modern recorders use a special kind of pressure-sensitive chart paper. This paper is chemically treated so that when pressure is applied by a stylus or some other sharp instrument, a molecular change occurs which produces a visible mark. The mark occurs only at points of contact, thus assuring a clean, distinct trace.

Some recorders use electro-sensitive chart paper, which changes color wherever electric current is passed through it. In instruments of this type, current flows from the stylus through the electrically conductive paper. The trace is produced when the electrical energy of the current causes a chemical change in the paper. Writing current is provided by a special circuit within the recorder.

Other methods used in recorders for producing a trace include the thermal technique and the ink-writing technique. The *thermal* technique makes use of heat-sensitive paper and a stylus that functions as an electric heater. Wherever the hot stylus touches the paper, a mark is produced. In *ink-writing* systems, perhaps the oldest recorder method, the stylus is actually a pen equipped with a supply of ink. The visible image is thus an ordinary ink trace on the chart paper. Although ink-writing systems are very simple and economical, they have certain disadvantages. An obvious one is that the ink supply must be replenished periodically. Another is that they usually can be operated only in one (level) position due to the requirements of the ink-feed system. In addition, ink-writing systems always pose the hazards of leaking, spilling, or clogging, which often can have disastrous results.

Depending on the type of recorder, the trace may be continuous, in which case the stylus remains in contact with the chart throughout the recording operation, or it may consist of a loosely spaced series of dots. In the latter case, the stylus is brought briefly into contact with the chart at definite intervals, such as every five seconds. Both types are shown in Figure 2-16.

In a unit that produces a dot-type trace, the writing medium makes no contact with the chart paper during the "spaces" (between the dots.) In a unit that produces a continuous trace, however, the force of friction must be constantly overcome. As a result, the continuous type requires a meter movement with a greater motor torque—and hence less sensitivity—than the intermittent type. The disadvantage of the intermittent type, however, is that transients cannot be followed.

Feeding the chart paper

The chart paper in a strip-chart recorder must move at a precise speed. This movement is provided by a mechanical transport mechanism driven by a geared synchronous motor. Synchronous motors are used because of their excellent timing characteristics. They are the kinds of motors used in electric clocks. The output speed of the motor is geared to provide the required chart speeds. Chart speeds that may be needed cover a wide range. The chart speed that is best for a particular application depends on how rapidly measurement values change. In general, the faster you expect the changes to be, the faster the chart speed should be.

A diagram of a typical dot trace recorder and its major parts is shown in Figure 2-17. The recorder shown employs pressure-sensitive chart paper, and the trace is in the form of a sequence of dots.

The electrical signal being measured is applied to the meter movement (A), just as it is in a standard indicating meter. The magnitude of the signal

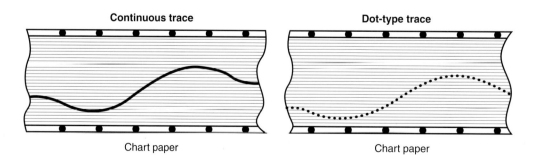

FIGURE 2-16. *Continuous and dot-type traces*

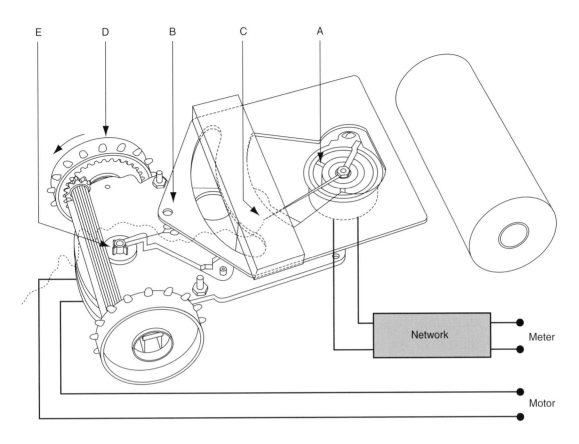

FIGURE 2-17. *Dot trace recorder*

determines the angular position of the meter pointer. A recording of the pointer's deflection is obtained by a lift plate (B), which presses the stylus (C) against the underside of the chart paper, causing a dot to appear on the top side of the chart, which in turn is being pressed against a glass plate.

After the stylus is released by the lift plate, the meter movement is free to deflect the pointer to a new position, should the input signal vary. During this release time, the transport mechanism (D), which is driven by the drive assembly (E), advances the chart paper. As this sequence is repeated, a series of very closely spaced dots is printed on the chart—producing, in effect, a nearly continuous line trace.

The speed at which the chart paper moves through the recorder, and the speed with which the impressions are made by the stylus, should be taken into consideration when selecting a recorder for a specific application. Since chart paper can be fed through the recorder at almost any given rate, from many inches per second to fractions of an inch per day, each application must be carefully analyzed. How long can the recorder be left unattended? What is the expected frequency of deviation of the variable?

There are continuous trace recorders that are ideally suited for applications in which a transient or unexpected instantaneous signal might have to be sensed. However, this is not the case in most applications. Thus, sensing the measured variable once every five seconds or so may be sufficient. If the variable being measured is relatively stable over a considerable period of time, a chart speed of one inch every few hours might be desirable, since it will enable the recorder to operate unattended for long periods of time on a single roll of chart paper. The proper selection of recorder sensing speed and chart feed rate can result in a considerable savings in cost.

CURRENT AND VOLTAGE RECORDERS

Strip-chart recorders can be designed to measure and display any variable, providing a transducer can convert the variable to an electrical signal. The three most common types of recorders are those for recording current, voltage and temperature. This Lesson deals only with current and voltage recorders.

Recording ammeters

A *recording ammeter* measures and records variations in current. Both the meter face and the chart paper of an ac recording ammeter are marked in units of current, in order to help you interpret readings quickly and accurately.

Recording ammeters are available in a wide variety of styles. Usually, the most important consideration in selecting a particular instrument is the amount of current to be measured. If it is known that the current will always be small, then an instrument with a single current range of from 0 to 5 A is suitable. However, if large currents of 1,000 A or more are to be measured, a unit with a much greater current-measuring capability (such as 0 to 1,500 A) is required. A problem arises when a wide range of currents is to be measured. What should you do, for example, when you need to go as low as 1 A and as high as 1,000 A?

Two separate recorders could be used—one for small current measurements, and the other for large current measurements. However, this approach can be expensive, since two complete recorders must be purchased. A single recorder with a range of 0 to 1,000 A could be used. But its accuracy when measuring small currents would be very poor, because accuracy is expressed as a percentage of full-scale capability. The problem can be solved by using a *dual-range* recording meter—one that has scales, for example, for measuring from 0 to 100 A and from 0 to 1,000 A. With such an instrument, currents anywhere from 1 to 1,000 A can be measured with maximum accuracy merely by selecting the proper range before making a measurement.

40

The clamp-on current transducer of a recording ammeter eliminates the need to shut down equipment and interrupt service. The range switch is located on the recorder itself. Some units have a range switch built into the transducer.

Recording voltmeters

The ac *recording voltmeter* is similar to the recording ammeter, except that it measures voltage instead of current—and, therefore, has its meter scale and chart paper marked in units of voltage. The meter portion of the instrument is, of course, a voltmeter. When you select a voltmeter recorder for a particular job, the most important consideration is the range of voltage to be measured. When the voltages you need to measure cover a wide range, the most practical choice is to select a multi-range instrument. As with the recording ammeter, this approach combines the required measuring capability with maximum accuracy. Figure 2-18 shows one type of recording voltmeter.

In many applications, both voltage and current must be recorded at one time or another. Here, too, separate instruments could be used—one for voltage and one for current. However, it is possible to do both jobs with a single instrument. A type of instrument called a *volt/ammeter recorder* can record both voltage and current. For applications in which the ranges of voltage and current to be recorded vary widely, volt/ammeter recorders designed to measure multiple ranges should be used. A conveniently located switch on the recorder can be set to select the desired type and range of measurement.

Current transformers

Just as there are accessories for clamp-on meters, strip-chart recorder manufacturers offer accessories for use with their recorders. Perhaps the most useful of these accessories is the *current transformer*. Typically, the current transformer is placed around the conductor to be monitored and connected to a basic 5-A recorder. Each transformer has a specific maximum current rating, but is designed so that the maximum input on the primary will induce only

FIGURE 2-18. *Recording ac voltmeter*

5 A on the secondary. Thus, the 5-A recorder becomes a very versatile and multi-scaled instrument when used with a current transformer and appropriately marked chart paper.

Connecting recorders

Before using any recorder, *always* read the manufacturer's instructions carefully. Some recorders have spring motors that drive the chart, others operate on either line voltage or battery power. Before connecting electrically driven recorders, carefully check the voltage required to operate the recorder. Some recorders must be connected to the power supply before they can be zero adjusted.

Prior to connecting any instrument for use, you must make certain that the instrument is capable of measuring the variable. If you know that the variable is within the range of the instrument, and if the instrument is a multi-range unit, always start reading on the highest range. Switch to a lower range only if the initial reading indicates that the variable is within the lower range.

Connecting the sensing element to an ammeter recorder is usually done by means of plug or screw terminals. Be sure to note whether the terminals on the recorder are marked to indicate polarity. If they are, make certain that the connections on the sensing element are matched to the terminals on the recorder. Connecting a clamp-on ammeter to a circuit is simpler—the transducer jaws need only be clamped around a single conductor (one leg of the circuit). Insulation on a wire will not interfere with its reading. If you clamp the jaws around both legs of a circuit, the instrument will *not* read. Voltmeters, whether they are the recording type or not, are always connected in *parallel* with the circuit component to be tested.

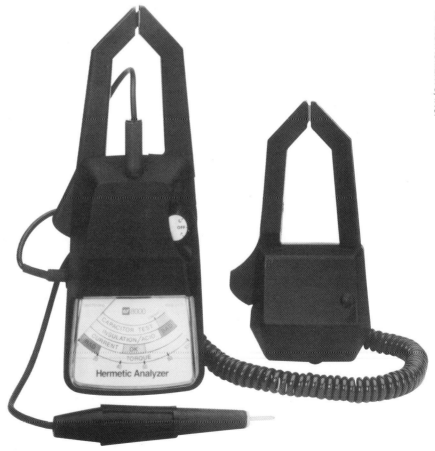

FIGURE 2-19. *Hermetic compressor analyzer*

COMPRESSOR ANALYZERS

There are many different models of *hermetic compressor analyzers* on the market today. These hand-held devices use computer electronics to help the service technician find the source of a problem quickly and easily, eliminating the need for "trial-and-error" part substitutions. Some compressor analyzers have clamp-on sensors, as shown in Figure 2-19, so that no wire disconnections are required. Some of the things that a typical hermetic compressor analyzer allows you to check for include:

- starting torque

- acid in refrigerant

- insulation breakdown

- mechanically frozen compressor

- capacitor open or shorted

- capacitor microfarads

- open start or run windings

- open relays.

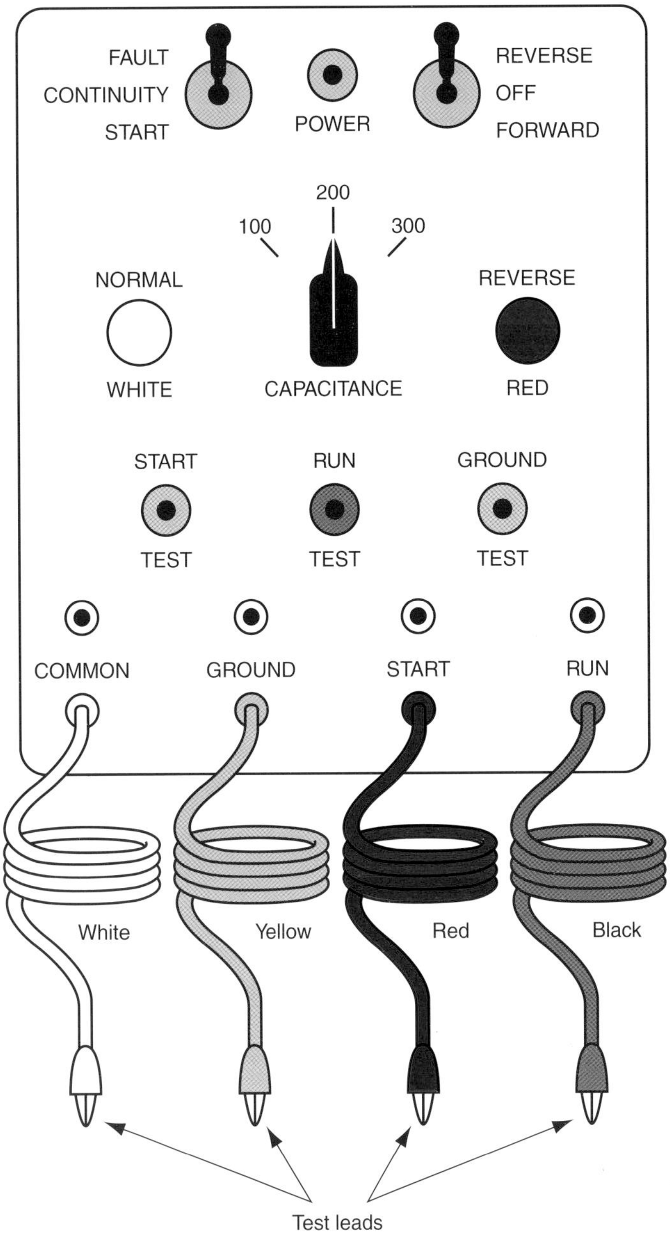

FIGURE 2-20. *GHCA-120/220*

This portion of the Lesson leads you step-by-step through a procedure using a generic analyzer. A fictitious model of test equipment, the GHCA-120/220, has been created strictly for learning purposes. Features from several manufacturers' instruments were combined to make this possible. As illustrated in Figure 2-20, this "Generic Hermetic Compressor Analyzer" is intended to provide the service technician with an example of an easy-to-use, reliable test instrument. To obtain the maximum benefit from any specific test equipment, be sure to read the manufacturer's instructions.

Warning: Under some test conditions, line voltage may be present at the test cables. Refer to the operation section of the tester.

The GHCA-120/220 includes the following features:

- indicates continuity

- indicates ground faults

- frees locked rotors by reversing motor action

- provides test jacks to facilitate VOM measurement of voltage and resistance

- dual 120/240-V ac operation

- current range: 25 A

- color-coded leads for easy use.

Controls and switches

POWER. This is a combination "power ON" switch and a circuit breaker.

CAPACITANCE. This switch selects one of the three starting capacitor ranges listed below:

Position	Range
100 μF	88 to 108 μF
200 μF	161 to 193 μF
300 μF	249 to 301 μF

REVERSE/OFF/FORWARD. This switch determines the mode of operation of the compressor. In the FORWARD (sustained) position, power is applied to the run winding of the compressor motor, and the start capacitor is connected to the START cable. In the REVERSE (momentary) position, power is applied to the start winding of the compressor motor and the start capacitor is connected to the RUN cable. In the OFF (sustained) position, the power supply circuit to the motor is broken.

FAULT/CONTINUITY/START. This is a multi-function switch. The FAULT (momentary action) position is used to check for shorts between the frame and the run and start windings. The CONTINUITY (sustained action) position is used to check for ground, run, and start continuity. In the START (momentary action) position, the start capacitor is connected to the compressor motor through the REVERSE/OFF/FORWARD switch.

GROUND TEST. The GROUND TEST (yellow) switch is a push-button switch that tests for grounds and continuity between the system ground and the frame of the compressor being tested.

Note: The GHCA-120/220 introduces a "false ground" to make it possible to test for short circuits between the motor winding and the shell of a compressor that may not be directly grounded. For example, units with two-wire power cords would not be connected to the system ground (unless a separate ground connection were present).

START TEST. The START TEST (red) switch is a push-button switch that tests two conditions, depending on the position of the FAULT/CONTINUITY/START switch:

Switch position	Condition tested
FAULT	Short between start winding and shell
CONTINUITY	Continuity of start winding

RUN TEST. The RUN TEST (black) switch is a push-button switch that also tests two conditions, depending on the position of the FAULT/CONTINUITY/START switch:

Switch position	Condition tested
FAULT	Short between run winding and shell
CONTINUITY	Continuity of run winding

Indicator lights

The NORMAL (white) and REVERSE (red) lights are used to indicate the condition of the power source to which the GHCA-120/220 is connected. The various combinations possible are:

Line voltage	Indicator lights	Status
110 V ac	NORMAL on, REVERSE off	Normal
110 V ac	NORMAL off, REVERSE on	Neutral wire and hot wire are reversed at power receptacle (Refer to the "Caution" in the section on 110-V ac operation.)
110 V ac	NORMAL on, REVERSE on (half intensity)	System ground open or not connected at power receptacle
220 V ac	NORMAL on, REVERSE on (full intensity)	Normal

Test points

Each of the four test points is connected directly to the test cable of the corresponding color:

COMMON . . . White
GROUND . . . . Yellow*
START . . . . . . Red
RUN . . . . Black

The purpose of the test points is to facilitate resistance and voltage readings. Voltmeter and ohmmeter test leads can be connected to the compressor motor circuit simply by inserting them into the appropriate jacks on the front panel. (*Note that since the GROUND cable is a "false" or artificial ground line, it is yellow instead of green.)

GHCA-120/220 OPERATION

The following procedures have been constructed to help you gain a thorough understanding of the operation sequence of a compressor analyzer. In practice, the following tests may be performed very quickly. Every effort has been made to make the GHCA-120/220 a safe and versatile tester. Remember, however, that under some circumstances line voltage may be present at the test cables when the control switches are in the OFF position.

110-V ac operation

 CAUTION: The GHCA-120/220 is wired so that the COMMON (white) test cable is connected to the neutral side of the line. The START (red) and RUN (black) cables are connected to the "hot" side of the line by the POWER and REVERSE/OFF/FORWARD switches. If the wiring of the 110-V ac receptacle has accidentally been reversed, the COMMON (white) cable will be "hot" as soon as the GHCA-120/220 is plugged into the power receptacle. To warn against such a condition, the red REVERSE indicator will light as soon as the GHCA-120/220 is plugged into a grounded receptacle. In this case, follow procedure "B" for reversed-line operation.

A. Test procedure for normal operation

1. The REVERSE/OFF/FORWARD switch must be in the OFF position.

2. Plug the GHCA-120/220 into a grounded 110-V ac receptacle and turn on the push-button POWER switch. The white NORMAL indicator should light. (If the receptacle is ungrounded, both the NORMAL and the REVERSE indicators will light, but at half intensity. The absence of a grounded line will not prevent any of the following tests from being made.)

Note: You can verify that the receptacle is not reverse-wired by measuring the voltage between the COMMON (white) cable and a ground connection. A reversed line will measure 110 V ac. A normal line will measure 0 V. If the receptacle is reverse-wired, follow procedure "B."

3. Remove power to the unit that is to be tested.

4. Remove and identify the connectors leading to the common, start, and run terminals of the compressor motor.

5. Connect the test cables of the GHCA-120/220 to the compressor motor as follows:

   a. yellow GROUND cable to the compressor motor frame

   b. red START cable to the start terminal

   c. black RUN cable to the run terminal.

   (Leave the white COMMON cable disconnected until Step 7.)

6. Flip the FAULT/CONTINUITY/START switch to the FAULT position and hold it there while pressing the red START TEST and black RUN TEST pushbuttons in turn. If either the START indicator or the RUN indicator lights, there is a short between that winding and the frame. *Stop* the test and replace the unit.

7. Connect the white COMMON cable to the common terminal of the compressor motor.

8. Press, in turn, the GROUND TEST, START TEST, and RUN TEST buttons. Continuity in the circuit being tested is verified when the appropriate indicator lights. *Note*: To test for ground continuity, the appliance must be plugged into a grounded 110-V ac receptacle, or be grounded through an external connection. If the test indicates that either the run winding or the start winding is open, *stop* the test and replace the unit.

9. Select the appropriate motor start capacitor.

10. Flip the FAULT/CONTINUITY/START switch to the START position and hold it there while throwing the REVERSE/OFF/FORWARD switch to the FORWARD position. If the compressor starts, release the START switch. The compressor will continue to run. The compressor may be stopped by returning the REVERSE/OFF/FORWARD switch to the OFF position.

11. If the compressor does not start immediately, the rotor may be locked. Release the START switch and return the REVERSE/OFF/FORWARD switch to the OFF position.

12. To "bump" the compressor, flip the FAULT/CONTINUITY/START switch to the START position and hold it there while throwing the REVERSE/OFF/FORWARD switch to the REVERSE position. If the compressor starts immediately, release both switches.

13. Repeat Step 10 to ensure that the compressor will run in the forward direction. If the compressor does not start immediately in reverse, then release both switches. A locked rotor will result in excessive current being drawn by the compressor.

14. Steps 10 through 13 may be repeated a few times in an attempt to free a locked rotor, but be careful not to overheat the motor windings. If the compressor still does not start, it should be replaced.

15. Push the POWER switch off. Disconnect the GHCA-120/220 test cables from the motor.

B. Test procedure for reversed-line operation

If the 110-V ac receptacle is reverse-wired, the main thing to remember is that the white COMMON cable will be "hot." This will be true regardless of any GHCA-120/220 switch setting. Therefore, you must be sure to exercise extreme caution.

Follow the same Steps 1 through 6 as described in procedure "A" for normal operation, but keep the white COMMON cable isolated to prevent accidental contact with it. Before proceeding to Step 7, unplug the GHCA-120/220 from the power receptacle, connect the white COMMON cable to the common terminal of the motor, and then plug the GHCA-120/220 into the power receptacle. Then continue with the tests outlined in Steps 8 through 12 of procedure "A" for normal operation.

220-V ac operation

⚠️ **CAUTION: The white COMMON cable will be "hot" as soon as the GHCA-120/220 line cord is connected to 220 V ac. In order to avoid a potentially dangerous situation, *always* make sure that power to the GHCA-120/220 is shut off before connecting the analyzer's cables to a compressor motor operating on 220 V ac.**

1. Both the REVERSE/OFF/FORWARD switch and the POWER switch must be in the OFF position.

2. Remove power to the unit that is to be tested.

3. Some compressor units have fans mounted in the same housing as the compressor. If possible, either turn down the thermostat or disconnect the fan, so that the fan will not operate during the compressor tests. The fan noise could make it difficult to listen to the action of the compressor.

4. Remove and identify the connectors leading to the common, start, and run terminals of the compressor motor.

5. Connect the test cables of the GHCA-120/220 to the compressor motor as follows:

    a. yellow GROUND cable to the compressor motor frame

    b. red START cable to the start terminal

    c. black RUN cable to the run terminal.

    (Leave the white COMMON cable disconnected until Step 10.)

6. Use an adapter cord of at least No. 14 AWG wire size to connect the GHCA-120/220 to the 220-V ac input terminals.

7. Turn on the power to the GHCA-120/220.

Note: Remember to keep the white COMMON cable out of the way. It will have 110 V ac on the clip.

8. Push the POWER switch to the ON position. Both line indicators (NORMAL and REVERSE) will light.

9. Flip the FAULT/CONTINUITY/START switch to the FAULT position and hold it there while pressing the red START TEST and black RUN TEST buttons in sequence. If either the START indicator or the RUN indicator lights, there is a short between that winding and the frame. *Stop* the test and replace the unit.

10. Turn off the 220-V ac power source to the GHCA-120/220. Then connect the white COMMON cable to the common terminal of the compressor motor.

11. Press, in turn, the GROUND TEST, START TEST, and RUN TEST buttons. Continuity in the circuit being tested is verified when the appropriate indicator lights. If the test indicates that either the run winding or the start winding is open, *stop* the test and replace the unit.

12. Select the appropriate motor start capacitor.

13. Flip the FAULT/CONTINUITY/START switch to the START position and hold it there while throwing the REVERSE/OFF/FORWARD switch to the FORWARD position. If the compressor starts, release the START switch. The compressor will continue to run. The compressor may be stopped by returning the REVERSE/OFF/FORWARD switch to the OFF position.

14. If the compressor does not start immediately, the rotor may be locked. Release the START switch and return the REVERSE/OFF/FORWARD switch to the OFF position.

15. To "bump" the compressor, flip the FAULT/CONTINUITY/START switch to the START position and hold it there while throwing the REVERSE/OFF/FORWARD switch to the REVERSE position. If the compressor starts immediately, release both switches.

16. Repeat Step 13 to ensure that the compressor will run in the forward direction. If the compressor does not start immediately in reverse, then release both switches. A locked rotor will result in excessive current being drawn by the compressor.

17. Steps 13 through 16 may be repeated a few times in an attempt to free a locked rotor, but be careful not to overheat the motor windings. If the compressor still does not start, it should be replaced.

18. Turn off the 220-V ac power source to the GHCA-120/220. Disconnect the GHCA-120/220 test cables from the motor compressor.

1. Electric power is measured with a(n) _____.

2. How does an electrodynamometer-type instrument differ from a galvanometer-type instrument?

3. The fixed coils of a wattmeter are _____ coils, and the movable coil is the _____ coil.

4. The stationary coils of a wattmeter are connected in _____ with the load.

5. Why does the potential coil of a wattmeter generally have a high-resistance resistor connected in series with it?

6. Does the reading on a wattmeter indicate whether the coils are being overheated?

7. The watt-hour meter is an instrument used for measuring _____.

8. How do you read a watt-hour meter?

9. The power factor of a circuit is the ratio of _____ to _____.

10. Power incapable of producing work is called _____ power. It is measured in _____.

11. What are instrument transformers used for?

12. Why should the secondary of a potential transformer always be grounded at one point?

13. In wiring diagrams, a dot on the primary or secondary of an instrument transformer identifies terminals that have the same _____.

14. What instrument is used primarily for measuring insulation resistance?

15. A permanent, continuous record of equipment operation over an extended period of time can be obtained by using a(n) _____.

16. A device that converts a signal of one kind into a corresponding signal of another kind is called a(n) _____.

17. What are some of the conditions that a typical hermetic compressor analyzer can check for?

Resistors

SELECTING AN OHMMETER

There is such a wide variety of ohmmeters on the market today that deciding which one to purchase can be a difficult task. Before making such a decision, you should be familiar with how ohmmeters function. This Lesson uses a generic "analog" ohmmeter and a generic "digital" ohmmeter to explain the basics of operation. Stand-alone ohmmeters do exist, but the ohmmeter function frequently is incorporated in a multimeter. Ultimately, a more important question than *What ohmmeter should I use?* is *What measurement range should I use—and why?*

USING AN ANALOG OHMMETER

 CAUTION: Before making *any* resistance measurements, turn off all power to the circuit being tested.

As explained in Lesson 1, all analog ohmmeters have two controls. They are the *range switch* and the *zero adjust control*. These are illustrated in Figure 3-1 on the next page.

The *range switch* allows the technician to use different ranges of resistance values by selecting different dial settings. The meter depicted in Figure 3-1 shows seven different ranges, labeled R × 1, R × 10, R × 100, R × 1,000, R × 10,000, R × 100,000, and R × 1 meg. In order to determine the value of the resistance being measured, the technician must read the value indicated on the scale by the pointer, and then multiply that number by the number on the range switch.

The main purpose of the *zero adjust control* is to compensate for battery age and for differences in resistance in the internal components of the ohmmeter. Note the location of the zero (which corresponds to full-scale deflection) on the scale shown in Figure 3-2 below. A typical ohmmeter has the zero on the right (low-resistance) end of the scale. The left (high-resistance) end of the scale displays the symbol for *infinity* (∞).

Assume that you have a resistor rated at 1,000 Ω (1 kΩ), with a tolerance of ±5%, and you wish to verify that the resistance value actually is within that range (950 to 1,050 Ω). First, set the range switch to the R × 1 function, and touch the test leads together. Then use the zero adjust control to set the meter needle to the zero reference position, as shown in Figure 3-3A.

Next, place the resistor to be tested across the test leads of the ohmmeter, as shown in Figure 3-3B. It may be difficult to tell exactly where the needle is pointing, because the increment markings are very close together at the far left end of the scale. Where the scale is "crowded," a much smaller portion of the scale represents a much larger resistance—and, therefore, there is a greater

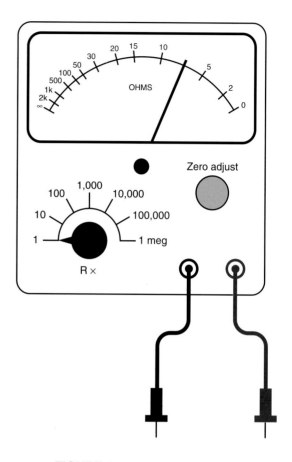

FIGURE 3-1. *Analog ohmmeter*

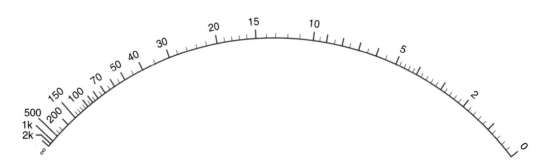

FIGURE 3-2. *Typical analog ohmmeter scale*

chance of inaccuracy and uncertainty. If the pointer appears to be indicating "1k," then the reading would be 1,000 Ω. (Because the range is set at R × 1, the resistance value indicated on the scale is interpreted as 1 × 1,000 Ω.) But the uncertainty of the reading in this case is more than ±5%.

To avoid the uncertainty that comes from taking a reading in this "compressed" region of the scale, a good strategy is to try using a range switch setting with a higher multiplier—say, R × 100. As shown in Figure 3-3C, the needle is now pointing at "10" on the scale. This also results in a reading of 1,000 Ω (derived by multiplying the resistance value indicated on the scale by the range setting multiplier, or 10 Ω × 100). A reading in the middle portion of the meter scale is much easier to read, and much less uncertain. You can tell, for example, whether the pointer is less than half a scale division on either

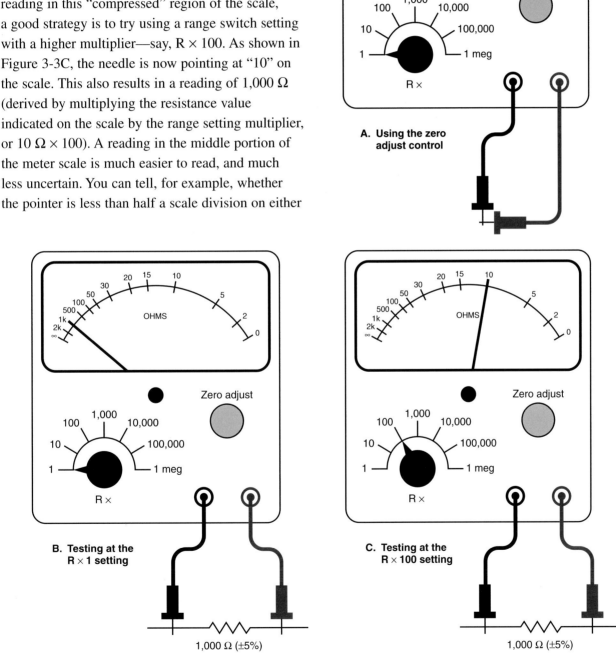

A. Using the zero adjust control

B. Testing at the R × 1 setting

C. Testing at the R × 100 setting

FIGURE 3-3. *Testing a 1,000-Ω resistor with an analog ohmmeter*

side of the "10" mark. And if the pointer is between 9.5 and 10.5 Ω, then (again using the range setting multiplier) your measurement is within ±5% of the resistor's 1,000-Ω rating.

As another example, suppose you wish to test a resistor rated at 1 MΩ (1,000,000 Ω) to verify that its resistance is within ±5 % of its indicated value. After using the zero adjust control as previously described, you place the resistor to be tested across the test leads of the ohmmeter. Figure 3-4A shows that if you set the range selector to R × 1, the pointer will indicate a resistance of near "infinity" (∞). A normal analog meter is not designed to read such high resistances on the R × 1 range setting.

Again, a good strategy for overcoming the uncertainty of such a reading is to set the range selector to another position—one that will enable you to obtain a reading near mid-scale. As shown in Figure 3-4B, if you use the R × 100,000 setting, the reading will be near "10," and 10 Ω times 100,000 (the range setting multiplier) is 1,000,000 Ω. As you can see, a reading near the middle of the scale is both easier to read and more reliably accurate.

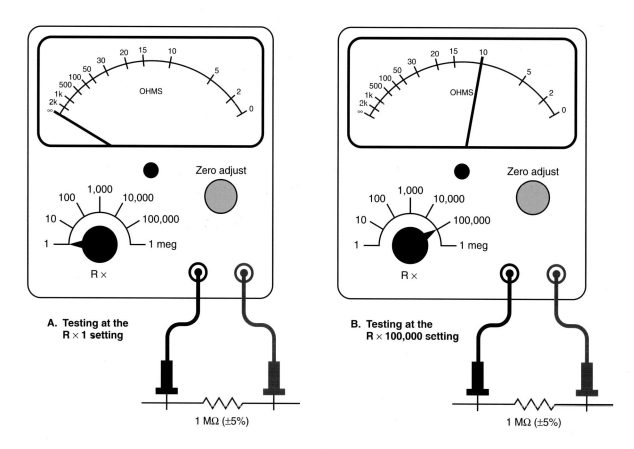

FIGURE 3-4. *Testing a 1-MΩ resistor with an analog ohmmeter*

In summary, because the scale of an analog ohmmeter is not *linear*, it can be difficult to obtain accurate readings for very high or very low resistances. This is why it is important to make a range selection that will cause the value of the resistance being measured to appear near the middle of the scale. (There are specialized ohmmeters that will measure very high or very low resistances, but most service technicians are not required to carry these.)

USING A DIGITAL OHMMETER

Advances in electronics have led to a great deal of change in the instruments used by HVACR service technicians. One result of this change is the development of the digital ohmmeter, which is probably the easiest piece of test equipment to use. Figure 3-5 depicts a typical digital ohmmeter. As you can see, there is a range switch similar to that depicted for the analog ohmmeter, but this meter does not require a zero adjust control. Notice that there are only three numerical places on the digital readout display.

Digital ohmmeters are said to be *auto ranging* in some modes. This means that the meter will display exactly what is being measured, so you do not need to estimate the relative position of a pointer between two scale division marks.

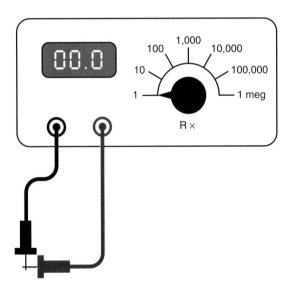

Like the range switch on an analog ohmmeter, the range switch on a digital ohmmeter allows the technician to use different ranges of resistance values by selecting dial settings with different multipliers. Assume, for example, that you are testing a resistor rated at 1,000 Ω (1 kΩ) with a tolerance ±5%. First, set the range switch to the R × 1 function. Place the test leads of the ohmmeter across the resistor to be tested, as shown in Figure 3-6A on the next page.

As you can see, the reading on the digital readout is "OL," or "over the limit" of the ohms scale. This is because the average digital ohmmeter set to the R × 1 range will read only up to 99.9 Ω. If you move the range selector switch to the R × 10 position, as shown in Figure 3-6B on the next page, the reading will still be "OL." This is because the average digital ohmmeter set to the R × 10 range will read only up to 999 Ω.

FIGURE 3-5. *Digital ohmmeter*

Since the resistor under test has a tolerance of ±5 %, the value of the resistance can be expected to be between 950 and 1,050 Ω. However, since the second

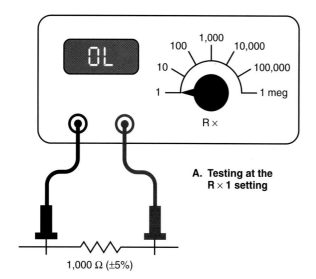

A. Testing at the R × 1 setting

1,000 Ω (±5%)

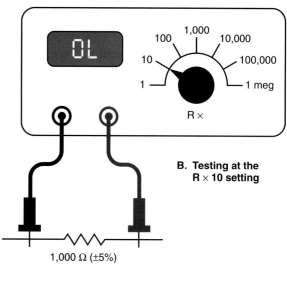

B. Testing at the R × 10 setting

1,000 Ω (±5%)

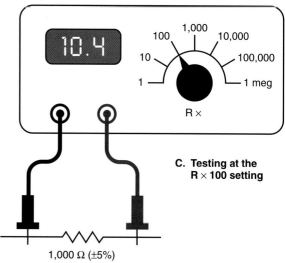

C. Testing at the R × 100 setting

1,000 Ω (±5%)

FIGURE 3-6. *Testing a 1,000-Ω resistor with a digital ohmmeter*

reading was "OL," the resistor must be on the "plus" side of the 5% tolerance—that is, more than 1,000 Ω. If you advance the range switch to R × 100, as shown in Figure 3-6C, the digital display reads "10.4," which corresponds to 1,040 Ω (10.4 Ω × 100). Obviously, each time the range switch is moved to the next higher range, the decimal point will move one place to the left in the digital display.

Now assume that you wish to test a resistor rated at 1 MΩ (1,000,000 Ω) to verify that its resistance is within ±5 % of its indicated value. If the range switch is set to the R × 1 position, and the resistor to be tested is placed across the test leads of the ohmmeter, as shown in Figure 3-7A, the meter reading is "OL." As stated before, this is because the average digital ohmmeter set to the R × 1 range will read only up to 99.9 Ω.

Advance the range switch to R × 10, as shown in Figure 3-7B, and the reading is still "OL." The average digital ohmmeter operating at the R × 10 setting will read only up to 999 Ω. Now advance the range switch to R ×100, as shown in Figure 3-7C. Once again, the reading is "OL." When the range selector is set to R × 100, the meter will read only up to 9,990 Ω.

Advance the range switch to R × 1,000, as shown in Figure 3-7D, and you obtain a reading of "970." Because the multiplier is now set to 1,000 (R × 1,000), the value of the resistance being measured is 970,000 Ω. This is on the "minus" side of the resistor's ±5% tolerance (that is, between 950,000 and 1,000,000 Ω).

Finally, advance the range switch one more notch, to the R × 10,000 setting. As shown in Figure 3-7E, the reading now becomes slightly more precise. A readout of "97.2" means that the actual value of this resistor is 97.2 Ω × 10,000, or 972,000 Ω.

Note: If an analog meter reads infinity (∞) or a digital meter reads "OL" on all scales, the resistor is *open*, and it is bad.

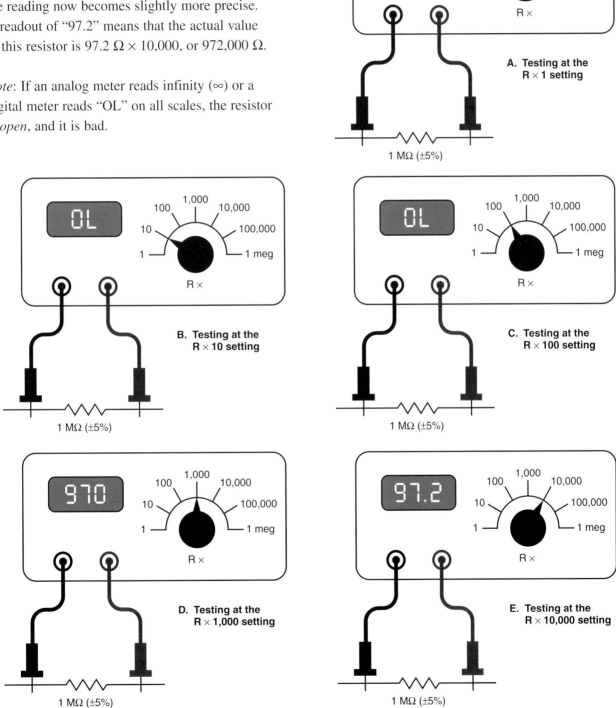

FIGURE 3-7. *Testing a 1-MΩ resistor with a digital ohmmeter*

RESISTORS

Fixed and adjustable resistors

Resistors come in a wide variety of sizes. Their size determines the amount of current that they can handle and how much heat they can dissipate. A *fixed* resistor is constructed so that its resistance value does not change. Most fixed resistors made today are of two types. *Carbon composition* resistors, which have a limited power-handling capacity, have a resistance element made primarily of carbon and sealed in a plastic case. *Wire-wound* resistors, which have a higher power-handling capability, are made of high-resistance wire wound around an insulated ceramic core and covered with a protective coating.

All small carbon resistors (from ⅛ W to 2 W) are marked with colored bands that indicate the resistance value. The color coding system is shown in Figure 3-8. (The carbon resistor in the illustration is not shown to true scale.) The color of the first band (working from left to right) indicates the value of the first digit of the resistance value of the resistor. The second band indicates the value of the second digit. The third color band represents a multiplier by which the first two digits must be multiplied. The last band indicates the tolerance—that is, the manufacturer's allowable deviation from the numerical value that you calculate from the first three bands.

Larger wire-wound resistors normally have the resistance value imprinted on the body of the resistor. Figure 3-9 is a representation of a typical wire-wound resistor. (Again, this is for illustration purposes only, and is not shown to scale.)

Sometimes it is necessary to have several different resistances packaged together. This is accomplished by using a large wire-wound resistor with *taps*, or contacts, at various points on it. Figure 3-10 shows the profile of a fixed tapped resistor.

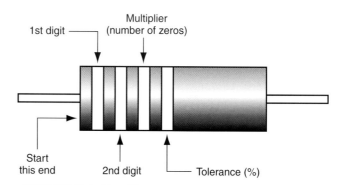

Color	Digits	Multiplier	Tolerance
Black	0	1	±20%
Brown	1	10	±1%
Red	2	100	±2%
Orange	3	1,000	±3%
Yellow	4	10,000	—
Green	5	100,000	±5%
Blue	6	1,000,000	±6%
Violet	7	10,000,000	±12.5%
Gray	8	0.01	±30%
White	9	0.1	±10%
Gold	—	0.1	±5%
Silver	—	0.01	±10%
No color	—	—	±20%

FIGURE 3-8. *Color coding for resistors*

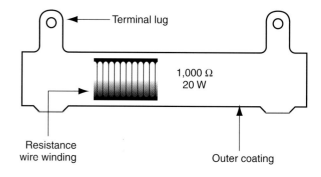

FIGURE 3-9. *Wire-wound resistor*

An *adjustable* resistor is similar in construction to a fixed wire-wound resistor, but with a metal band or collar that slides up and down the body of the resistor to make the tap adjustable. Note in Figure 3-11 that the resistance material is exposed, so that the metal collar will make contact at the desired point when the screw is tightened. Loosen the screw completely before moving the collar so that you do not damage the wire. Make sure that the power is off before adjusting the sliding contact.

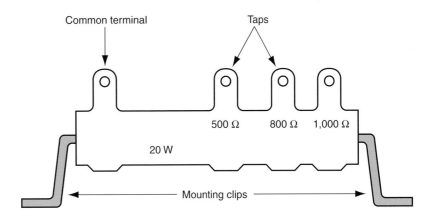

FIGURE 3-10. *Tapped resistor*

Variable resistors

There are two basic types of *variable* resistors. One is called a *potentiometer*, and the other a *rheostat*. Both have a resistance element, usually circular in shape, mounted in a case. Contact can be made to any point of the element by means of a rotating slider. The primary difference between them is that the potentiometer usually has *three* terminals, two fixed (one at each end of the resistance element) and one movable (for the sliding contact). The rheostat has only *two* terminals, one at one end of the element and one for the sliding contact. Figure 3-12 shows a potentiometer.

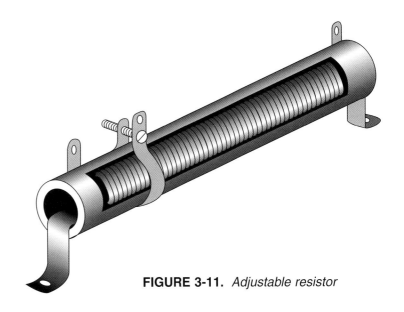

FIGURE 3-11. *Adjustable resistor*

TESTING TAPPED AND ADJUSTABLE RESISTORS

Note: Before testing any tapped or adjustable resistor with an ohmmeter, first disconnect the resistor from its circuit. A tapped or adjustable resistor is tested like any other resistor, with the exception that the tap, or slider, must be tested at both ends of the resistor. As an example, suppose that you are testing a 500-Ω resistor with the tap set at 225 Ω. (The tolerance rating for 90% of all power resistors is ±20%. Assume this to be true for this example.)

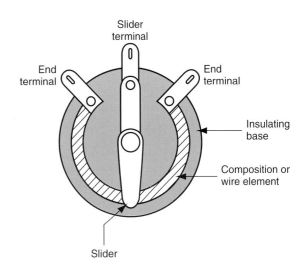

FIGURE 3-12. *Potentiometer*

First test the resistor at both ends, as illustrated in Figure 3-13A. Because the component being tested is a 500-Ω resistor, the ohmmeter range switch is set at R × 10. Note that the ohmmeter reading is "51.0." By applying the multiplier of 10, you can calculate the actual resistance to be 510 Ω. This is well within the specified 20%.

The next step is to determine whether the tap is actually connected. In the first step, you proved that the resistor is good—that is, the correct resistance was measured from one terminal to the other. Now move one test lead to the tap, as shown in Figure 3-13B, and leave the other test lead connected to one end of the resistor.

It does not make a difference *which* end of the resistor you choose, because a simple calculation will determine which is closest to the intended 225 Ω. Notice that the digital display now reads "23.6," or 236 Ω, well within the specified 20%. If you move the test probe to the other end of the resistor, you will obtain a reading of 264 Ω (500 − 236 = 264).

You can use the same procedure to test an adjustable resistor, but it is quite possible that the slide will be corroded. It may even be unstable in its position, resulting in unwanted movement and an inaccurate reading.

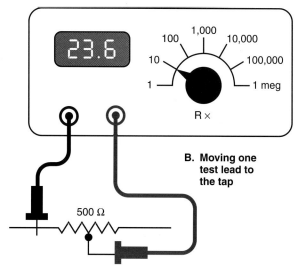

A. Testing the resistor at both ends

B. Moving one test lead to the tap

FIGURE 3-13. *Testing a tapped resistor*

TESTING VARIABLE RESISTORS

When you test potentiometers and rheostats, be aware that the center terminal, or arm, is movable, and can be positioned at any point on the resistor. As an example, consider a standard wire-wound 135-Ω control potentiometer, with the arm positioned at one end of the control. (Again, assume the tolerance rating to be ±20%.)

As always, first disconnect the resistor from its circuit. Then test the potentiometer at both ends, as shown in Figure 3-14A. Because the potentiometer is rated at 135 Ω, the ohmmeter range switch is set at R × 10. Note that the ohmmeter reading is "13.8." By applying the multiplier of 10, you can calculate that the actual resistance being measured is 138 Ω. This is well within the specified 20%.

To determine whether the arm is making good contact with the potentiometer, place one of the test leads on the arm and leave the other lead in place, as shown in Figure 3-14B. In this step, because both test probe connections are at essentially the same point on the potentiometer, the digital display reads "00.0."

By moving the arm to the midpoint of the potentiometer, you can expect the reading to increase to some value that is indicative of about half the total resistance. As shown in Figure 3-14C, the meter now reads "7.0," or 70 Ω.

TESTING BLEEDER RESISTORS

A *bleeder resistor* draws a fixed current and is often used, as a safety measure, to discharge a capacitor when power is no longer being supplied to it. The typical bleeder resistor is permanently connected to a capacitor, and can be difficult to remove. It is connected in parallel with the capacitor's terminals, and you may get a false reading if the capacitor is defective. Most bleeder resistors are rated at 15,000 Ω (brown-green-orange in Figure 3-8), with a ±20% tolerance. If you set the ohmmeter's range selector switch at R × 1,000, you should obtain a reading of "15." If you are in doubt about the condition of a bleeder resistor, remove it. Replace the bleeder resistor or the capacitor, or both.

TESTING THERMISTORS

A *thermistor* is a solid-state device that changes resistance with changes in temperature. Thermistors come in a many different sizes and shapes, but only two basic classifications. The first is the NTC (*negative temperature coefficient*) thermistor. As the temperature around or through the NTC thermistor increases, its resistance decreases. The second is the PTC (*positive temperature coefficient*) thermistor. When the temperature around or through the PTC thermistor increases, its resistance also increases. Both NTC and PTC thermistors are used as protective devices for motors and compressors, as sensors in thermostats, and as remote sensors for temperature-testing equipment.

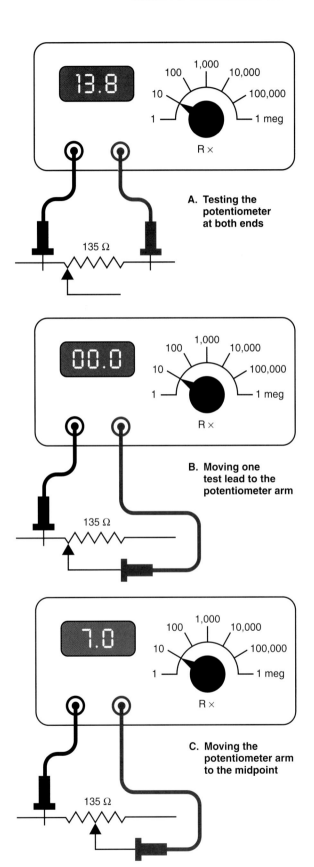

A. Testing the potentiometer at both ends

B. Moving one test lead to the potentiometer arm

C. Moving the potentiometer arm to the midpoint

FIGURE 3-14. *Testing a potentiometer*

To test a thermistor, you first must remove it from its associated circuits in order to prevent inaccurate readings. Check the manufacturer's specifications for the particular device that you are testing. As an example, consider a thermistor that the manufacturer has specified as having a resistance of 1,000 Ω at 32°F. Figure 3-15 shows a thermistor placed in a glass of ice water (32°F), with the range selector switch of the ohmmeter set at R × 100. (In reality, the thermistor would be much smaller in relation to the glass of water.)

After waiting for at least ten minutes, check the ohmmeter reading. In this case, the digital display reads "10.0," which means that the resistance is indeed 1,000 Ω. This indicates that the thermistor is good. If the reading was less than "9.9" or greater than "10.1," the thermistor would be considered defective. Most thermistors are extremely accurate (to within ±1%).

Thermistor manufacturers generally supply a chart similar to the one depicted in Table 3-1. It shows data for a PTC thermistor, the type that undergoes an increase in resistance with an increase in temperature.

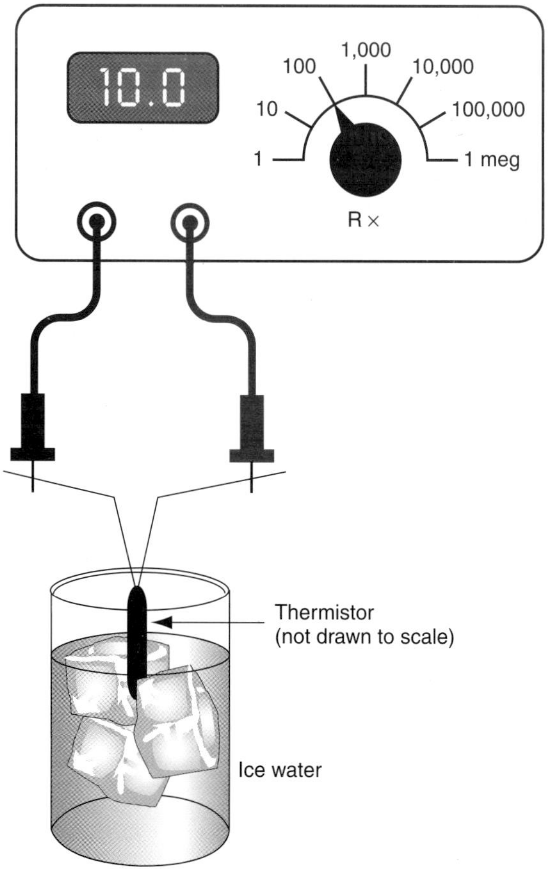

FIGURE 3-15. *Testing a thermistor*

PTC start-assist devices

A form of PTC thermistor is frequently used as a "start-assist" device. The PTC start-assist device is installed on a compressor to aid in starting the compressor under low-voltage conditions. There are many of these PTC start-assist devices on the market today.

When start-assist devices are hot, or when current is passing through them, their resistance is high—usually in the range of several thousand ohms. When they are cold, their resistance is low—anywhere from 12 to 100 Ω. Contact the manufacturer for the correct values. Once again, when you test one of these devices, first disconnect it from the circuit and turn off the power.

TESTING DIODES AND RECTIFIERS

There are special testers on the market that can be used to check the breakdown voltages of most diodes. Generally speaking, most digital ohmmeters do not accurately read diode resistances. The following paragraphs explain how to use an analog ohmmeter for testing the resistance of a diode.

Temperature, °F	Resistance, Ω	Temperature, °F	Resistance, Ω
−20	896	+70	1076
−18	900	+72	1080
−16	904	+74	1084
−14	908	+76	1088
−12	912	+80	1092
−10	916	+82	1096
−8	920	+84	1100
−6	924	+86	1104
−4	928	+88	1108
−2	932	+90	1112
0	936	+92	1116
+2	940	+94	1120
+4	944	+96	1124
+6	948	+98	1128
+8	952	+100	1132
+10	956	+102	1136
+12	960	+104	1140
+14	964	+106	1144
+16	968	+108	1148
+18	972	+110	1152
+20	976	+112	1156
+22	980	+114	1160
+24	984	+116	1164
+26	988	+118	1168
+28	992	+120	1172
+30	996	+122	1176
+32	1000	+124	1180
+34	1004	+126	1184
+36	1008	+128	1188
+38	1012	+130	1192
+40	1016	+132	1196
+42	1020	+134	1200
+44	1024	+136	1204
+46	1028	+138	1204
+48	1032	+140	1212
+50	1036	+142	1216
+52	1040	+144	1220
+54	1044	+146	1224
+56	1048	+148	1228
+58	1052	+150	1232
+60	1056	+152	1236
+62	1060	+154	1240
+64	1064	+156	1244
+66	1068	+158	1248
+68	1072	+160	1252

TABLE 3-1. *Temperature-resistance chart for PTC thermistor*

Conduction test

As you know, a diode conducts current in one direction only. To check for the conduction of current through a diode, use an analog ohmmeter set at the R × 1,000 range. You do not need to know the polarity of the test leads for this quick test:

1. Disconnect the diode being tested from its circuit.

2. Place the test leads across the diode, as shown in Figure 3-16A.

3. Note whether the meter reads high or low.

4. Reverse the leads of the diode, as shown in Figure 3-16B, and you should get an opposite meter reading.

You can tell that the diode has been turned around because the banded and rounded end of the diode in the drawing is now facing left instead of right. (Diodes are marked to distinguish the cathode end from the anode end. The banded and/or rounded end designates the cathode end of a diode.)

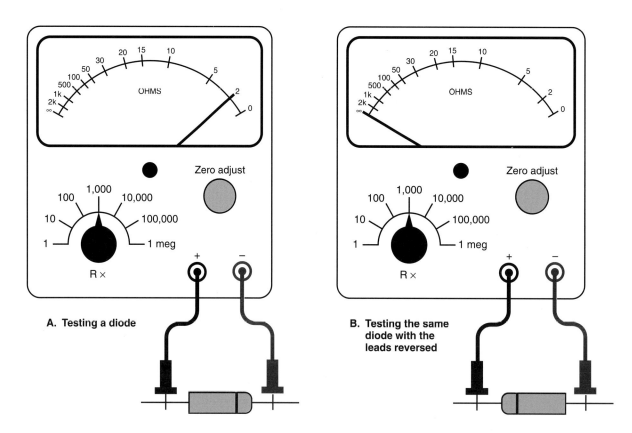

A. Testing a diode

B. Testing the same diode with the leads reversed

FIGURE 3-16. *Diode conduction test*

There is no conduction, of course, when the meter indicates an infinite resistance. In this example, then, the orientation of the diode shown in Figure 3-16A is such that it permits conduction. There is no conduction through the diode as it is shown being tested in Figure 3-16B.

A test of this kind on a diode will reveal one of four different results. The diode may be good, open, short, or leaking (that is, there is high resistance in both directions).

Polarity test

As stated earlier, diodes conduct current in one direction only. There are many times when it is important for you to know the actual direction of the current through a diode. To correctly identify the diode's characteristics, you must know the polarity of the test leads of the meter that you are using. All analog ohmmeters are battery-operated, but not all manufacturers connect the negative terminal of the battery to the negative test lead. To make this distinction, you need a good diode with visible markings.

Recall that a forward-biased diode conducts current, and a reverse-biased diode does not. Figure 3-17A shows the negative terminal of a battery (–) connected to the cathode of a diode (K), and the positive terminal of the battery (+) connected to the anode (A). This is a *forward-biased* diode. In Figure 3-17B, the negative terminal of the battery is connected to the anode, and the positive terminal of the battery is connected to the cathode. This is a *reverse-biased* diode. Current will not pass through a reverse-biased diode unless the diode is shorted or leaking.

Once you know the direction of current in the ohmmeter, you can determine the polarity of the test leads and mark them accordingly. Figure 3-18A on the next page shows the negative lead of the ohmmeter placed on the cathode end of the diode (the end with the band or arrow), and the positive lead on the anode end. You would normally expect this to be a forward bias. But note that the ohmmeter's needle is not deflected—and, therefore, the diode is not conducting.

Figure 3-18B on the next page shows the diode connected in reverse fashion (that is, the negative lead of the ohmmeter is connected to the anode, and the positive lead is connected to the cathode). This would appear to be a reverse bias, but the meter now shows deflection, meaning that there is conduction.

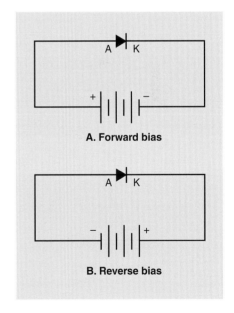

A. Forward bias

B. Reverse bias

FIGURE 3-17. *Forward-biased and reverse-biased diodes*

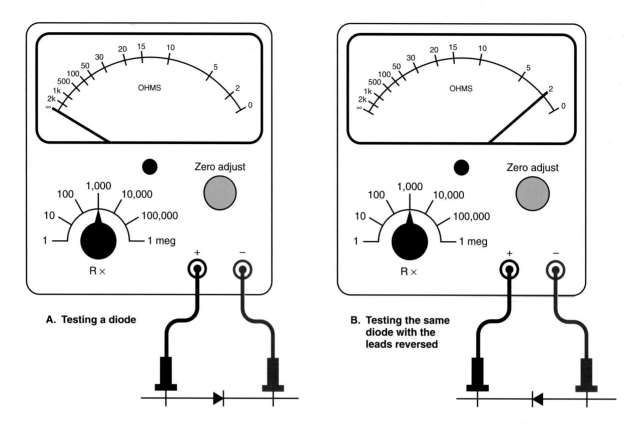

A. Testing a diode

B. Testing the same diode with the leads reversed

FIGURE 3-18. *Diode polarity test*

Because there is conduction when the positive lead is placed on the cathode, you can conclude that the negative terminal of the meter's battery is connected to the positive test lead. This will not be true in all cases, but it is a frequent occurrence.

Test results

As stated earlier, tests on diodes may reveal any of four different conditions:

- **Good.** A *good* diode shows high resistance in the reverse-bias mode, and low resistance in the forward-bias mode. This was illustrated in Figures 3-16A and 3-16B.

- **Open.** An *open* diode is one that has a break in the junction, or in the wires that connect to its elements. When you test an open diode, the ohmmeter will read infinity (∞), regardless of the direction of the applied bias.

- **Shorted.** A *shorted* diode is one in which there has been a breakdown in the *P* and *N* materials—that is, the two different materials that the diode is made of have fused together because of excessive voltage or excessive heat. When you test an shorted diode, the ohmmeter will read 0 Ω (or show a very low reading), regardless of the polarity of the test leads.

- **Leaky.** A *leaky* diode is one in which there has been a small breakover in the junction, or in the wires that connect to its elements. When you test a leaky diode, the ohmmeter will indicate a very high resistance, no matter which way the probes are applied.

MISCELLANEOUS TESTS

Ohmmeters make very good continuity testers. They can be used to find shorts and breaks in wiring, and to test relay points and contactor contacts. They also can be used to test other devices, such as motor windings, relay coils, and transformer windings. These uses will be covered in future Lessons.

1.   What must you do before making any resistance measurements?

2.   What is a range switch multiplier?

3.   The zero is located at the far _____ end of an analog ohmmeter's scale, and the symbol for infinity is at the far _____ end.

4.   Why is it a good idea to use a range switch setting that results in a reading in the middle portion of the meter scale?

5.   What is the advantage of *auto ranging* in the display characteristics of a digital ohmmeter?

6.   Suppose that a digital ohmmeter is used to measure a 1-MΩ resistor with a tolerance rating of ±5%. If the meter's range switch is set at R × 100,000, and the digital display reads "9.6," is the resistor's actual value in agreement with the manufacturer's specifications?

7.   The average digital ohmmeter set to the R × 1 setting will read only up to _____ Ω.

8.   When a digital ohmmeter reads "OL" on all scales, the resistor under test is _____.

9.   What is the rated value of a resistor with the following colored bands, in order from left to right: orange, black, blue, silver?

10.   What is the primary difference between a potentiometer and a rheostat?

11.   What type of resistor is usually connected in parallel with a capacitor?

12.   What is a *thermistor*?

13.   The resistance of an NTC thermistor _____ as its temperature increases. The resistance of a PTC thermistor _____ as its temperature increases.

14.   What are thermistors used for?

15.   Is the resistance of a cold PTC start-assist device high or low?

16.   When you test a diode, what does it mean if the resistance reading indicates an infinite resistance?

17.   What does it mean if there is conduction through a diode when the negative lead of an ohmmeter is connected to the anode and the positive lead is connected to the cathode?

18.   What are the four different conditions that tests on diodes might reveal?

19.   A good diode shows _____ resistance in the forward-bias mode.

20.   An ohmmeter will read _____ when you test an open diode in either bias.

Capacitors

TYPES OF CAPACITORS

This Lesson deals with capacitors used in the HVACR field. There are numerous types of capacitors, but not all of them pertain to the HVACR industry directly. As a service technician, you will usually find two types of capacitors in your daily work—the *start* capacitor and the *run* capacitor. Both are considered ac-only capacitors.

Of the two types, the *start* capacitor usually has a higher capacitance value and a lower voltage rating. The capacitance of a typical start capacitor ranges from 50 to 380 μF. Its voltage rating is usually in the 110 to 330-V range. It is normally encased in a plastic container. Figure 4-1 on the next page shows typical start capacitors.

Most start capacitors have a foil/paper/foil construction. The paper is usually coated with film or paste that increases both the dielectric strength and the capacitance. Because these capacitors can generate heat if left in a circuit too long, a fuse hole or "pop-out" hole in the top of the capacitor is designed to release any gases that could be built up from heat.

A *run* capacitor usually has a lower capacitance value and a higher voltage rating. The capacitance of a typical run capacitor ranges from 5 to 50 μF.

Its voltage rating is usually in the 370 to 440-V range. A run capacitor is normally encased in a metal container, although newer run capacitors are now being manufactured in plastic containers. Figure 4-2 shows typical run capacitors.

Almost all run capacitors use oil and paper as the dielectrics. At one time, the capacitors were filled with PCBs (polychloride biphenyls). When these chemical compounds were discovered to cause cancer, all manufacturing of this type of capacitor was stopped and oil was once again used as the dielectric. Because of the hazards involved with oil, a system of protection was devised to prevent fires from occurring within the equipment. Figure 4-3 shows how a fusing device is incorporated into the capacitor. This safety feature is designed to prevent an explosion or fire that could result from a shorted capacitor, but it can also create a service problem if the capacitor is not discharged correctly.

MALLORY

Bleeder resistor

Pop-out hole

FIGURE 4-1. *Typical start capacitors*

TESTING CAPACITORS

CAUTION: Before making *any* capacitance measurements, turn off all power to the circuit being tested. Disconnect the capacitor and then discharge it correctly.

Discharging a capacitor

A capacitor can hold a charge for several days (depending on its size and capacitance value). The old "tried and true" method of discharging a capacitor was to use a screwdriver or jumper wire to short across the capacitor's terminals. Today's run capacitors have internal fusing, as shown in Figure 4-3. If you were to place a direct short across the terminals, you could possibly destroy a good capacitor. To prevent this, capacitor manufacturers recommend that a bleeder resistor be used as a discharging device. A 15,000-Ω, 2-W (brown, green, orange) resistor with jumper clips is the easiest and safest way to discharge a capacitor. If you are in doubt about whether a capacitor is charged or not, simply bridge the capacitor with the resistor.

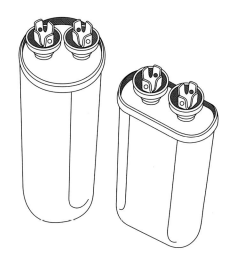

FIGURE 4-2. *Typical run capacitors*

There are four main problems that you may encounter when you test capacitors:

- an *open* capacitor, which occurs when one of the wires or terminals becomes disconnected from the foil or plate of the capacitor

- a *shorted* capacitor, which occurs when the dielectric between opposing plates breaks down and there is a direct short circuit from one plate or layer of foil to the other

- a *leaking* capacitor, which occurs when a partial breakdown of the dielectric allows a high-resistance path for a small current to pass between foils or plates of opposite polarity

- a capacitor that has *changed value*, which occurs when either the dielectric or the foil changes size due to excessive heat or overvoltage.

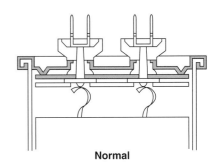

Normal

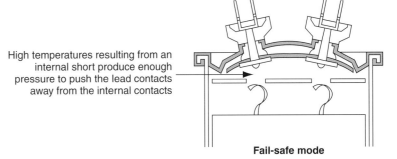

High temperatures resulting from an internal short produce enough pressure to push the lead contacts away from the internal contacts

Fail-safe mode

FIGURE 4-3. *Run capacitor safety*

The last condition can be measured only with a digital direct-reading capacitance meter, like the one shown in Figure 4-4 on the next page, or with a bridge-style capacitance meter. The various types of instruments used for testing capacitors are discussed below.

TYPES OF CAPACITANCE TESTERS

The types of capacitance testers with which you should be familiar include:

- neon light tester

- analog ohmmeter

- digital direct-reading capacitance meter

- bridge-style capacitance meter

- ammeter/voltmeter.

TIF INSTRUMENTS, INC.

NEON LIGHT TESTERS

A *neon light tester* is the least expensive unit to buy, and does an adequate job of testing capacitors. It will test fairly close to value, and it will discharge the capacitor when you have finished the test. Figure 4-5 is a simplified schematic of a typical neon light tester. Notice that there are three ranges of capacitors that can be tested. The paragraphs that follow explain the operation of a neon light tester.

Normal. If a good capacitor is placed across the test leads and the unit is plugged into a 115-V ac outlet, the neon light will glow when the test switch is pressed. This occurs because the capacitor is charged to its value by the range resistor. How long the light glows depends on the range switch setting and on the capacitance value of the capacitor. Usually it is a very brief period of time—perhaps 1 or 2 seconds. Then the capacitor is discharged through the limit resistor. The combination of capacitance and resistance in the circuit determines the *time constant*, which is the time it takes the capacitor to discharge.

FIGURE 4-4. *Digital capacitance meter*

Open. If an open capacitor is placed across the test leads and the unit is plugged into a 115-V ac outlet, the neon light will not glow at all when the test switch is pressed, regardless of where the range switch is set. This occurs because the capacitor is not connected in any part of the circuit.

Shorted. If a shorted capacitor is placed across the test leads and the unit is plugged into a 115-V ac outlet, the neon light will glow continuously when the test switch is pressed, regardless of where the range switch is set. This occurs because the capacitor is acting as one part of a complete circuit, together with the limit resistor and the neon light.

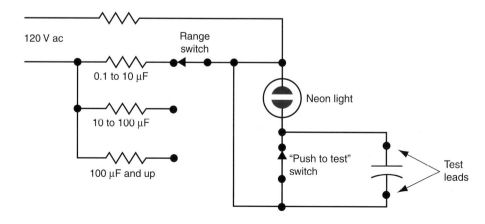

FIGURE 4-5. *Neon light tester*

Leaking. If a leaking capacitor is placed across the test leads and the unit is plugged into a 115-V ac outlet, the neon light will glow when the test switch is pressed, but it will "flicker." The light may continue to flicker for a long time before it goes out completely. This occurs regardless of where the range switch is set, because the capacitor is acting as a resistive part of the circuit.

Changed value. Most neon light testers will not be able to distinguish a capacitor that has changed value, unless the change is a drastic one. In field work, this is not normally the case.

ANALOG OHMMETERS

Figure 4-6 shows an analog ohmmeter connected to a run capacitor. When you test a capacitor with an analog ohmmeter, it is best to use the R × 10,000 setting of the range switch (or, if that is not available, the highest setting possible).

Normal. When you use an analog ohmmeter to test a good capacitor, the needle will swing first toward the low end of the scale, and then slowly move back toward the high (infinity) end. This occurs because the capacitor is charged to its value by the battery in the ohmmeter, and then discharged through the circuit in the meter. Reversing the test leads will repeat the process, so that again the needle will swing first toward the low end of the scale, and then back toward the high end.

Open. When you use an analog ohmmeter to test an open capacitor, the needle will not deflect at all, regardless of where the range switch is set. This occurs because the capacitor is not, in effect, connected to the meter.

Shorted. When you use an analog ohmmeter to test a shorted capacitor, the needle will deflect to the low end of the scale (it will probably read 0 Ω). This will occur for all range settings of the ohmmeter. Remember that run capacitors can also short to the case. The outside foil is connected to the terminal marked with a dot, and this side of the capacitor needs to be connected to the line side of the circuit. To test for a short to the case, place one test lead against the side of the case. Then, with the other test lead, touch each of the terminals in turn.

Leaking. When you use an analog ohmmeter to test a leaking capacitor, you will get a steady resistance reading. This may

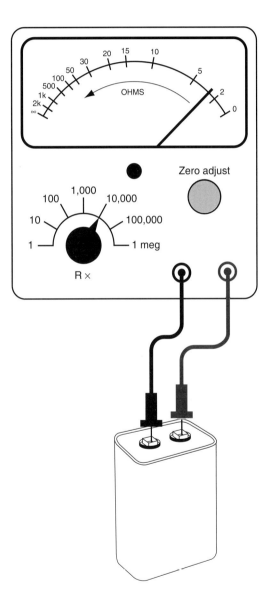

FIGURE 4-6. *Testing a run capacitor with an analog ohmmeter*

79

be a high-resistance leakage or a medium-resistance leakage. (A low-resistance reading indicates a shorted capacitor.)

Changed value. Analog ohmmeters will not be able to distinguish a capacitor that has changed value.

DIGITAL CAPACITANCE METERS

There are several varieties of digital direct-reading capacitance meters. Some are combination instruments that measure not only capacitance, but voltage, resistance, and inductance as well. Figure 4-7 depicts a typical digital meter used to measure capacitance only. Note that the dial settings of this meter start at 10 pF (a *picofarad* is a millionth of a millionth of a farad) and go to 1,000 µF. This is typical of digital capacitance meters, although the ranges will vary according to the particular instrument being used. As was the case with the digital ohmmeters discussed in

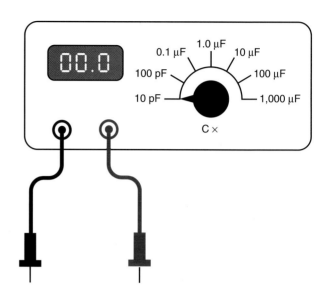

FIGURE 4-7. *Digital capacitance meter face*

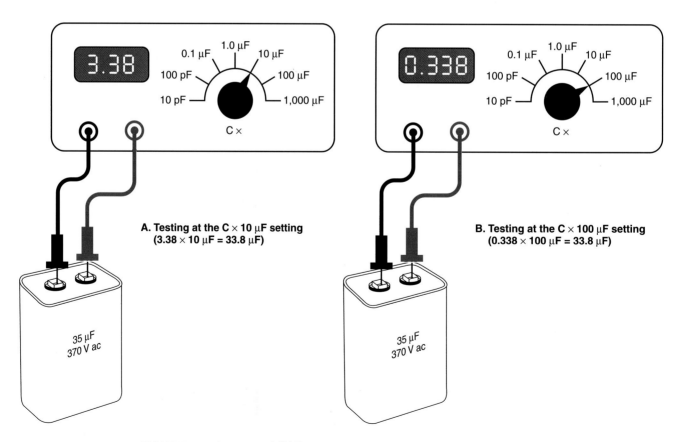

A. Testing at the C × 10 µF setting
(3.38 × 10 µF = 33.8 µF)

B. Testing at the C × 100 µF setting
(0.338 × 100 µF = 33.8 µF)

FIGURE 4-8. *Testing a run capacitor with a digital capacitance meter*

the previous Lesson, the digital readout must be multiplied by the number on the range selector.

Testing a run capacitor

Figure 4-8A shows a 35-μF, 370-V ac run capacitor under test. When the range switch is set to C × 10 μF, the digital readout ("3.38" in this example) should be multiplied by 10 μF (3.38 × 10 μF = 33.8 μF). Most ac run capacitors have tolerance ratings of ±10 to ±15%. In this example, the actual capacitance value of 33.8 μF is well within the ±10% range, which would be from 31.5 to 38.5 μF.

By moving the range switch to the C × 100 μF setting, as shown in Figure 4-8B, the decimal point is moved one place to the left, and the reading on the digital display is now "0.338" (0.338 × 100 μF = 33.8 μF).

Most digital capacitance meters will display a "1" or a "1x" if a capacitor is *shorted*. This is illustrated in Figure 4-9. If the capacitor is *open*, most digital capacitance meters will indicate all zeros ("00.0"). If the capacitor is *leaking*, the display will usually flash, or may indicate the capacitor to be shorted.

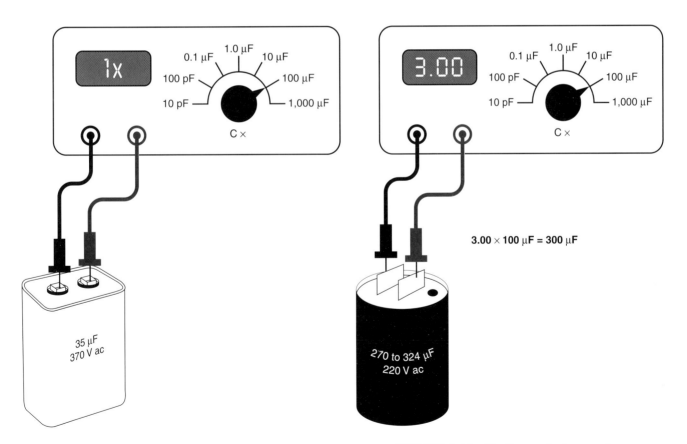

FIGURE 4-9. *Shorted capacitor*   **FIGURE 4-10.** *Testing a start capacitor*

Testing a start capacitor

Start capacitors, as stated earlier, usually have much higher capacitance values than run capacitors. They also have higher tolerance ratings (usually ±20 to ±25%). Figure 4-10 on the previous page depicts a start capacitor with a capacitance in the 270 to 324-μF range. Again, note the wide tolerance range of start capacitors. The meter in the illustration is reading 300 μF (3.00×100 μF), which is well within the tolerance range of the capacitor.

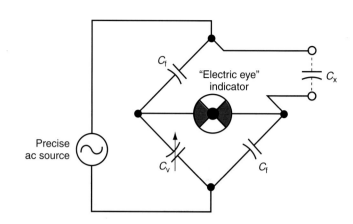

FIGURE 4-11. *Bridge-style capacitance meter*

Faulty start capacitors produce meter readings that are similar to those previously described for faulty run capacitors. That is, if a start capacitor is shorted, the digital readout will display a "1" or a "1x." If the capacitor is open, the display will read all zeros. If the capacitor is leaking, the display will usually flash, or may indicate the capacitor to be shorted.

BRIDGE-STYLE CAPACITANCE METERS

A *bridge-style* capacitance meter operates on the Wheatstone bridge principle. That is, a capacitor of unknown value is placed across a bridge circuit, and some form of indicator is used to show when the capacitance equals a standard value.

Figure 4-11 is a schematic of a typical bridge-style capacitance meter. In this circuit, a capacitor of unknown value (C_x) is placed across a bridge. When its capacitance is matched by C_v, the indicator shows a balanced or "null" (zero) effect—in this case, the "electric eye" closes. This type of instrument, now largely obsolete, had limited use, because it employed vacuum tubes and therefore required the use of a line voltage. It was, however, a very accurate device, and an extremely useful tool on the bench.

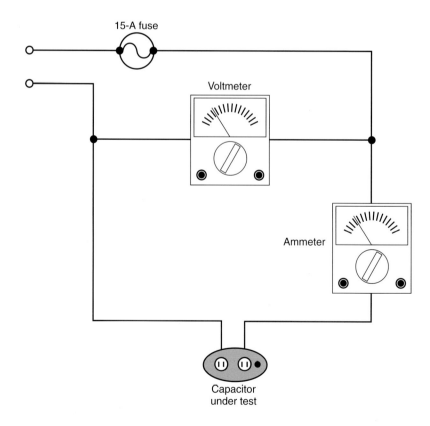

FIGURE 4-12. *Testing a capacitor with voltmeter and ammeter*

AMMETER/VOLTMETERS

Another method for testing capacitors uses a combination of a voltmeter and an ammeter. Figure 4-12 shows a typical circuit that can be used if there are no capacitance meters available.

To measure the value of a capacitor, set the voltmeter's range switch to the proper voltage setting and read the line voltage. Then set the ammeter to the appropriate current range and read the capacitor current. During the test, keep the capacitor connected for a very short period of time, because motor-starting electrolytic capacitors are rated for intermittent duty. The capacitance (in microfarads) can be computed by substituting the voltage and current readings in the following equation, which is good for 60-Hz power:

$$\mu F = \frac{2,650 \times A}{V}$$

Assume, for example, that you have a voltmeter reading of 240 V and an ammeter reading of 3 A. When these values are substituted in the equation, you can calculate the capacitance as follows:

$$\mu F = \frac{2,650 \times 3 \text{ A}}{240 \text{ V}}$$

$$= \frac{7,950 \text{ A}}{240 \text{ V}}$$

$$= 33 \ \mu F$$

An *open* capacitor will be evident if there is no current indication in the above test. A *shorted* capacitor will blow the fuse when the line switch is turned on. Therefore, the recommended practice is to use an ohmmeter to check for shorts before attempting this test. A clamp-on ammeter may be used in place of the normal ammeter for this test.

CAPACITOR SELECTION GUIDELINES

Table 4-1 lists typical capacitance ratings for start capacitors (used in capacitor-start motors and split-phase motors). Since design factors vary widely, these figures are intended merely to give an *approximation* of typical capacitor values. Always check the voltage of the capacitor, and *never* use a value lower than that specified by the equipment manufacturer.

Motor rating, hp	Capacitance, μF
1/8	75 to 90
1/6	88 to 108
1/4	108 to 120
1/4	124 to 138
1/3	161 to 180
1/2	216 to 240
3/4	324 to 420
1	400 to 480
1 1/2	485 to 540

TABLE 4-1. *Typical values for start capacitors*

Motor rating, hp	Capacitance, μF	Motor rating, hp	Capacitance, μF
$1/100$	2 to 3	$1/3$	14 to 15
$1/40$	2 to 3	$1/2$	10 to 15
$1/20$	3	$3/4$	15 to 20
$1/12$	5	1	15 to 20
$1/8$	5	$1 1/2$	25 to 30
$1/6$	7.5	2	30 to 35
$1/4$	7.5 to 10		

TABLE 4-2. *Typical values for run capacitors*

Table 4-2 lists typical capacitance ratings for run capacitors (used in permanent split-capacitor motors). Since capacitors usually operate at a voltage higher than the line voltage, always take the precaution of selecting a capacitor with a voltage rating that is the same as (or higher than) the voltage rating of the capacitor being replaced. Again, these guidelines are to be used as suggestions only—to prevent any problems with the motor, *always follow the equipment manufacturer's recommendations*.

1.   What are the typical ranges of capacitance and voltage for a start capacitor?

2.   Why do start capacitors have a fuse hole?

3.   What are the typical ranges of capacitance and voltage for a run capacitor?

4.   Why should you use a resistor instead of a screwdriver to discharge a capacitor?

5.   What is the recommended value (in ohms) of a resistor used to discharge a capacitor?

6.   What are the four main problems associated with capacitors?

7.   What happens when a capacitor becomes shorted?

8.   When you use a neon light tester to test a capacitor, what is the significance of a continuously glowing light?

9.   What will happen when you use an analog ohmmeter to test a good capacitor?

10.   What will happen when you use an analog ohmmeter to test an open capacitor?

11.   The terminal of a capacitor marked with a dot should always be connected to the _____ side of a circuit.

12.   What is a *picofarad*?

13.   When you use a digital capacitance meter, what reading is displayed if the capacitor being tested is shorted?

14.   When you use a digital capacitance meter, a reading of "00.0" indicates a(n) _____ capacitor.

15.   Start capacitors have typical tolerance ratings of _____%.

16.   When you use the ammeter/voltmeter method to determine capacitance, what is the approximate value of the capacitor if the ammeter reads 2.5 A and the voltmeter reads 245 V?

17.   What should you do *before* performing the ammeter/voltmeter test?

18.   Is a 5-μF run capacitor appropriate for use with a ¾-hp motor?

Relays, Contactors, and Starters

BASIC COMPONENTS OF A RELAY

Relays are electrically operated control switches, and may be classified as either *power relays* or *control relays*, according to their use. Power relays are frequently called *contactors*. Control relays are usually known simply as *relays*. This Lesson will examine troubleshooting techniques for relays, contactors, and starters used in the HVACR field. Figure 5-1 shows a typical pilot-duty relay. A *pilot-duty* relay usually controls less than 2 A of current at its contacts. Some relays, however, have more than one set of contacts. As you can see in Figure 5-1, there are four basic parts to the relay. The *coil* of wire becomes magnetized when a voltage or current is applied to it. The *armature* is connected to the *contacts*. (Generally, the armature and the contacts are electrically isolated from one another.) The *spring* keeps the relay in its normally open or normally closed position when no power is applied.

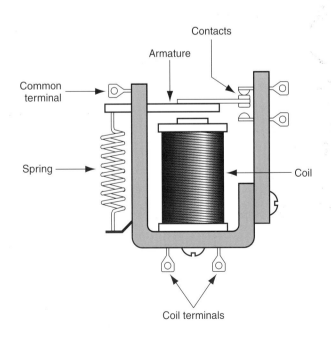

FIGURE 5-1. *Basic relay*

87

COMMON FAULTS

There are at least four common faults that you may encounter in working with relays:

- **Stuck armature.** This occurs when the armature (the moveable part of the device) becomes mechanically caught within the housing or frame of the relay.

- **Shorted coil.** This occurs when the windings in the coil have either shorted together, or to the frame of the relay.

- **Open coil.** This occurs when the wire has broken or has burned off due to excessive voltage being applied to the relay.

- **Burned or welded contacts.** This occurs when the relay has cycled too many times, or when too large a current has passed through the contacts, causing the metal points to fuse together.

TESTING PILOT-DUTY RELAYS

Testing the contacts

Most pilot-duty relays are housed in plastic containers. It may be difficult to see whether the contacts are burned or pitted, because the container is usually riveted together. If there are no visible marks indicating that the relay has burned or pitted contacts, most technicians will replace the suspected relay.

You can use an ohmmeter to determine if a set of contacts or points are welded (fused) together. As an example, look at the schematic of an SPDT relay shown in Figure 5-2. (Many manufacturers print the schematic diagram of the relay on the side of the relay itself.) In this case, numbers have been assigned to the terminals to make it easier to follow the testing procedure. In the normal position of the relay—that is, when no power is applied—terminals 1 and 2 are normally closed (NC) and terminals 1 and 3 are normally open (NO). When power is applied to the coil, these configurations will be reversed.

To test for a welded set of points or contacts, first make a diagram of the wiring, then disconnect *all* the wires. For the relay in Figure 5-2, use an ohmmeter to measure the resistance between terminals 1 and 2 (with no power applied). Your reading should be 0 Ω. If you measure anything other than 0 Ω, replace the relay. When you measure the resistance between terminals 1 and 3, you should get a reading of infinity (∞). If you get any other reading, replace the relay.

As stated previously, Figure 5-2 shows an SPDT (single-pole, double-throw) relay. Recall that there are numerous other contact configurations for pilot relays. Figure 5-3, for example, shows a DPDT (double-pole, double-throw) relay.

Testing the coil

With power applied to the relay, place a voltmeter across its coil. If voltage is detectable and the relay is not energized, it is the possible that the coil is *open*. To test for an open coil, first turn off the power, then disconnect the coil from all of its associated circuits. With an ohmmeter (either analog or digital), test the continuity of the coil. Because most small pilot relay coils are wound with very fine wire, the resistance may be anywhere from 5 Ω to several hundred ohms. If your ohmmeter displays an infinity reading on any scale, the relay coil is open, and you must replace the relay.

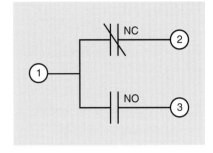

FIGURE 5-2. *SPDT relay*

Testing for a *shorted* coil is a little more difficult. Most technicians in the field will not know the actual dc resistance of the relay in question. However, if the control circuit fuse has blown, or if you do a voltage test across the coil and the voltage goes below 30% of its rated value, then you can assume that the coil is shorted. Depending on the type of relay, the average current draw of a pilot-duty relay ranges from 5 to 20 VA. This rated value can be obtained from the manufacturer's literature, and can be converted to amperes by dividing the volt-ampere rating by the control voltage.

Example. For an SPDT pilot relay with a 24-V coil and a sealed VA rating of 15 VA, calculate the current draw as follows:

$$A = \frac{15 \text{ VA}}{24 \text{ V}} = 0.208 \text{ A}$$

If this relay were to draw more than about 0.25 A, the coil could possibly have a short between the windings. (*Note*: The *sealed* VA is the VA rating for the relay when the armature is pulled all the way down on the coil.) Remember, though, that these are *typical* readings. It is recommended that the manufacturer's literature be consulted for each device that you encounter.

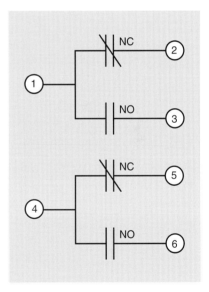

FIGURE 5-3. *DPDT relay*

TESTING LINE-DUTY RELAYS

A typical *line-duty* relay (also called a *switching* relay) has contacts rated from 8 to 12 A. Testing a line-duty relay is similar to testing a pilot-duty relay, but it is important to check for resistance between all terminal combinations. Most line-duty relays are DPST (double-pole, single-throw) devices. They control small motors or small compressors that have internal line protection. Figure 5-4 shows a general-purpose switching relay. This type of relay differs from a contactor in that the contactor is a repairable device, whereas a faulty line-duty relay must be replaced. Figure 5-5 is a schematic of a typical line-duty relay and its controlling coil.

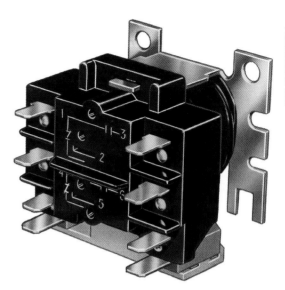

FIGURE 5-4. *General-purpose switching relay*

Testing the contacts

Most line-duty relays are *open* relays, which allows for visual inspection of the contacts. It is easy to see if they are burned or pitted. Almost all relay contacts are silver-plated over steel or cadmium. Any pitting or burning can increase resistance in the circuit. This additional resistance generates unwanted heat, and also may create a voltage drop across the contacts, thus reducing the voltage supplied to the motor.

Testing the coil

As was the case with the pilot-duty relay, the coil of a line-duty relay may be either open or shorted. To test for an *open* coil, first turn off the power, then disconnect the coil from all of its associated circuits. With an ohmmeter (either analog or digital), test the continuity of the coil. Because most line-duty relay coils are wound with heavier wire, the resistance normally will be low (anywhere from 0.5 Ω to several ohms), depending on the relay's construction and application. If your ohmmeter displays an infinity reading on any scale, the relay coil is open, and you must replace the relay.

Testing a line-duty relay for a *shorted* coil is similar to testing a pilot-duty relay. If the control circuit fuse has blown, you can assume that the coil is shorted. Depending on the type of relay, the average current draw of a line-duty relay ranges from 20 to 50 VA. Again, the rated value can be converted to amperes by dividing the volt-ampere rating by the control voltage.

Example. For a DPST line-duty relay with a 120-V coil and a sealed VA rating of 60 VA, calculate the current draw as follows:

$$A = \frac{60 \text{ VA}}{120 \text{ V}} = 0.5 \text{ A}$$

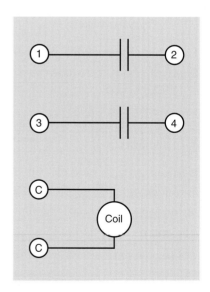

FIGURE 5-5. *Line-duty relay and coil*

If this relay were to draw more than about 0.5 A, the coil could possibly have a short between the windings. Always consult the manufacturer's literature for the ratings of a specific relay.

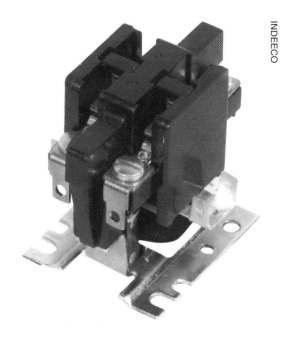

INDEECO

BASIC COMPONENTS OF A CONTACTOR

Figure 5-6 shows a typical contactor. A *contactor* is a heavy-duty power relay with contacts that are usually rated for 15 A or higher. The function of a contactor is to use a relatively small amount of electric power to control the switching of a larger amount of power. Constructed of the same four basic parts as a relay, a contactor can have as few as one set of contacts, or as many as five sets. Contactors are normally open—that is, they do not close until power is applied to the coil. Because a contactor can have more than one set of extra heavy-duty contacts, more power is required to pull in the armature.

FIGURE 5-6. *Typical magnetic contactor*

TESTING CONTACTORS

Contactors can be visually inspected for burned contacts, burned coils, and cracked cases. If you see any of these symptoms, replace the contactor. It is also a good practice to replace the contactor whenever the compressor or motor that the contactor controls has been replaced.

A contactor's mating contacts are sometimes referred to as *poles* (that is, a "three-pole" contactor has three sets of contacts). Figure 5-7 is a schematic of a typical three-pole contactor. Note that the terminals are marked T1, T2, T3, and L1, L2, L3. The "L" represents the line side, and the "T" represents the load side. (The "T" actually stands for the "transformer" side of the system in an older terminology.)

Many manufacturers in the past few years have found it economical to use single-pole contactors in single-phase residential equipment, and two-pole contactors in three-phase equipment. When you have to replace a single-pole contactor, it is advisable to use a two-pole contactor wherever possible. In three-phase systems, replace two-pole contactors with three-pole contactors.

Testing the contacts

If you are in doubt about the condition of the contacts, a simple test with a voltmeter will provide you with enough evidence to

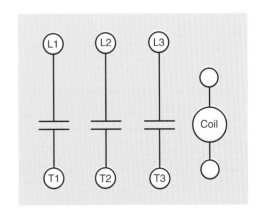

FIGURE 5-7. *Three-pole contactor and coil*

help you decide whether to keep the contactor or replace it. As stated earlier, contactors are designed to handle higher currents and voltages than control relays. Contactors are used mostly in line-voltage systems of 208-1-60, 230-1-60, 208-3-60, 360-3-60, and 575-3-60. Figure 5-8 illustrates the best way to tell if the contacts are good or bad.

The 20-V reading in Figure 5-8 is excessive. The maximum voltage drop across the contacts should be no more than 3% of the rated line voltage. If this is calculated for a 208-V system, the maximum voltage drop should be no more than about 6 V (0.03 × 208 V = 6.24 V). Thus, a voltage drop of 20 V tells you that the contactor must be replaced.

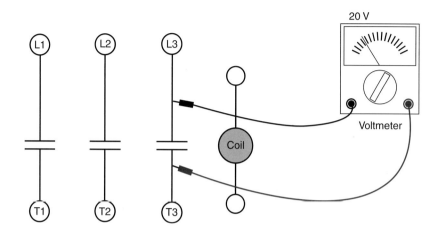

FIGURE 5-8. *Measuring voltage drop across the contacts*

Testing the coil

Like the coil of a control relay, the coil of a contactor is subject to two faults— it may be either open or shorted. To test for an *open* coil, first turn off the power, then disconnect the coil from all of its associated circuits. With an ohmmeter (either analog or digital), test the continuity of the coil. Most contactor coils are wound with heavy wire, and the resistance normally will be low (anywhere from 0.5 Ω to several ohms), depending on the contactor's construction and application. If your ohmmeter displays an infinity reading on any scale, the coil is open, and you must replace the contactor.

When you test for a *shorted* coil, it is doubtful whether you will know the actual dc resistance of the contactor in question. However, if the control circuit fuse has blown, you can assume that the coil is shorted. Depending on the type of contactor, the average current draw of a contactor ranges from 50 to 200 VA. You can obtain the proper figure from the manufacturer, and convert the rated value to amperes by using the same equation as you did for a control relay.

Example. For a two-pole contactor with a 120-V coil and a sealed VA rating of 150 VA, calculate the current draw as follows:

$$A = \frac{150 \text{ VA}}{120 \text{ V}} = 1.25 \text{ A}$$

If this contactor were to draw more than about 2 A, the coil might have a short between the windings. Always consult the manufacturer's literature for the specifications of a given contactor.

BASIC COMPONENTS OF A STARTER

A magnetic *starter* is the same thing as a contactor, but with some form of protection built into it. An *overload protector* is usually a thermally operated switch. As the current passes through the overload protectors, they get hot and open a switch in the starter's control circuit. The full current of the device being controlled is normally passed through them. Figure 5-9 is a picture of a three-pole starter that shows the overloads, contacts, and coil. Figure 5-10 is a schematic diagram of a three-pole starter that shows how the overloads and the coil are wired. As with all control circuits, they are wired in series.

FIGURE 5-9. *Full-voltage starter*

TESTING MAGNETIC STARTERS

Troubleshooting a magnetic starter is similar to testing a contactor. However, the overloads can create problems if they have been cycled too many times. They begin to lose their current-carrying capabilities, and tend to trip prematurely. The overloads are normally closed switches, and open when the overload element overheats. To test for an open overload, turn off the power, disconnect the switch from the circuit, and take a reading with an ohmmeter.

POTENTIAL RELAYS

Potential (or voltage) relays are used to assist in starting motors, and are also called "start" relays. Used in conjunction with a start capacitor, a potential relay consists of a coil and a set of normally closed contacts. A certain amount of voltage, called the *pickup* voltage, is required to open a potential relay. Once the motor attains full speed, the relay will be held in the open position. The *holding* voltage is considerably less than the pickup voltage. The relay will close again when the voltage drops to a certain level, called the *dropout* voltage.

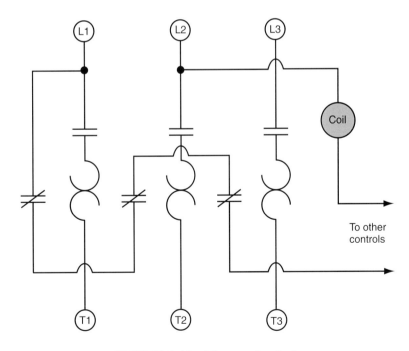

FIGURE 5-10. *Three-pole starter*

Figure 5-11 depicts a potential relay. The terminal numbers (1, 2, and 5) are always the same, regardless of the manufacturer. The terminals are connected as follows:

- Terminal 1 is always connected to the start capacitor.

- Terminal 2 is always connected to the start terminal.

- Terminal 5 is always connected to the common terminal.

There are as many designs of potential relays as there are relay manufacturers. It is beyond the scope of this Lesson to cover each of them. The following paragraphs refer to a "typical" or "generic" potential relay.

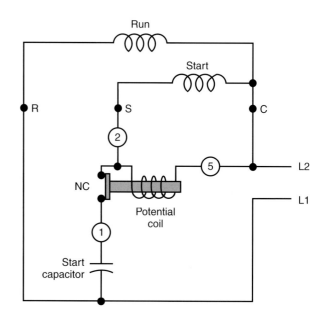

FIGURE 5-11. *Potential relay*

TESTING POTENTIAL RELAYS

You can use an ohmmeter to test a potential relay. A voltmeter can be used to measure the pickup and dropout voltages.

First turn off the power to the device, and disconnect all the wires from the relay. Place the test leads of your ohmmeter across terminals 1 and 2. You should read continuity. If you do not, the contacts are open and the relay must be replaced.

Testing the coil of a potential relay can be difficult, because there are a number of different coil voltages that must be considered—pickup, holding, and dropout. The resistance of most potential relay coils can range from a few ohms to several hundred ohms. This is because the pickup voltage can range from 160 to 310 V, the holding voltage can range from 110 to 250 V, and the dropout voltage can range from 40 to 150 volts. However, if you measure infinite resistance between terminals 2 and 5, the coil is open and you must replace the relay. When you have to replace a potential relay, it is a good idea to replace the start capacitor as well.

Using a relay tester

There are several commercial relay testers on the market. Some models can be used on both 120-V and 240-V circuits. By means of indicator lights, such a device can show you the relay's pickup, holding, and dropout voltages. It can also tell you if the contacts are fused together, or if they are open. Because there are so many different types of relays, this Lesson cannot describe how to test all of them. However, with a relay tester and the information that you can obtain from the manufacturer's literature, you can test most potential relays simply and efficiently.

CAUTION: When you test potential relays, be aware that there may be very high voltages present.

Testing the relay in operation

The next test requires the equipment to be powered. Set your voltmeter to the highest ac scale and clip the test leads to terminals 2 and 5. The initial voltage reading will be the pickup voltage—the voltage at which the relay will open, taking the start capacitor out of the circuit. As the motor comes up to speed, the voltage will decrease to the holding voltage—the voltage at which the relay will stay open. Make a note of these voltages, and then check the manufacturer's specs to see if the relay is opening and closing at the proper voltages.

CURRENT RELAYS

Current relays are also "start" relays, but it is the current through the motor's run winding that operates the relay. Current relays are normally open relays, usually found on smaller-horsepower motors. In some cases, a start capacitor is used in conjunction with a current relay. You can recognize a current relay by the coil of heavy wire wound around the armature. Figure 5-12 depicts a current relay. It shows the armature, coil, and normally open contacts.

The terminals on a current relay are connected as follows:

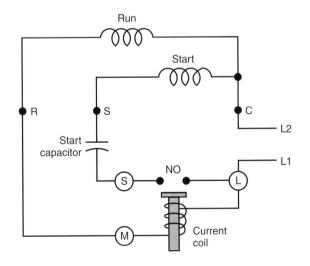

FIGURE 5-12. *Current relay*

■ The "L" terminal is connected to the line voltage.

■ The "M" (for *main*) terminal is connected to the motor's run winding.

■ The "S" terminal is connected to the motor's start winding.

A current relay works in one position only. The "top" of the relay is usually marked or identified in some way. If the relay is not mounted in a straight up-and-down position, the movable armature may rub against the sides of the relay body.

TESTING CURRENT RELAYS

When you test a current relay out of the circuit, make sure that you keep the relay in the correct position. Place the test leads of your ohmmeter across terminals "S" and "L," and you should read infinity (an open set of contacts). If any other resistance is indicated between these two terminals, replace the relay. In order to test the relay mechanically, try turning the relay upside down while the ohmmeter is still connected. The contacts should close and the meter will read 0 Ω. If the contacts do not close, replace the relay.

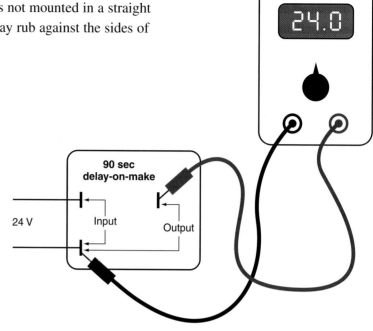

FIGURE 5-13. *Testing a delay-on-make relay*

Because the coil is made of very heavy wire, its resistance is very low. For this reason, it is difficult to test the coil's resistance accurately. (The wire has to be heavy because the coil is connected in series with the run winding of the motor, as shown in Figure 5-12.) It is not practical to test current relays in the field, unless you have a current relay tester. A typical current relay tester will measure the current at which the relay closes, and the current at which it opens again.

TIME-DELAY RELAYS

A *time-delay* relay is a relay in which there is an interval of time between the energizing or de-energizing of the coil and the movement of the armature. Most time-delay relays are low-voltage devices (usually 24 V), so it is relatively easy to test them. However, you must know if the relay under test is a *delay-on-make* or a *delay-on-break* type. With a delay-on-make relay, the timer will not start its delay until power is *applied* to the circuit. A delay-on-break relay will not start its delay until power has been *removed* from the circuit.

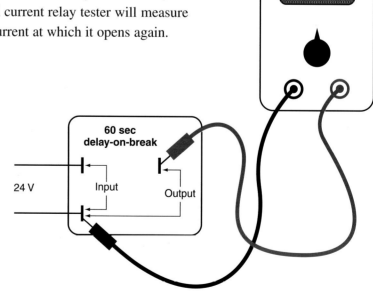

FIGURE 5-14. *Testing a delay-on-break relay*

Figure 5-13 shows a delay-on-make relay under test. When power is applied to the timer, the timing period begins. This relay is normally open, and has a 90-second delay. Therefore, if you disconnect all the wires from the relay, connect a voltmeter as shown, and apply 24 V to the input, you should read 24 V at the output for 90 seconds (plus or minus 5 seconds). If the relay does not close after 90 seconds, or does not close at all, replace it.

Figure 5-14 shows a delay-on-break relay under test. This relay is normally closed. When power is removed from the relay, the timing period (60 seconds in this example) begins. Therefore, if you disconnect all the wires from the relay, connect a voltmeter as shown, apply 24 V to the input and then remove it, you should read 0 V at the output for 60 seconds (plus or minus 5 seconds). If the relay does not open after 60 seconds, or does not open at all, replace it.

1.   A pilot-duty relay usually controls a load that draws less than _____.

2.   Name the four basic components of a relay.

3.   List four common faults that you may encounter with relays.

4.   What is the "normal" position of a relay?

5.   When testing for a welded set of points or contacts, what should you do before disconnecting all the wires?

6.   If there is a measurable voltage across the coil of a relay, but the armature is not pulled in, the trouble may be a(n) _____ coil.

7.   If you test a the coil of a relay with an ohmmeter and find that the reading is infinity, what can you conclude?

8.   When you test the coil of a relay, what does it mean if the voltage goes below 30% of its rated value?

9.   If a relay with a VA rating of 20 VA has a control voltage of 24 V applied to its coil, what current does it draw when the armature is pulled all the way down?

10.   What does the term "sealed VA" refer to as it applies to relays?

11.   What are the consequences of burned or pitted relay contacts?

12. What is the maximum acceptable voltage drop across the contacts of a contactor?

13. What is the difference between a magnetic starter and a contactor?

14. The contacts of a potential relay are normally _____.

15. The voltage required to open a potential relay is called the _____.

16. What is the *holding* voltage for a potential relay?

17. What is the voltage at which a potential relay closes?

18. A potential relay has three active terminals. How are they numbered, and how are they connected?

19. The contacts of a current relay are normally _____.

20. Describe the terminal wiring connections for a current relay.

21. What are the differences between a *delay-on-make* time-delay relay and a *delay-on-break* time-delay relay?

Transformers

BASIC COMPONENTS OF A TRANSFORMER

A *transformer* is a device that can be used to increase ("step up") or decrease ("step down") voltage and current levels. The principal parts of a transformer are two coils of wire, called the *primary winding* and the *secondary winding*, wound on some type of *core* material. An *enclosure* protects the internal components from dirt, moisture, and mechanical damage. Figure 6-1 shows a schematic diagram of a simple transformer.

COMMON DEFECTS

There are at least five common faults that you may encounter in working with transformers:

- **Open primary.** This occurs when the coil of wire in the primary breaks or separates from the leads or terminals of the transformer.

- **Open secondary.** This occurs when the coil of wire in the secondary breaks or separates from the leads or terminals of the transformer. This condition also results from a blown internal fuse.

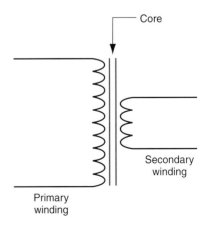

FIGURE 6-1. *Basic transformer*

- **Winding-to-winding short.** This occurs when the insulation on the coil of wire in the primary or secondary breaks down, and current can pass from one winding to the other.

- **Winding-to-case short.** This occurs when the insulation on the coil of wire in the primary or secondary breaks down, and current can pass directly to the case or ground.

- **Overheated transformer.** This occurs when the load or demand on the transformer is too great. This condition can be detected by discoloration of the winding area of the transformer.

TRANSFORMER RATINGS

A transformer is rated according to its primary voltage, secondary voltage, and power-handling capacity. The power-handling capacity of a transformer is measured either in watts or volt-amperes (VA). You can determine the maximum current that a transformer can safely handle by using a "rule of thumb" for converting volt-amperes to amperes. Simply divide the volt-ampere rating of the transformer by the secondary voltage.

Example. For a 40-VA transformer with a 120-V primary and a 24-V secondary, calculate the current draw as follows:

$$A = \frac{40 \text{ VA}}{24 \text{ V}} = 1.66 \text{ A}$$

The VA rating of the controlled devices must not exceed the VA rating of the transformer. If the total VA draw is greater than the transformer's rating, the secondary voltage can drop drastically, and the transformer will overheat. If you must replace a transformer, make sure that you select a transformer with a volt-ampere rating equal to or greater than that of the transformer being replaced.

RESIDENTIAL TRANSFORMERS

Figure 6-2 shows a typical low-voltage transformer with wire leads. This type of transformer is normally found in residential equipment. The primary voltage of such a transformer will vary according to whether the transformer is placed in a condensing unit or a furnace. If the transformer is in a condensing unit, the primary voltage is 230 V. If it is in a furnace, the primary voltage is 120 V. The secondary voltage will range from 24 to 28 V. Most residential transformers have VA ratings of 20 or 40 VA. Some may go as high as 75 VA for very large systems.

Figure 6-3 shows a typical low-voltage transformer with screw terminals and a dual-voltage or tapped secondary. The schematic diagram for this transformer is shown in Figure 6-4. This type of transformer is also found in residential equipment. In the past, it was frequently used where a lower voltage was required for some form of glow coil ignitor in a heating system.

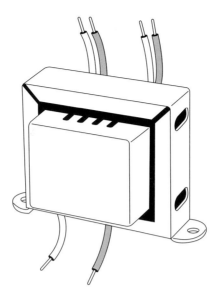

FIGURE 6-2. *Low-voltage residential transformer with wire leads*

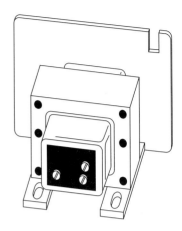

FIGURE 6-3. *Low-voltage residential transformer with screw terminals*

TRANSFORMER FUSING

Transformers with VA ratings of 40 VA and above usually have an *internal* fuse built into the secondary windings. This makes it imperative for the service technician *not* to short across the secondary with a screwdriver (to see if it "sparks"). If the secondary is shorted for any reason, the fuse will open and the transformer will have to be replaced. This can be a costly mistake. The schematic diagram for a transformer with an internal fuse is shown in Figure 6-5.

A number of newer transformers, especially the general replacement types, have an *external* fuse. Some local codes require external fusing, and some manufacturers make transformers with external fuses in order to meet UL approval. An external fuse may be an in-line type or a chassis-mounted type.

Regardless of the type of fuse, remember that if you find an open fuse, *something* must have caused the excessive current. Look for the trouble elsewhere in the circuit.

TESTING RESIDENTIAL TRANSFORMERS

To test a transformer, first turn off the power supply. Remove all the controlling circuits, and place a voltmeter across the terminals on the secondary side of the transformer, as shown in Figure 6-6 on the next page. Turn the power back on. The voltage read across the secondary, with no load, is called the *open circuit voltage* (OCV). The OCV is usually about 5 to 10% higher than the nameplate voltage. If no voltage is read, turn off the power, disconnect the

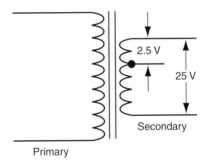

FIGURE 6-4. *Low-voltage transformer*

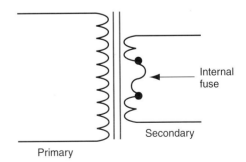

FIGURE 6-5. *Transformer with internal fuse*

transformer, and do a continuity test of the transformer's primary and secondary.

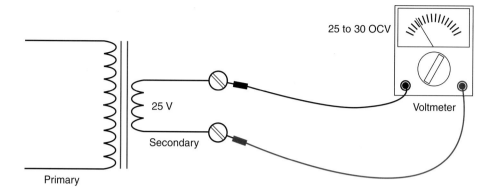

FIGURE 6-6. *Testing a residential transformer*

If there is a short in the secondary, usually the fuse will open, or the winding itself may be found open. If there is a short to the case or ground of the transformer, usually a circuit breaker will be open or a line fuse will have blown. This is because there is a potential difference between the primary and secondary windings of the transformer. As a result, a current is allowed to pass from the grounded case to the neutral wire of the transformer's primary winding. This is illustrated in Figure 6-7.

MULTI-TAPPED PRIMARY TRANSFORMERS

Some transformers have additional connections, called *taps*, made to the windings at points other than the ends of the windings. A number of residential replacement transformers have multi-tapped primaries. Figure 6-8 is a schematic of a typical multi-tapped primary transformer. The availability of multiple voltages makes this type of transformer ideal for replacement purposes. (The colors shown in Figure 6-8 may not pertain to all transformers out in the field. They are for example only.)

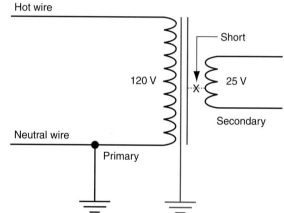

FIGURE 6-7. *Transformer with a short in the secondary*

TESTING MULTI-TAPPED PRIMARY TRANSFORMERS

 CAUTION: When you test multi-tapped primary transformers, be aware that there may be very high voltages present.

When testing or replacing a multi-tapped primary transformer, be sure that the leads that are *not* being used are taped off from each other, and cannot come in contact with the chassis or cabinet of the unit. There are very high voltages on the leads not being used. Look at Figure 6-8, for example. If a voltage of 120 V is applied across the white and black wires, 208 V will be present across the white and orange wires, 230 V across the white and brown wires, and 460 V across the white and red wires.

COMMERCIAL TRANSFORMERS

Commercial control transformers are usually larger physically and have greater power-handling capacities than their residential counterparts. Figure 6-9 shows a typical commercial control transformer. Transformers of this type can usually be identified by their open frame housings. They normally have spade or solder terminals.

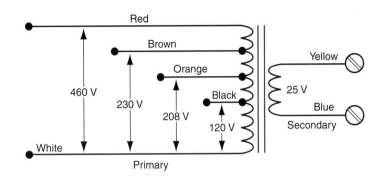

FIGURE 6-8. *Multi-tapped primary transformer*

Larger equipment requires more accessories. As a result, the VA ratings of commercial transformers are correspondingly higher—usually in the 500 to 2,000-VA (0.5 to 2-kVA) range. Large control transformers do not always have 24-V secondaries. A number of manufacturers utilize 120-V or even 220-V control circuits, especially if a three-phase power supply of 460 or 575 V is being used. Figure 6-10 is a schematic diagram of a typical transformer that has a 460-V, three-phase line primary and a 120-V secondary control circuit.

This type of transformer is very easy to troubleshoot. There is usually an external fuse in the secondary circuit and, if there is a problem in the controls circuit, the fuse will open and protect the transformer.

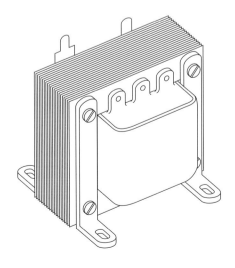

FIGURE 6-9. *Commercial control transformer*

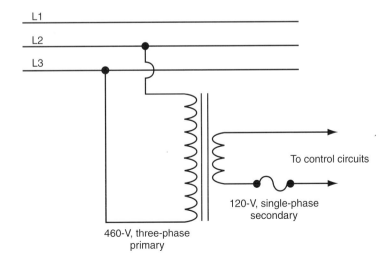

FIGURE 6-10. *High-voltage transformer*

MULTI-VOLTAGE COMMERCIAL TRANSFORMERS

Some large control transformers are used primarily to change three-phase line voltage to a lower single-phase voltage. These are multiple-winding transformers used to control fan motors and other devices that draw a heavy current but need a lower control voltage. The VA ratings for such transformers can range from 1 to 10 kVA. Figure 6-11 is a schematic diagram of a typical multi-voltage control transformer. Note the voltage variations on the primary and secondary windings of the transformer.

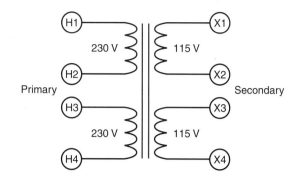

FIGURE 6-11. *Multi-voltage control transformer*

This transformer can be used for a number of different applications. By wiring together certain leads, you can obtain a variety of voltages. Figure 6-12 illustrates this by showing how the transformer can be wired with a 460-V primary and a 230-V secondary.

The terminals marked "H" are normally used for the primary windings, located on the high-voltage side of the transformer. The terminals marked "X" are normally used for the secondary windings, located on the low-voltage side of the transformer. However, this arrangement can be reversed with no adverse effect on the transformer as long as the circuit that the transformer is controlling operates at a voltage lower than the transformer's rated capacity. Additional versatility of this type of transformer is shown in Figure 6-13.

TESTING COMMERCIAL CONTROL TRANSFORMERS

 CAUTION: When you test commercial control transformers, be aware that line voltages will be present.

Control transformers vary considerably from one equipment manufacturer to another. However, the only three pieces of test equipment that you need for testing these transformers are a voltmeter, an ammeter, and an ohmmeter. First determine if there is voltage present at the transformer. If there is no voltage across the secondary, check the voltage across the primary. If there is voltage across the primary, then turn off the power and disconnect the transformer from all of

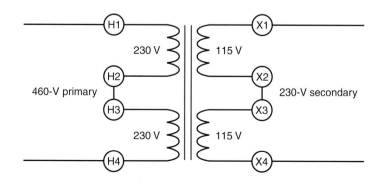

FIGURE 6-12. *Wiring a multi-voltage transformer for different voltages*

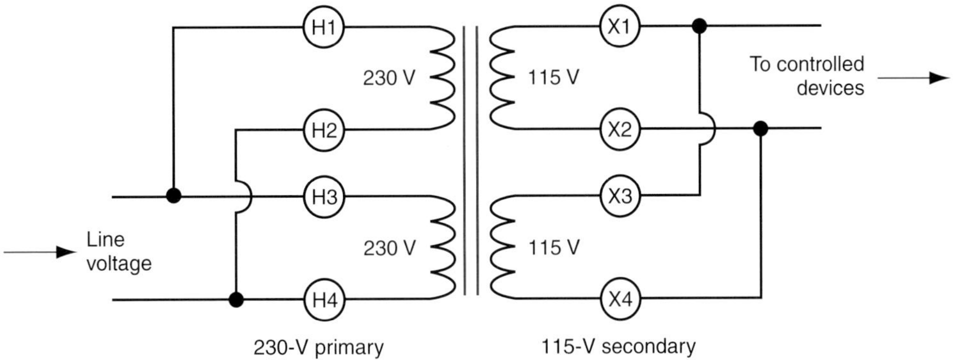

FIGURE 6-13. *Another wiring option for a multi-voltage transformer*

the controls. Use an ohmmeter to determine whether the primary or secondary windings are open. Of course, if you find an open winding, you must replace the transformer.

If there was a reason for the transformer to overheat without blowing the fuse, you can use an ammeter to determine the current draw of each of the items that are being controlled. Then use the same equation that you used before to find the current-carrying capacity of the transformer (i.e., divide the VA rating by the secondary voltage).

Example. For a 0.75-kVA transformer with a 115-V secondary, calculate the current draw as follows:

$$A = \frac{750 \text{ VA}}{115 \text{ V}} = 6.52 \text{ A}$$

The total load that this transformer can safely handle is 6.52 A. Any current greater than this will cause the transformer to overheat. This can happen when there are too many devices on the control circuit. There also could be a defective relay or contactor coil. Find the cause and repair it, or replace the transformer if necessary.

1. Name five common defects found with transformers.

2. How can you tell if a transformer has been overheated?

3. How are transformers rated?

4. How much current can a 60-VA transformer with a 24-V secondary safely handle?

5. What will happen if the VA rating of a transformer is exceeded?

6. The primary voltage of a residential transformer is either 120 or 230 V. What is the normal secondary voltage?

7. Transformers rated at over 40 VA are usually protected by a(n) _____.

8. What should you do when you find an open fuse in the transformer circuit?

9. What is the *open circuit voltage* of a transformer?

10. A transformer's open circuit voltage is usually _____% higher than the loaded secondary voltage.

11. What should you do when you test a transformer and there is no OCV?

12. What normally happens when there is a short in the secondary of a transformer?

13. What normally happens when there is a ground (short to case) in the secondary?

14. What precautions should you take when testing a multi-tapped transformer?

15. What are the typical VA ratings for commercial control transformers?

16. The primary terminals of a multi-voltage commercial control transformer are usually identified by the letter _____, and the secondary terminals are usually identified by the letter _____.

17. What three test instruments do you need for checking a transformer?

18. When checking a transformer, what tests should you perform, and in what order?

Thermostats

BASIC COMPONENTS OF MECHANICAL THERMOSTATS

Thermostats are probably the most common control devices found in heating and cooling systems. A thermostat consists of a temperature-sensing device and a control mechanism that turns the system on or off when preset temperature conditions are met. (Some thermostats *modulate*—that is, they act to increase or decrease a condition rather than starting or stopping a system.) Although thermostats exist in a wide variety of styles and shapes, it can be said that there are two general categories of thermostats—those that operate mechanically and those that operate electronically. The first part of this Lesson will discuss mechanical thermostats.

Figure 7-1 shows a very common style of space thermostat. This one happens to be round—others are square or rectangular in shape. Some thermostats have the switches that control heating, cooling, and/or fan operations built into them, and others have the control switches built into a *subbase* on which the thermostat is mounted. The latter approach is more versatile, because various combinations of thermostats and subbases can be used. This makes possible a greater number of different control applications. The thermostat acts as the sensing unit, and the subbase provides the necessary circuitry.

HONEYWELL INC.

FIGURE 7-1. *Typical space thermostat*

111

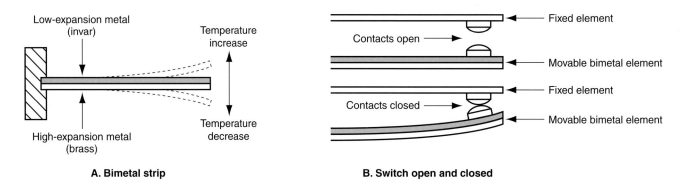

| A. Bimetal strip | B. Switch open and closed |

FIGURE 7-2. *How a bimetal strip works*

Many mechanical thermostats use a *bimetal strip* as the element that reacts to changes in temperature. A bimetal strip, as its name suggests, is composed of two different metals fused together. A common combination, shown in Figure 7-2A, is brass and invar (a steel alloy that contains 36% nickel). A bimetal element of this kind operates on the principle that equal lengths of the two metals, when heated to the same temperature, will expand at different rates.

Brass has a higher coefficient of expansion than invar. Therefore, when heated, the brass expands faster than the invar, which causes the strip to warp or bend. This warping of the bimetal is used to control the switching action of the thermostat. As shown in Figure 7-2B, the bimetal strip acts as the movable element of an electrical switch. That is, a moving contact is attached to the bimetal, and a fixed contact is attached to the thermostat base. Whenever the temperature of the conditioned space rises or falls, the bimetal responds by warping in one direction or the other. At a point determined by the thermostat's heating and cooling settings, the bimetal either "makes" (completes) or "breaks" (disconnects) an electric circuit, thus turning heating or cooling on or off.

Bimetal strips come in several different configurations. They may be straight, curved, or—more commonly—wound in a spiral in order to provide greater surface area. The contacts may be exposed or sealed in glass. When the contacts are exposed, a permanent magnet is often used to provide the "snap" action that makes it possible for the contacts to open and close quickly and precisely. This is shown in Figure 7-3. Depending on the thermostat application, either an increase or a decrease in temperature causes the bimetal to warp toward the fixed contact. When it is close enough, the magnet pulls the contacts firmly

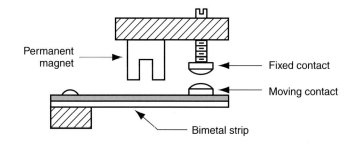

FIGURE 7-3. *Permanent magnet used to snap contacts together*

together. To break the contacts, the bimetal must warp enough in the opposite direction to overcome the magnetic field. When it does, they snap apart.

Contacts exposed to the air are also exposed to dust, lint, and moisture, and subject to corrosion. Hermetically sealed contacts eliminate these problems, and have the added advantage of being silent. *Mercury-tube* contacts are housed in a sealed glass tube mounted on one end of a bimetal arm. Inside the tube is a ball of liquid mercury. When the temperature changes, the position of the bimetal element also changes, tilting the tube up or down. This in turn causes the mercury to flow in one direction or the other, either completing or breaking the connection between the two electrodes, as shown in Figure 7-4A.

 WARNING: Mercury is a hazardous material, and must be disposed of properly.

Some mercury tubes have a third electrode, permitting them to act as a single-pole, double-throw (SPDT) switch. This arrangement, shown in Figure 7-4B, is often used in heating/cooling thermostats. Depending on how the bulb is tilted, the mercury can complete a circuit between the common contact and either the heating or cooling contact (but not both heating and cooling at the same time).

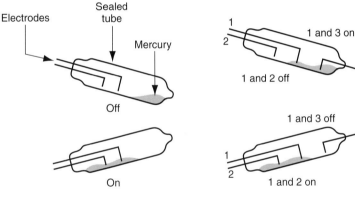

A. Two-electrode mercury switch   **B. Three-electrode mercury switch**

FIGURE 7-4. *Sealed mercury tubes*

In some configurations, a magnet is attached to the bimetal coil and the sealed glass bulb contains a spring-biased switch with the moving contact made of ferrous metal. Such an arrangement can be designed to operate on either a rise or fall in temperature. In Figure 7-5 on the next page, an increase in temperature causes the bimetal to expand, moving the magnet closer to the glass tube. The magnet attracts the moving contact, which then completes the circuit with the stationary contact. As the temperature decreases, the bimetal coil contracts and the magnet moves away from the tube. When the magnetic force is too weak to keep the contacts together, the spring returns the moving contact to its previous position. The key point to remember is that, regardless of the type of contacts, the switching action in a thermostat that uses a bimetal sensing element depends on the warping of the bimetal as it is heated or cooled.

Basically, a thermostat can be defined as a temperature-sensitive switch. Figure 7-6 shows simple schematic symbols used to depict thermostats. In Figure 7-6A, the temperature-sensitive element contracts as the temperature falls, and the switch is pulled downward to close the circuit. This is why the switch line is drawn *above* the open contact point. If the switch were to close due to rise in temperature, the switch line would be drawn *below* the open contact point, as shown in Figure 7-6B.

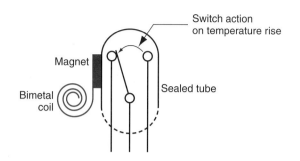

FIGURE 7-5. *Magnet attracts moving arm*

ANTICIPATORS

A mechanical thermostat may produce wide variations in the temperature of the conditioned space, whether the application calls for heating or cooling. For more precise control, a process called *anticipation* is used.

Heat anticipation

Heat anticipation is defined as "the addition of heat to the sensing element of a thermostat to prevent excessive temperature changes in the conditioned space." In practice, anticipation adds "artificial" heat to the thermostat's temperature-sensing element to reduce the effect of a sluggish mechanical differential.

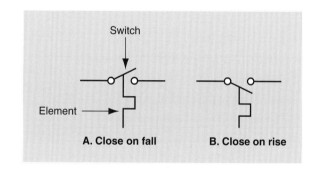

FIGURE 7-6. *Schematic symbols for thermostats*

Assume that the desired temperature that you wish to maintain (the *setpoint*) is 72°F. If the furnace turns on at 72°F and off at 74°F, there is a *differential* of 2°F. But what actually happens? When the thermostat closes its heat switch at 72°F, it takes the equipment some time before it can begin to provide heat to the space. This delay, called *lag*, allows the space temperature to continue to drop. Let's say it drops one more degree, to 71°F, before the space starts to warm up. When the space temperature reaches 74°F and the heat switch turns the equipment off, residual heat in the furnace causes the temperature to continue to rise. This increase in the ambient temperature above the cut-off point is called *overshoot*. If the temperature rises about one more degree, to 75°F, then instead of the desired 2°F space temperature swing (from 72 to 74°F), you have a swing of approximately 4°F (from 71 to 75°F).

To compensate for this, extra heat is added to the thermostat to "fool" it into "thinking" that the space is warmer than it really is. A *heat anticipator* generates the very small amount of additional heat needed inside the thermostat. The heat anticipator is an adjustable resistor placed near the bimetal sensing element. As shown in Figure 7-7, the resistor is wired in series with the heating contacts of the thermostat, and therefore is energized only during a "call for heat" period. Because the bimetal senses a temperature higher than the actual temperature in the room, it shuts off the heating unit sooner, which reduces both the overshoot and the resulting temperature swing. When the thermostat is no longer artificially heated, it senses a drop in room temperature faster. As a result, the furnace cycles on and off more often, but overall ON time is reduced, and a much more efficient control of the space temperature is achieved.

The heat anticipator is adjusted to match the current rating of the primary control device, which may be a relay or some other type of control. When adjusting the anticipator, remember that a higher setting reduces anticipator heat, while a lower setting increases it. Adjustable anticipators allow a thermostat to be used with a number of different heating devices, as long as the current rating of the primary control is within the anticipator adjustment range.

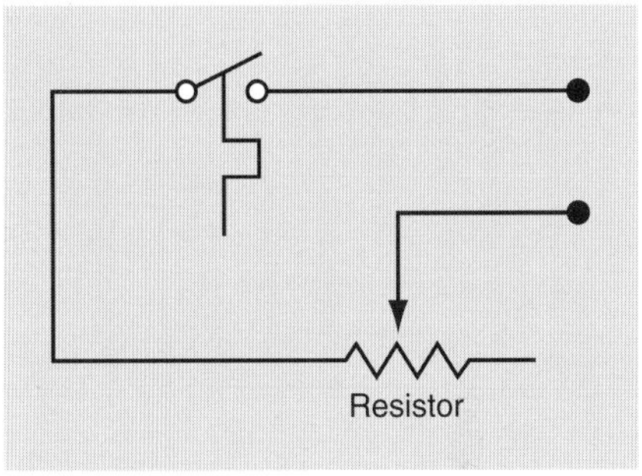

FIGURE 7-7. *Heat anticipator in series with contacts*

Cooling anticipation

Anticipation can be added to the cooling cycle in much the same manner—heat generated by a resistor is applied to the sensing device. A *cooling anticipator*, sometimes called a "cooling compensator," is wired in parallel with the cooling contacts of the thermostat, as shown in Figure 7-8. This means that the cooling anticipator *is* energized during the cooling OFF cycle, and is *not* energized during the cooling ON cycle. Again, extra heat is added to the thermostat to "fool" it into "thinking" that the temperature of the conditioned space is higher than it actually is. Given the additional heat, the bimetal warps more rapidly than it otherwise would, thus causing the cooling unit to come on slightly sooner. This prevents the conditioned space from getting too warm before cooling starts.

Unlike a heat anticipator, a cooling anticipator is *not* adjustable. Because a cooling anticipator is powered when the cooling system is off, it is the only load in the circuit. As a result, it is not dependent on other devices. Its own fixed resistance determines the amount of current that passes through it and, therefore, the amount of heat it generates. The resistance value is selected by the manufacturer to provide the best performance.

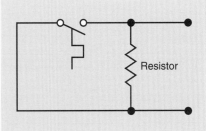

FIGURE 7-8. *Cooling anticipator in parallel with contacts*

SWITCHING AND TERMINAL NOMENCLATURE

Whether a thermostat is self-contained or connected to a subbase, there are certain terminal identifications used in the HVACR industry that are accepted as "standards." Look at the examples of typical wiring diagrams shown in Figures 7-9 and 7-10. Figure 7-9 shows a single-stage heating/cooling thermostat in schematic form. Figure 7-10 depicts a basic heating/cooling system. Note the terminal designations. Thermostat terminal identification often indicates the color coding of the low-voltage wire used:

C   common to all devices

G   green—fan relay connection

R   red—24-V ac input (transformer connection)

W   white—heating (single-stage)

Y   yellow—cooling (single-stage).

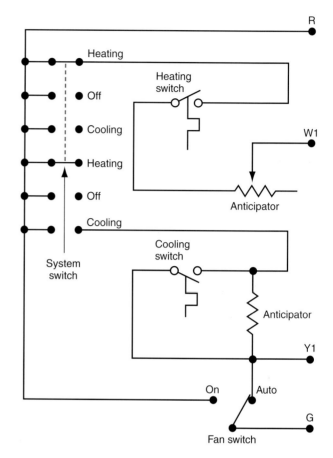

FIGURE 7-9. *Single-stage heating/cooling thermostat*

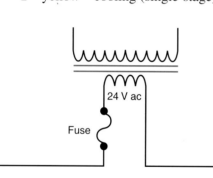

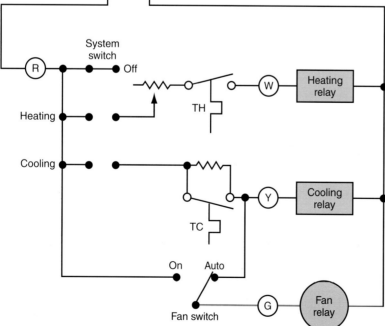

FIGURE 7-10. *Typical heating/cooling system*

The fastest way to identify a single-stage thermostat, whether it is used for heating only, cooling only, or a heating/cooling combination, is to note that there is only *one* mercury bulb or *one* switch for each function. The switch may be configured for SPST or SPDT operation, depending on the application. *Note*: If a schematic drawing represents a multistage thermostat, then numbers are added to the letters to denote the stages of heating or cooling (W1, W2, Y1, Y2, etc.). Also, be aware that some transformer connections may be labeled "RC" and "RH" (to distinguish the cooling input from the heating input).

MULTISTAGE THERMOSTATS

As illustrated in Figure 7-9, a single-stage system provides one level of heating and/or cooling. *Multistage* systems generally are more efficient, because heating or cooling comes on in stages, as needed. A multistage thermostat operates two or three circuits in sequence, and can be designed to control either heating (close on temperature fall) or cooling (close on temperature rise).

Figure 7-11 shows a simplified schematic of a heat pump thermostat circuit in the heating mode. It is one of many possible examples of a multistage system. The first stage in this two-stage heating process is initiated by the temperature falling below the heating setpoint. The upper contacts of the thermostat (TH1) close, turning on the compressor and fan, and producing compression (or "reverse cycle") heat. If the temperature continues to fall, the lower or secondary contacts of the thermostat (TH2) close, energizing the electric resistance heaters, which will supplement compression heat.

Two-stage cooling operates in a similar manner, with the second stage coming on if the first stage cannot satisfy the demand for cooling. The secondary contacts

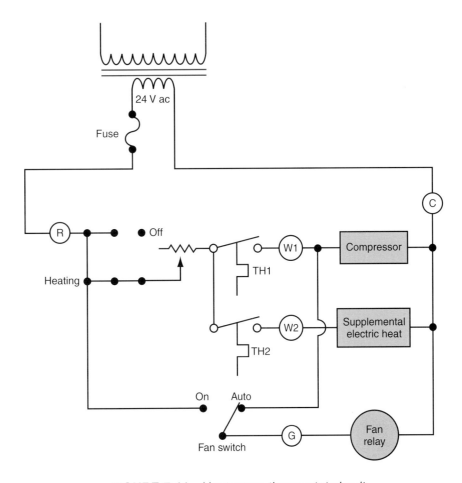

FIGURE 7-11. *Heat pump thermostat circuit*

117

might speed up the compressor or fan, or might even switch on an additional compressor, depending on the unit and the application.

Figure 7-12 shows a basic schematic of a two-stage combination (heating/cooling) thermostat. The easiest way to identify a multistage thermostat is by the number of its mercury bulbs or switches. There may be two, three, or four switching arrangements, depending on the application. Figure 7-13 shows a typical multistage thermostat.

AUTOMATIC CHANGEOVER

Some combination thermostats "change over" (from heating to cooling or back again) automatically, and others must be switched manually. In order to understand automatic changeover, recall the earlier discussion of the term "differential." Simply stated, the *differential* of a thermostat is the difference (in degrees Fahrenheit) between its opening and closing points. This differential is typically 2°F. In other words, if the heating setpoint is 72°F, the heat will be turned on at 72°F, and shut off when the temperature of the conditioned space reaches 74°F.

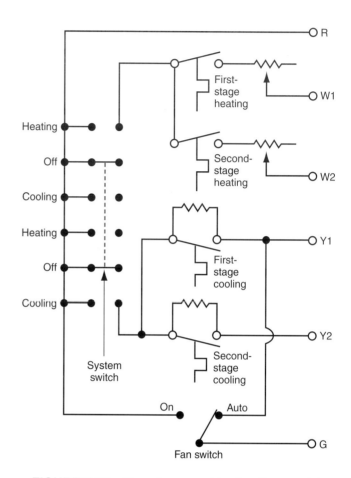

FIGURE 7-12. *Two-stage combination thermostat*

In a thermostat with automatic changeover, the differential can pose a problem—it might cause constant cycling between heating and cooling. Imagine, for example, that the heating setpoint is 72°F and the cooling setpoint is 74°F. Then, when the temperature reaches the heating cut-off point of 74°F, the heating will shut off—but the cooling will turn on. The cooling equipment will run until the temperature is reduced by 2°F—but at 72°F the heating will turn on again! To prevent this constant cycling, something must be added to the design of the thermostat.

The additional feature is called the *minimum interlock setting*, or *deadband*. It is designed into all thermostats with automatic changeover. *Deadband* is defined as the range of values through which a variable (temperature, in this case) can change without initiating a response. For example, if the deadband for the thermostat described in the preceding paragraph is 3°F, it simply means that the difference between the heating and cooling setpoints cannot be *less* than 3°F. Thus, when the heating ON point is 72°F, the cooling ON point will be 75°F. Since the heating will shut off at 74°F (because of the 2°F differential), there is no conflict. The design of the thermostat makes it physically impossible to override the deadband setting.

COMMON DEFECTS

There are several common faults that you might encounter in working with mechanical thermostats:

- **Open heat anticipator.** This occurs when someone shorts the primary controller or gas valve with a screwdriver, to see if it "sparks." This puts the full 24 V across the anticipator resistor. The thermostat must be replaced.

- **Broken wire leading to the switch.** This occurs when the one of wires breaks off from the mercury bulb or the thermostat switch. The thermostat must be replaced.

- **Bad connections between the thermostat and the subbase.** This occurs when the screws from the thermostat to the subbase are not sufficiently tightened.

- **Broken or shorted wires at the subbase.** This occurs when the wires that attach to the subbase are installed incorrectly, or are touching each other.

- **Broken or shorted wires between the unit and the subbase.** This occurs when the wires that attach to the subbase are touching each other, or have a nail driven through them.

- **Dirty switches at the subbase.** This is self-explanatory, and occurs when contacts are exposed to dirt and dust.

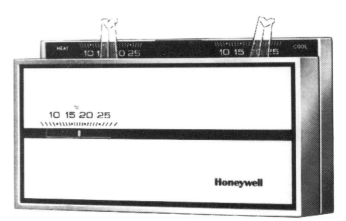

FIGURE 7-13. *Typical multistage thermostat*

HONEYWELL INC.

- **Thermostat not calibrated.** This occurs when the thermostat is not leveled, and may cause the thermostat to read inaccurately.

TESTING MECHANICAL THERMOSTATS

Because mechanical thermostats are basically switches that are activated by changes in temperature, it is fairly easy to test them with a voltmeter or an

Function	Switch rating		Anticipator rating		Fan and system switches
Heating	1.5 A	A D J	Stage 1 2	0.10 to 1.2 A 0.10 to 1.2 A	2.5 A
Cooling	1.5 A	F X D	Stage 1 2	5,100 Ω 10,000 Ω	2.5 A

TABLE 7-1. *Typical electrical characteristics of low-voltage (24-V) mechanical thermostats*

ohmmeter. Table 7-1 lists some of the common characteristics of generic low-voltage thermostats.

Voltmeter method

To test a heating thermostat with a voltmeter, you must have access to the wired connections of the unit or subbase while the system is powered. Set the meter's range switch to the 60-V setting. Place one of the test leads on the "R" terminal, and the other on the "W" terminal. Move the thermostat from a higher to a lower setpoint, and the voltmeter will tell you when the switch is open by indicating a voltage. When the switch closes, the voltage will drop to zero. This is illustrated in Figure 7-14.

The same basic test can be used to check a cooling thermostat and the fan switches. By keeping one test lead on the "R" terminal and moving the other from the "Y" terminal to the "G" terminal, the same effect will be seen.

If you get no reading at any time, it is possible that the power to the thermostat has been interrupted. This must be traced back to the transformer or control device.

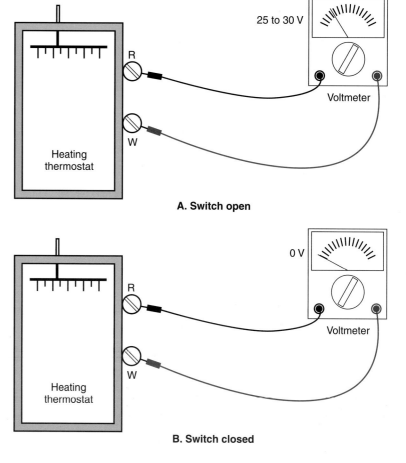

FIGURE 7-14. *Testing a heating thermostat with a voltmeter*

Ohmmeter method

You can also use an ohmmeter to test the continuity of a thermostat—however, the power must be disconnected from the thermostat before this test can be done. Remember, when you use an ohmmeter to check the continuity of a thermostat, the resistance of the anticipator will affect your reading. As you did with the voltmeter, use the "R" and "W" terminals of the thermostat (but first disconnect all the wires from them).

Figure 7-15 shows an example of how to test a heating thermostat with an ohmmeter. When the thermostat's switch is closed, as shown in Figure 7-15A, you will obtain a reading of 0 Ω, regardless of the scale used on the ohmmeter. (Because the anticipator's resistance is extremely low—on the average of 0.1 to 0.5 Ω—most ohmmeters will not register it.) When the thermostat's switch is open, as shown in Figure 7-15B, you will obtain a reading of infinity (∞), regardless of the scale used. (Because the switch is open, there can be no resistance.)

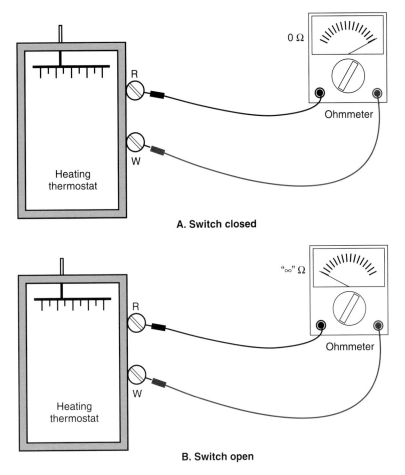

A. Switch closed

B. Switch open

FIGURE 7-15. *Testing a heating thermostat with an ohmmeter*

Figure 7-16 on the next page shows an example of how to test a cooling thermostat with an ohmmeter. When the thermostat's switch is open, as shown in Figure 7-16A, you will obtain a reading of 5,000 to 6,000 Ω because of the placement of the anticipator resistor in the circuit. When the thermostat's switch is closed, as shown in Figure 7-16B, you will obtain a reading of 0 Ω, regardless of the scale used on the ohmmeter. Note that you must use the "R" and "Y" terminals when testing a cooling thermostat. However, you must disconnect all the wires from them first.

TESTING ANTICIPATORS IN MECHANICAL THERMOSTATS

Unless there is physical evidence of an open anticipator (usually burned), the easiest way to test an anticipator is to use an ammeter. Because a heat anticipator is wired in series with the heating contacts of the thermostat, it must be adjusted to match the heating circuit current. The heating circuit current draw can be measured with an ammeter (or a clamp-on ammeter).

To use a clamp-on ammeter, first remove the thermostat from its subbase, then run ten turns of wire around the jaws, as shown in Figure 7-17. Connect one end of the wire to the "R" terminal, and the other end to the "W" terminal. The anticipator setting must match the current draw of the heating system's R-W circuit. Divide the current reading on the ammeter by 10 to obtain the heating circuit current draw. For example, if the ammeter reading is 5 A, you should set the heat anticipator at 0.5 A (5 A ÷ 10).

Caution: It is possible to burn out the anticipator if the current value is set too low, or if the heating cycle is operated with the primary control jumpered out.

Note that the heat anticipator may be adjusted further to achieve slightly longer or shorter system ON times. To *decrease* the system cycles per hour (and achieve a *longer* ON time), go to a *higher* setting. Move the pointer in increments of 0.05. For example, if the original setting is 0.55 A, adjust the desired setting to 0.60 A, and then check system operation. To *increase* the system cycles per hour (and achieve a *shorter* ON time), go to a *lower* setting. Again, use increments of 0.05. For example, if the original setting is 0.55 A, adjust the desired setting to 0.50 A, and then check system operation. *Do not exceed four cycles per hour.*

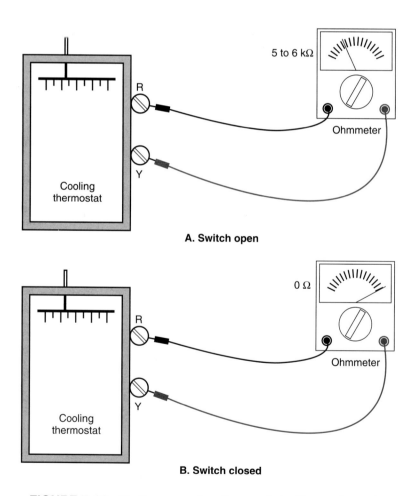

FIGURE 7-16. *Testing a cooling thermostat with an ohmmeter*

Under certain conditions, bimetal thermostats that have anticipation may show a characteristic known as "droop." *Droop*, in this case, refers to more than the normal offset between setpoint and control point—it is an undesirable and excessive deviation from the setpoint. It may be caused by an improperly sized anticipator, or by other factors that can affect the anticipator. These may include heat buildup in the thermostat from the wall on which the thermostat is mounted, inadequate circulation of room air through the thermostat, and excess voltage applied to the contacts.

Excessive heat generated in the thermostat causes a short ON cycle. Because the bimetal senses more heat from the anticipator than from the room air, the temperature of the conditioned space progressively decreases, with the result that the setpoint is never reached. Conversely, with *insufficient* heat anticipation, the bimetal lags behind room temperature change. This causes longer ON and OFF periods, and larger room temperature variations. Extended operating ON times can occur in installations where units are grossly undersized, and therefore must operate most of the time in an attempt to maintain the desired temperature. Droop may occur during either the heating or cooling cycle. However, its effect on cooling is minimal. Droop does not occur in systems that use electronic thermostats.

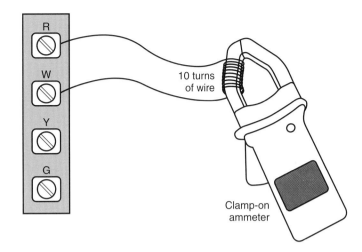

FIGURE 7-17. *Measuring current in a thermostat circuit*

MAINTENANCE PROCEDURES

Some very simple maintenance procedures will help you keep a mechanical thermostat in good operating condition:

- Check the terminals to make sure that they are tight and free of corrosion.

- Clean the surface of the bimetal coil.

- Clean the contacts. (This does not apply to sealed types, of course). Never use abrasives to clean the contacts—a business card or matchbook cover will work quite well. Separate the contacts just enough to pass the card between them. Then slide the card between the contacts, using only the natural spring force to supply the needed friction for cleaning.

CALIBRATION

Most thermostats are calibrated by the manufacturer with precision instruments. Normally, little or no recalibration is needed. Thermostats should be located in areas with natural air circulation, where no sources of heat or cold (such as heating or cooling ducts, a fireplace, or even a television) can affect them. If you think that recalibration is required, first make sure that the thermostat is level (if it contains a mercury bulb). Then:

- Place an accurate test thermometer near the thermostat.

- Turn the thermostat setting up until the heater turns on. (Listen for an audible snap of the thermostat switch.)

- When the thermostat switch makes contact, note the temperature on the test thermometer. If the thermostat setting is about the same, recalibration is not needed.

- If the thermostat setting differs from the thermometer reading, then recalibrate.

To recalibrate, you must have the temperature of the conditioned space at the desired setpoint (as measured by your test thermometer). Remove the thermostat cover and slowly rotate the adjustment screw or nut until the thermostat switch snaps closed. Sometimes a small screwdriver or a very small wrench is all that is required for this procedure.

COMMERCIAL MECHANICAL THERMOSTATS

There are three primary differences between residential mechanical thermostats and commercial ones:

- First, almost all commercial thermostats are line-voltage devices. Therefore, all of the contacts are heavier, and there can be multiple pairs of contacts for different stages.

- Second, a commercial thermostat usually does *not* include anticipation, since it uses a gas- or liquid-filled bulb or bellows. The temperature control method does not consider lag or overshoot times.

- Third, the contacts of a typical commercial thermostat can handle currents that range from 5 to 20 A. The contacts usually are self-cleaning at these currents.

Commercial thermostats are adjustable, and are used in a variety of applications, ranging from low-temperature freezers to high-temperature flower cases. A commercial thermostat has two setpoints—the *cut-in* point is the point at which the thermostat switch closes, and the *cut-out* point is the point at which the switch opens. The differential between these two points is typically 2 to 8°F. In other words, if the unit is turned on when the temperature of the conditioned space reaches 36°F (the cut-in point), and shut off when the temperature of the conditioned space reaches 34°F (the cut-out point), then the differential is 2°F.

Sometimes a commercial thermostat will lose its charge, or a bulb or cap tube will break, preventing the switch from operating. This kind of physical evidence normally can be gained from a visual inspection. Testing a commercial thermostat may require ice water to determine if the switch is opening and closing at its prescribed temperatures. Because most commercial thermostats work at line voltages, it is best to disconnect them and then use an ohmmeter to check the cut-in and cut-out points.

ELECTRONIC THERMOSTATS

The energy crisis of recent years, which saw heating costs more than double, created a demand for energy efficiency. At the same time, the development and rapid improvement of solid-state micro-electronic circuits made it possible to replace electromechanical thermostats (like the bimetal devices discussed in the preceding portions of this Lesson) with *electronic* thermostats that provide greater accuracy and higher reliability. Microprocessor-based "smart" thermostats can control temperatures precisely, and can be programmed to respond to different conditions and different times of day.

There are as many different types of electronic thermostats on the market as there are manufacturers. It is beyond the scope of this Lesson to cover them all. However, you should be familiar with some of the "basics" of these thermostats. Figure 7-18 shows a typical electronic thermostat. Like the model pictured, most electronic thermostats use an LCD (liquid crystal display) to show what functions the thermostat is performing.

Electronic thermostats are more compact than their electromechanical counterparts, and their lack of moving parts makes them less susceptible to failure. They can provide temperature control within 1°F or less, whereas mechanical thermostats are generally accurate within 2 to 3°F. In addition, electronic thermostats can measure extremely high and low temperatures. This capability makes them effective in applications where conventional thermostats cannot be used. Some electronic thermostats also can be controlled from remote locations (the sensor unit is installed in the conditioned space).

HONEYWELL INC.

FIGURE 7-18. *Typical electronic thermostat*

Electronic thermostats operate on the same principles as electromechanical thermostats do, but various functions, such as timing, sensing, and switching, are accomplished by electronic components. Thermistors generally are used to sense temperature changes, and thus to initiate heating and cooling operations. A *thermistor* is a solid-state semiconductor device whose electrical resistance varies with changes in temperature.

Electronic thermostats have other advantages over electromechanical models. They are not subject to the condition known as *droop*, which is especially common in line-voltage thermostats. (As discussed earlier, droop affects the response of the anticipator, causing the thermostat to shut off the heat before the setpoint is reached.) And, unlike thermostats with mercury bulbs, electronic thermostats do not have to be precisely leveled during installation.

Today, electronic thermostats are being made with more and more optional capabilities that are not available with other types of thermostats. For example, some electronic thermostats can automatically keep track of the number of hours that have passed since the filters or humidifier elements were replaced. They can indicate, with a visible or audible signal, when a component in a heating or cooling system has failed, and when maintenance is required.

Electronic thermostats are now available that can be programmed with variable start-up time delays. This allows a staggered start-up of equipment in a complex of many units, such as a hotel. Large units can be programmed for "ramped" start-up, to minimize large power drains during start-up. Many electronic thermostats are able to display the outside temperature, and to use changes in the outside temperature to anticipate the need for heating or cooling. This feature greatly improves comfort levels.

Programmable electronic thermostats

Programmable thermostats are equipped with a clock or timing device, and many of them have digital readouts for displaying temperature, time, day of the week, etc. Programming of the thermostat is usually done through a keypad that is accessed by opening the front cover. Figure 7-19 shows a programmable thermostat with the cover opened to reveal the controls. Because there are so many different manufacturers of electronic thermostats, gathering programming information for all of them would quickly fill a library. Try to get as much installation information as you can, however, from the literature furnished with the unit on which you will be working.

Briefly, programming options range from simple "night setback" to the selection of settings for various times of day for each day of the week. Most units are equipped with a battery backup to prevent the loss of programming in the event of a power outage. The battery is for emergencies only—it provides power to the microprocessor, but will not operate the thermostat.

There are versions of electronic thermostats that do not require a battery backup. These use *storage registers* built into the microprocessor to prevent the loss of programming in case of a power failure. This type of memory, called *non-volatile*, is being used more frequently in electronic thermostats. *Override* controls allow the temporary selection of special programming for occasions such as holidays and vacations, or other periods of time when the space will be unoccupied.

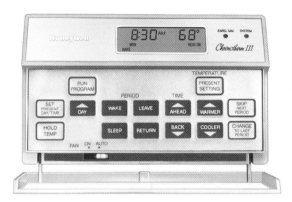

FIGURE 7-19. *Programmable electronic thermostat control panel*

HONEYWELL INC.

TROUBLESHOOTING ELECTRONIC THERMOSTATS

Some electronic thermostats have self-test procedures built into their microcomputer programs. By pressing the right buttons on the keypad, the service technician can cycle the system through all of its functions to verify proper operation, or to isolate a malfunction. In some cases, the thermostat will provide a feedback signal, usually through a flashing light or word on the display, to help in pinpointing the fault. The instructions provided with each thermostat will describe the use of such features.

There are a few common problems that will give the technician a hint as to where to look:

- If there is no display on the LCD, you can conclude that there is no power to the thermostat. The cause may be a broken wire, a bad transformer, or even a defective thermostat.

- If the display reads all zeros, and none of the keypad buttons have any effect, it is highly likely that the microprocessor has failed.

- If the clock on the thermostat does not keep the correct time, the problem may be the result of a power outage or a defective battery. Or, again, the thermostat may be defective.

- Some thermostats have the option of "locking out" the keypad—that is, there are controls on the thermostat that will prevent unauthorized personnel from tampering with the programming. Again, information about this will be found in the instructions that come with the unit.

Unlike most electromechanical thermostats, electronic thermostats require power to operate. Remember, the battery is for emergencies only, and in any case will only preserve the programming. Obviously, there must be some source of power. Most electronic thermostats now available are powered from the system control transformer (usually 24 V). Listed below are the general terminal connections used for a "generic" electronic thermostat:

R   24-V power

RH   24-V power (heating)

RC   24-V power (cooling)

Y   contactor coil (single-stage cooling)

Y1   contactor coil (first stage of multistage cooling)

Y2   contactor coil (second stage of multistage cooling)

W   heating control (single-stage heating)

W1   heating control (first stage of multistage heating)

W2   heating control (second stage of multistage heating)

G   indoor fan relay

O   reversing valve (heat pump energized in cooling)

B   reversing valve (heat pump energized in heating)

E   emergency heat (heat pump)

L   emergency heat light (heat pump)
(may also be a dirty filter indicator)

C   transformer common.

There are two basic precautions that you must remember to take into account when servicing or replacing electronic thermostats. First, when you run the thermostat wire, be sure to keep it away from all sources of electrical interference (ac and dc motors, fluorescent lighting, electronic air cleaners, etc.). Electrical interference may affect the accuracy of the timing functions. Second, although most electronic controls are protected from static electricity discharge, be aware that when a thermostat's case is open and the thermostat is being serviced or installed, the chances of static discharge damaging the thermostat are increased. To prevent damage from static discharge:

■ *Never* walk across carpeting while carrying a thermostat with the case open!

■ *Never* touch any exposed components while servicing or installing the thermostat!

"POWER-STEALING" ELECTRONIC THERMOSTATS

There are some four-wire electronic thermostats on the market today that do not require the "common" wire to power them. Instead of having a "C" terminal connection, they rely on drawing small amounts of power through the relays of the heating and cooling equipment for their operation. These so-called "power-stealing" thermostats can pose a compatibility problem with some hot-surface ignition and standing-pilot ignition systems. They may prevent the furnace microprocessor from functioning properly.

Heating-related problems that you may encounter with power-stealing thermostats include:

■ sporadic draft-inducer motor operation (the draft-inducer motor may operate when the thermostat is in the heating mode, but no call for heating exists)

■ low voltages (low-voltage measurements of less than 18 to 20 V ac at the furnace input terminals during the idle mode)

■ memory malfunctions (thermostat programming schedules or timing schedules may advance or become lost for no apparent reason)

■ overshoot (several degrees of temperature overshoot may occur because the furnace does not shut off immediately after the thermostat is satisfied)

■ general lack of control of furnace (the unit does not come on or shut off as per thermostat demand).

Cooling-related problems that you may encounter with power-stealing thermostats include:

- sporadic blower motor operation (the blower motor may operate when the thermostat is in the cooling mode, but no call for cooling exists)

- low voltages (low-voltage measurements of less than 18 to 20 V ac at the compressor contactor terminals during the idle mode)

- memory malfunctions (thermostat programming schedules or timing schedules may advance or become lost for no apparent reason)

- overshoot (several degrees of temperature overshoot may occur because the air conditioner does not shut off immediately after the thermostat is satisfied)

- general lack of control of air conditioner (the unit does not come on or shut off as per thermostat demand).

These are just a few symptoms of system incompatibility problems. Others could possibly appear as well. Not all power-stealing thermostats are incompatible with hot-surface ignition and standing-pilot ignition furnaces. However, various thermostat manufacturers offer their own recommendations of how to identify and correct incompatibility problems that might arise. Always follow the thermostat manufacturer's instructions.

TROUBLESHOOTING POWER-STEALING THERMOSTATS

A typical remedy for overcoming the types of problems described in the previous paragraphs is to place a resistor across the "R" and "W" terminals

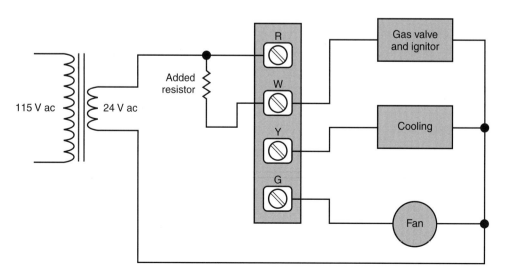

FIGURE 7-20. *Adding a resistor to a four-wire thermostat*

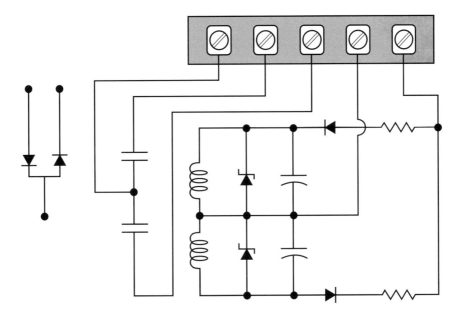

FIGURE 7-21. *Four-wire to five-wire conversion*

of the thermostat, as shown in Figure 7-20. The resistance value of the resistor depends on the manufacturer—however, a value of 1,500 Ω is a good starting point.

If you come across a four-wire electronic thermostat and adding a resistor does not work, you can change the four-wire thermostat to a five-wire configuration by adding an extra wire to connect to the "C" terminal. Observe the following terminal designations for proper five-wire operation:

R   24-V hot

C   24-V common

G   fan relay

W   heat relay

Y   cool relay.

Thermostat conversion kit

A device called a *thermostat conversion kit* has been developed for adding a fifth wire or replacing a broken wire in a four-wire thermostat system. It uses a back-to-back diode arrangement, shown schematically in Figure 7-21, that allows current to pass in one direction only.

A thermostat conversion kit is a 24-V ac accessory for converting a four-wire thermostat to five-wire operation. The following paragraphs discuss the use of a generic thermostat conversion kit. The colors used here are for reference purposes only. Always follow the manufacturer's wiring instructions.

These kits usually consist of two parts, as depicted in Figure 7-22 . Part A is a pigtail wire connection installed at the "Y" and "G" terminals of the thermostat. Part B is a small circuit board installed at the indoor equipment. A conversion kit of this kind is designed to use only one wire in sharing both the "Y" and "G" signals between the thermostat and the indoor equipment. *Note*: The kit must *not* be used to share the "R," "C," or "W" wires.

WARNING: Disconnect all power before proceeding. Make sure that the main electrical disconnect is in the OFF **position. Failure to follow this warning may result in personal injury or death.**

There are two steps to the installation procedure:

1. Install the pigtail (Part A) by connecting the yellow wire to the "Y" terminal and the green wire to the "G" terminal at the thermostat. Connect the opposite end (the blue wire) to the "Y/G" connection on the circuit board (Part B). Push excess

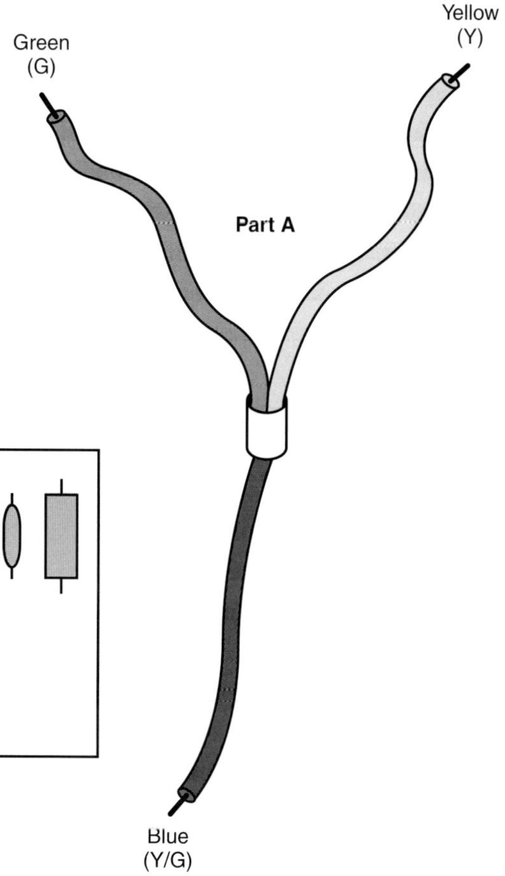

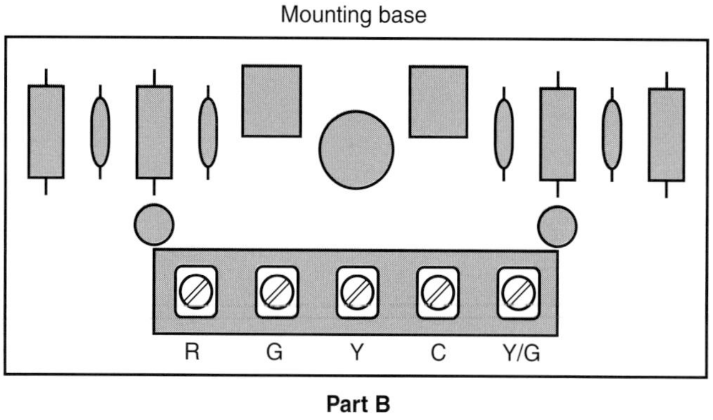

Green
(G)

Yellow
(Y)

Part A

Mounting base

R   G   Y   C   Y/G

Part B

Blue
(Y/G)

FIGURE 7-22. *Thermostat conversion kit*

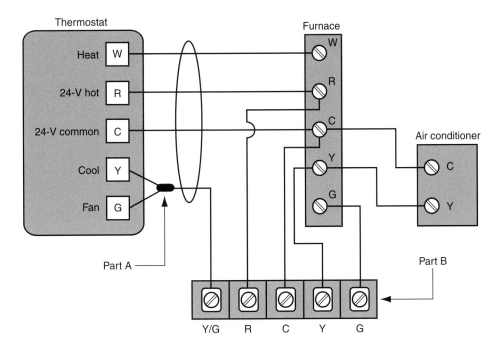

FIGURE 7-23. *Typical furnace and air conditioner installation*

wire from the pigtail into the wall, or tuck it neatly behind the
thermostat control board in the mounting base. See Figure 7-23
for a typical furnace and air conditioner installation.

2. Make the wiring connections to the circuit board (Part B). Mount
    the circuit board next to the indoor equipment low-voltage control
    assembly, and secure with screws. Do *not* install next to high-voltage
    wiring.

Caution: Do not connect any of the conversion kit's "Y," "G," or "Y/G" wires
to the "R" or "C" terminals of the thermostat or indoor equipment. Failure to
follow this caution may result in minor personal injury or product damage.

CONCLUSION

Because the number of electronic thermostats on the market is so great, it is a
good idea for the technician to start a library of technical information for each
thermostat that he or she encounters. The industry is changing very rapidly, and
many of thermostats in use today will quickly become obsolete. A well-prepared
service technician has as much information available as possible.

1. What happens to the bimetal strip in a mechanical thermostat when the temperature of the conditioned space rises or falls?

2. Bimetal elements come in various shapes or configurations. What is the most common?

3. In some thermostats, a(n) _____ is used to provide the "snap" action necessary for opening and closing contacts quickly and precisely.

4. How does a thermostat with hermetically sealed contacts work?

5. What determines the location of the switch line in the schematic symbol used to depict a thermostat?

6. The time elapsed after a thermostat closes and before heat is supplied to the conditioned space is called _____.

7. An increase in the temperature of the conditioned space above the heating cut-off point is called _____.

8. What is a heat anticipator?

9. What is the purpose of a heat anticipator?

10. What is a cooling anticipator?

11. When does a cooling anticipator operate?

12. What letters are used to identify a thermostat's heating and cooling terminals?

13.   What is a thermostat's *differential*?

14.   What is *deadband*?

15.   When you place the test leads of a voltmeter on the "R" and "W" terminals of a thermostat and a voltage is shown, the switch is

_____.

16.   What must you do before using an ohmmeter to test a thermostat?

17.   When you use an ohmmeter to test a cooling thermostat with the switch open (and all wires disconnected), what reading should you get from "R" to "Y"?

18.   How can you measure the current draw in a thermostat circuit with a clamp-on ammeter?

19.   How should you adjust a heat anticipator to increase the system cycles per hour?

20.   In systems that use bimetal thermostats with anticipation, an undesirable and progressive deviation from the setpoint is known as _____.

21.   What are the main differences between residential mechanical thermostats and commercial thermostats?

22.   List some of the advantages of electronic thermostats over mechanical thermostats.

23.   What is the function of the battery found in an electronic thermostat?

24.   Why should you *not* walk across carpeting while carrying an electronic thermostat with the case open?

25.   What is a "power-stealing" thermostat?

26.   What can be used to convert a four-wire thermostat to five-wire operation?

Motors

TYPES OF MOTORS

Although there are many different varieties of motors, those used in the HVACR industry can be grouped, for the purpose of organization, into nine basic categories. The first six motors on the list below are all *single-phase ac* motors. The seventh is a *three-phase ac* motor. The eighth is a *variable-speed* motor, and the last is a special dc motor called a *stepper* motor. The entire list is as follows:

1.   ac series (universal) motors

2.   shaded-pole motors

3.   permanent split-capacitor (PSC) motors

4.   split-phase (also called induction-start, induction-run) motors

5.   capacitor-start, induction-run (CSIR) motors

6.   capacitor-start, capacitor-run (CSCR) motors

7.   three-phase ac motors

8.   variable-speed motors

9.   dc stepper motors.

Alternating current (ac) motors are often grouped into *integral-horsepower* and *fractional-horsepower* classifications. The National Electrical Manufacturers Association (NEMA) defines an *integral-horsepower* motor as any motor rated at one horsepower (1 hp) or above, and a *fractional-horsepower* motor as any motor rated at less than 1 hp. The motor industry, however, tends to describe a fractional-horsepower motor as any ac induction motor built into a frame 6½ in. or less in diameter. Better insulation, new materials, and improved cooling systems have allowed motor manufacturers to build motors with higher horsepower ratings into smaller frames.

The first six motors listed on the previous page are all fractional-horsepower motors. They can be found in many kinds of applications, from portable tools and small fans to belt-driven blower assemblies and small compressors. Their *fractional* horsepower ratings range from $\frac{1}{200}$ hp to $\frac{3}{4}$ hp.

INSPECTING DEFECTIVE MOTORS

In order to determine whether a motor is defective or not, there are several things that you can look for. Start with a simple visual inspection. Physical evidence includes:

- burned windings

- stuck or worn bearings

- signs of overheating, including capacitors that have swelled, bulged, or split.

Electrical evidence includes:

- broken leads

- shorted capacitors

- open start and/or run windings.

Worn bearings are caused by a lack of lubrication. Shorted windings are usually the result of insulation breakdown, which in turn is caused by overheating. Motors must be kept clean, because dust, oil, and other contaminants can all contribute to unsatisfactory performance.

Once a motor has been found to be defective, you must determine what type of motor it is.

AC SERIES MOTORS

As you can see in Figure 8-1, the field coils in an *ac series* motor are wound on the stator and are wired in series with the armature. The electrical connections between the armature and the field windings are provided by carbon brushes and a ring of metal segments on the rotor called the *commutator*. The electric current passes directly through each coil in the motor—which is why the motor is called a *series* motor.

Motors of this type are also referred to as *universal* motors, because they can run on either alternating current or direct current. Universal motors normally are manufactured in fractional-horsepower sizes. They operate at speeds as high as 35,000 rpm. This makes them extremely versatile. They have high starting torques, and their ability to adjust to widely varying loads makes them ideal for powering electric shavers, drills, saws, sanders, blenders, vacuum cleaners, and other household appliances. Because universal motors have variable speeds, they are adaptable to use with speed-controlling devices, such as silicon-controlled rectifiers (SCRs).

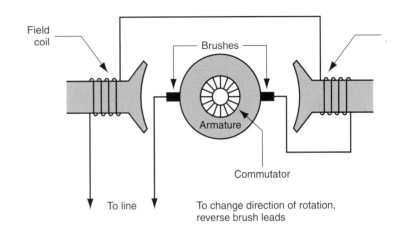

FIGURE 8-1. *ac series motor*

SHADED-POLE MOTORS

Figure 8-2 shows a typical *shaded-pole* motor. A shaded-pole motor is an induction motor that has no commutator, no brushes, no moving switch parts, and no capacitor. Its name derives from the fact that it uses loops of copper wire called *shading* coils to "shift" the starting current—that is, to produce the phase delay necessary for starting the motor. Shaded-pole motors generally are manufactured in very small sizes, and have low starting torques.

Regardless of the type of motor you are troubleshooting, two items of concern are

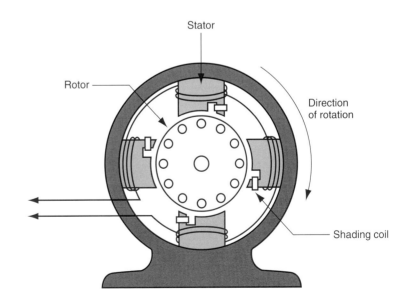

FIGURE 8-2. *Shaded-pole motor*

139

the direction of rotation and the speed of the motor. In shaded-pole motors, rotor *rotation* is always in the direction of the shaded pole, as shown in Figure 8-2. Most shaded-pole motors are not reversible. Only a few are made so that the direction of rotation can be reversed. If the motor is symmetrical, you can simply remove the end plates and reverse the rotor (so that the shaft extends from the opposite end of the motor), as shown in Figure 8-3. Another way to achieve the same effect is to remove the end plates and turn the stator poles 180°, as shown in Figure 8-4.

The *speed* of a fractional-horsepower motor is determined by the number of poles the motor has and the frequency of the current supplied to it. The following equation is used to determine the *synchronous* speed of an ac motor:

$$rpm = \frac{120 \times f}{p}$$

where *f* is the frequency (cycles per second) of the power supply, and *p* is the number of poles.

The shaded-pole motor shown in Figure 8-2 has four poles. Therefore, assuming a line frequency of 60 Hz, its synchronous speed is:

$$\frac{120 \times 60}{4} = \frac{7,200}{4} = 1,800 \text{ rpm}$$

However, because a motor usually operates under a load, its rotor does not rotate at exactly the synchronous speed. The difference between the synchronous speed and the lower actual speed is called *slip*, and is usually about 3 to 4% for fractional-horsepower motors.

Shaded-pole motors are very rugged and reliable, and their cost is relatively low. However, they have low starting torques and poor efficiency, and can be noisy in operation. Their primary use in the HVACR field is for direct-drive fans and blowers. Sleeve bearings are used to cut down on the noise. Maintenance of shaded-pole motors is usually limited to two fundamental problems:

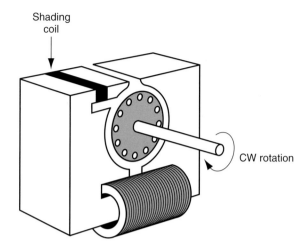

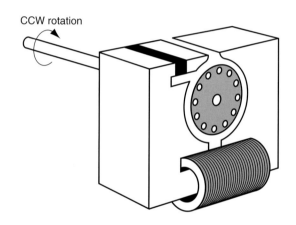

FIGURE 8-3. *To change direction, disassemble and reverse shaft*

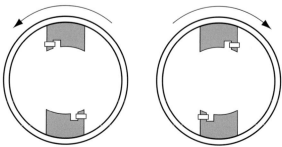

FIGURE 8-4. *Reversing direction of rotation*

- bad bearings (stuck, loose, or worn)

- open or shorted windings.

The first of these is of a mechanical nature, and should be dealt with accordingly. The second can be diagnosed easily with a voltmeter or an ammeter.

High-impedance motors

Some shaded-pole motors are called *high-impedance* motors. These motors are used for condenser fans and evaporator fans in condensing units, reach-in coolers and refrigerators, dehumidifiers, and small unit heaters. The term "high impedance" comes from the fact that the windings are wound with very fine wire, and use many more turns than normal motors. Because high-impedance motors are sealed and self-lubricating, they usually have long and reliable service lives. They can tolerate being "stalled" for long periods of time without burning out the windings. Such stalling can be caused by an evaporator coil freezing, for example, with the result that sufficient ice forms around the fan blade to stop the motor.

These types of motors are not rated in horsepower, but rather in watts of power consumed. The direction of rotation is visible from the rear of the motor, opposite the shaft end (OSE). Many of these motors (they are sometimes called "51 frame condenser fan motors") have operating data stamped into the end plate of the motor. This information may resemble the illustration below:

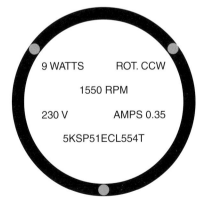

Table 8-1 on the next page lists common characteristics of high-impedance motors that are rated from 2 to 16 W. Motors in this range are always 3½ in. in diameter. There are some heavier high-impedance motors that are used in commercial applications. These larger motors are 3⅞ in. in diameter, and range from 25 to 50 W. Table 8-2, also on the next page, provides data for this style of motor.

Power, W	Voltage, V	Current, A	Speed, rpm	Direction of rotation
2	115	0.3	1300	CW
4	115	0.5	1550	CW
4	115	0.5	1550	CCW
6	115	0.6	1550	CW
6	115	0.6	1550	CCW
9	115	0.8	1550	CW
9	115	0.8	1550	CCW
9	230	0.4	1550	CW
9	230	0.4	1550	CCW
16	115	1.1	1550	CW
16	115	1.1	1550	CCW
16	230	0.8	1550	CW
16	230	0.8	1550	CCW

TABLE 8-1. *Characteristics of high-impedance motors (2 to 16 W)*

Power, W	Voltage, V	Current, A	Speed, rpm	Direction of rotation
25	115	1.1	1450	CW
25	115	1.1	1450	CCW
25	230	0.6	1450	CW
25	230	0.6	1450	CCW
35	115	1.4	1450	CW
35	115	1.4	1450	CCW
35	230	0.7	1450	CW
35	230	0.7	1450	CCW
50	115	1.7	1500	CW
50	115	1.7	1500	CCW
50	230	0.85	1500	CW
50	230	0.85	1500	CCW

TABLE 8-2. *Characteristics of high-impedance motors (25 to 50 W)*

Skeleton-frame motors

A type of shaded-pole motor sometimes referred to as a "skeleton-frame" motor is used primarily in domestic refrigerators and fan applications. It is an open-frame motor that can range in horsepower from $\frac{1}{200}$ to $\frac{1}{20}$ hp. Figure 8-5 shows an example of a two-pole skeleton-frame motor. Because there is very little load on this style of motor, its average synchronous speed is 3,000 rpm.

Other shaded-pole motors used in the HVACR industry range in size from 3½ to 5½ in. in diameter, depending on the application, and from ½₀₀ to ¼ hp. Table 8-3 shows the average size and horsepower range for various frame numbers.

Wiring shaded-pole motors

The wiring for a shaded-pole motor is relatively straightforward. There are no real "standards," but it is common practice to use white and black—and, if there is a third wire, green. Of course, the green wire is always used as the ground wire to the frame of the motor.

A typical color coding scheme used in wiring *dual-speed* shaded-pole motors is shown in Figure 8-6. The illustration depicts a 115-V dual-speed motor. Figure 8-7 on the next page shows a typical wiring diagram for a *dual-voltage* (115/230-V) shaded-pole motor. The examples shown in these two illustrations are for purposes of comparison only. Always consult the manufacturer's wiring diagram for more specific information.

PERMANENT SPLIT-CAPACITOR (PSC) MOTORS

A *permanent split-capacitor* (PSC) motor is more efficient than a shaded-pole motor. It has a greater starting torque, and usually draws less current. PSC motor currents are approximately half those of shaded-pole motor currents. For example, if you must replace a defective shaded-pole motor, a PSC motor that draws only 2.5 A can be used to replace a shaded-pole motor that draws 5 A. PSC motors are used for a variety of applications, including air conditioning and heating direct-drive blowers, small pumps, and small compressors.

Instead of using a shading coil for starting the motor, a PSC motor has two separate sets of windings—the *start* windings and the *run* windings—placed in slots in the stator frame. These windings are approximately 90° apart. A "run" capacitor is connected between the windings, and is wired in series with the start winding, as shown in

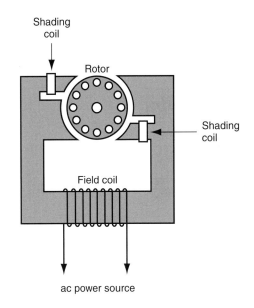

FIGURE 8-5. *Skeleton-frame motor*

Frame #	Diameter, in.	Horsepower range
59	3½	½₅₀ to ½₀
11	4	¼₀ to ⅟₁₅
29	5	½₀ to ¼
39	5½	⅟₁₀ to ¼

TABLE 8-3. *Shaded-pole motor sizes and capacities*

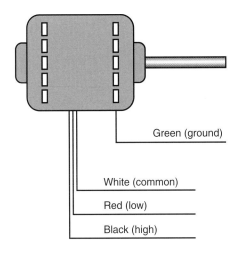

FIGURE 8-6. *Dual-speed shaded-pole motor*

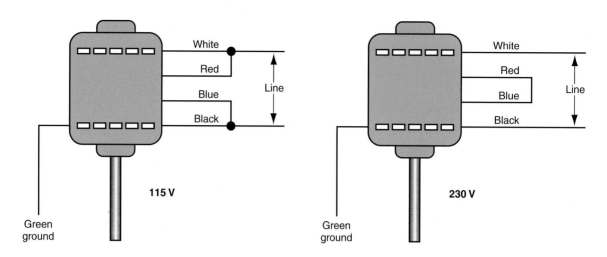

FIGURE 8-7. *Dual-voltage shaded-pole motor*

Figure 8-8. The run capacitor introduces the phase shift necessary for the motor to start every time power is applied. In a PSC motor, the start winding and the run capacitor remain in the circuit at all times.

The typical color code for wiring a 115-V PSC single-speed motor is:

- line (common)—white

- line (run)—black

- capacitor—brown or blue.

Sizes and capacities

PSC motors are more varied and versatile than shaded-pole motors, because they are electrically reversible, have multiple speeds, and can run on multiple voltages. Most PSC motors used in the HVACR industry, depending on the application, range in size from 3½ to 6½ in. in diameter, and have capacities ranging from 1/16 to ¾ hp. Table 8-4 shows the average size and horsepower range for various PSC motor frame numbers.

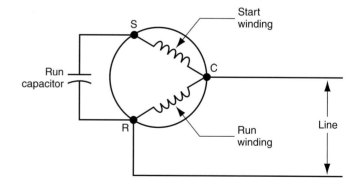

FIGURE 8-8. *PSC motor*

Troubleshooting PSC motors

With the right tools and knowledge, a PSC motor is easy to troubleshoot. The windings of the motor may become faulty due to overheating, overloading, or structural faults within the winding itself. A "bad" motor winding may be either shorted, open, or grounded. All of these problems can be checked easily with an ohmmeter. Service technicians must be careful in diagnosing problems with the windings of PSC motors, because such motors are often designed to provide several different operational speeds.

A bad capacitor can keep a PSC motor from starting, or can draw too high a current when running. You can check capacitors by using one of the methods covered in Lesson 4 of this Unit. In most cases, faulty PSC motors should be replaced, rather than repaired. When you replace a PSC motor, always replace the existing capacitor with a new one. There are two reasons for this. First, 99% of the time the replacement motor will require a different capacitance anyway. And second, the old capacitor may have changed value from what it was originally.

Frame #	Diameter, in.	Horsepower range
59	3½	⅛ to ½₀
11	4	¼₀ to ¹⁄₁₅
29	5	½₀ to ¼
39	5½	¹⁄₁₀ to ¼
43/49	6½	⅓ to ¾

TABLE 8-4. *PSC motor sizes and capacities*

Rotation

The direction of rotation cannot be determined from the windings on a PSC motor. If the motor does not have the direction of rotation stamped on the end plate, the best way to determine rotation is by direct observation of the driven fan. Figure 8-9 shows how dirt can accumulate on the leading edge of a fan blade—which, of course, serves an indication of the direction of rotation of the motor driving the fan.

The only other way to determine the direction of rotation of a PSC motor is to take it apart. Before dismantling it, make a scratch or mark on the case of the motor as a reminder of how the end plates are assembled (so that you can put everything back together the same way when you are finished working). If the motor has been in service for some time, it is often possible to determine the direction of rotation by inspecting the cooling fins cast onto the end of the rotor assembly. Dust, dirt, and grime will collect on the leading edge of the fin, as shown in Figure 8-10 on the next page.

Some PSC motors are reversible, either by making a change in their wiring or by placing a special plug on the outside of the motor that changes the way the stator is wired in relationship to the poles on the rotor.

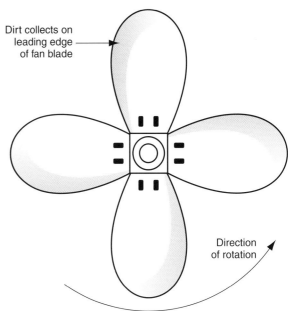

Dirt collects on leading edge of fan blade

Direction of rotation

FIGURE 8-9. *Inspect the fan blades to determine direction of rotation*

145

Speed

As is the case with a shaded-pole motor, the speed of a PSC motor is determined by the number of poles that the stator winding has. Typical speeds are as follows:

Number of poles	Speed, rpm
2	3,000 to 3,200
4	1,400 to 1,650
6	900 to 1,150
8	800 to 850

A so-called *multispeed* motor is really a *multi-horsepower* motor. The winding is tapped so that it generates less torque, and therefore runs slower under load. This is illustrated in Figure 8-11. At no load—for instance, when you are doing a bench test with nothing connected to the motor—there will be no difference in speed between any of the settings, because the motor will be running at idle. Nor will there be an appreciable difference in speed if the motor being used is too strong for the unit. If, for example, you are using a ½-hp 3-speed motor instead of a ¼-hp 3-speed motor, there will be no significant difference between the high, medium, and low settings. However, speed becomes imperative when air must be moved, as an air conditioning system must do when changing from cooling to heating.

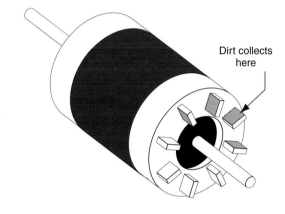

FIGURE 8-10. *Inspect the cooling fins to determine direction of rotation*

When replacing a PSC motor—whether it is a single-speed model or a multispeed model—the best practice is to replace the existing motor with another one just like it. Sometimes this may not be possible (the specific model may no longer be in production). If an exact replacement is not available, remember: although a shaded-pole motor can be replaced with a PSC motor, you *cannot* replace a PSC motor with a shaded-pole motor. Shaded-pole motors have the advantages of being inexpensive and reliable, but PSC motors are more energy-efficient.

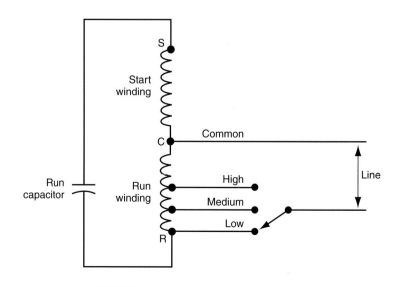

FIGURE 8-11. *Multispeed PSC motor*

SPLIT-PHASE MOTORS

A *split-phase* motor, also called an *induction-start, induction-run* motor, is a type of fractional-horsepower motor used for driving fans, centrifugal pumps, and refrigerator compressors. Like the PSC motor, a split-phase motor has two windings or sets of windings—start and run. However, the start winding is switched in and out of the circuit by a centrifugal switch attached to the motor shaft. When the motor reaches approximately 75 to 80% of its running speed, the switch opens and removes the start winding from the circuit. Figure 8-12 represents a typical split-phase motor.

Troubleshooting split-phase motors

The windings of a split-phase motor may become faulty due to overheating, overloading, or inherent defects. You can use an ohmmeter to determine whether a motor is shorted, open, or grounded. The centrifugal switch can cause problems if it does not disconnect the start winding from the circuit, or if it prevents the start winding from being energized when it should. A service technician can tell if a split-phase motor is operating correctly by the sound of the centrifugal switch opening as the motor comes up to speed. The switch will close when the motor is de-energized. Split-phase motors are not reversible in the field, and are never configured for multispeed operation. They are found in belt-drive blower assemblies and in some appliances.

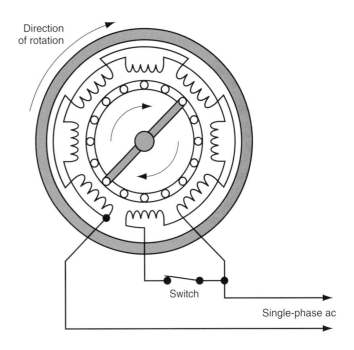

FIGURE 8-12. *Split-phase motor*

CAPACITOR-START, INDUCTION-RUN (CSIR) MOTORS

"Capacitor-start" motors are so-called because they require the additional assistance of a capacitor to get the rotor started. The fact that capacitors can be used in conjunction with split-phase motors broadens their scope of application. The use of capacitors also has a significant effect on construction costs, both for motor manufacturers and for producers of motor-driven devices.

There are many applications that require a relatively high *starting* load, but a relatively low (or normal) *operating* load. Without a "start" capacitor, more costly windings would have to be built into the motor in order to provide sufficient starting torque. In some applications (such as high-static residential air conditioning systems), the required starting torque is so high that even a split-phase motor capable of producing the best starting conditions may not be adequate. For example, the system may require a 1-hp motor to get the mechanism started, but only a ½-hp motor to keep it in operation.

Because of this and similar conditions, more motors are being designed today for specific applications than ever before. In addition, more consideration is being given to the starting and running torques of motors for particular applications than to the horsepower ratings of the motors. With the proper construction and selection of windings and capacitors, motor manufacturers can produce a motor for any unusual starting condition.

A *capacitor-start, induction-run* (CSIR) motor uses a start winding and start capacitor *only* during starting. Once the motor has attained about 75% of its full speed, the centrifugal switch opens, disconnecting the start winding and start capacitor. Then the unit continues to run as an induction motor. Figure 8-13 is a schematic representation of a CSIR motor.

Troubleshooting capacitor-start, induction-run motors

Troubleshooting a capacitor-start, induction-run motor is similar to troubleshooting a PSC motor. A bad capacitor can keep the motor from starting, or can draw a high current when running. You can check for shorted or open capacitors by using one of the methods covered in Lesson 4 of this Unit. If the capacitor is open, either the motor will not start or it will not attain a high enough speed to open the centrifugal switch and remove the start winding from the circuit. The motor windings then become subject to overheating. Overheating can lead to the eventual breakdown of insulation, and the windings can become shorted, open, or grounded. Of course, you can use an ohmmeter to check the condition of the motor windings.

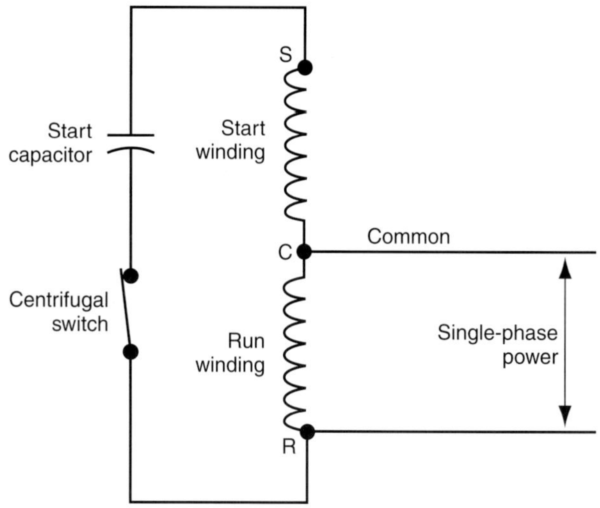

FIGURE 8-13. *Capacitor-start, induction-run motor*

The centrifugal switch can become dirty and may get stuck, either in the open or closed position, causing problems with the start capacitor and the start winding. If the start winding is not taken out of the circuit, or if it is not energized when it should be, the capacitor and/or the windings may fail. Again, you should be able to hear the centrifugal switch opening as the motor comes up to speed. The switch will close when the motor is de-energized.

In most cases, it is more cost-effective to replace a faulty CSIR motor with a new one than it is to attempt a repair. When you replace a CSIR motor, *always* replace the capacitor with a new one.

CAPACITOR-START, CAPACITOR-RUN (CSCR) MOTORS

As shown in Figure 8-14, a *capacitor-start, capacitor-run* (CSCR) motor uses two capacitors. The second capacitor, called a "run" capacitor, stays in the circuit all the time. Rather than improving starting torque, it is used to improve the power factor characteristics of the motor. Start capacitors are high-capacitance electrolytic capacitors designed for short-time starting duty only. A run capacitor, on the other hand, needs much less capacitance, but because it is always in the circuit while the motor is operating, it must be built to withstand continuous use.

The CSCR motor is essentially a combination of the permanent split-capacitor motor and the capacitor-start motor. It provides the high starting torque of the capacitor-start motor and the efficiency of the PSC motor. Of course, it is susceptible to the same

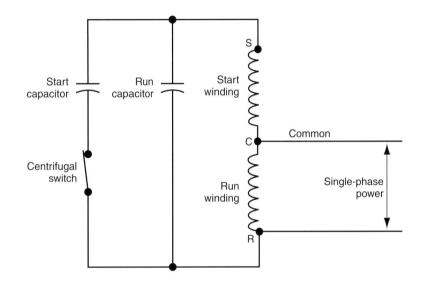

FIGURE 8-14. *Capacitor-start, capacitor-run motor*

problems as any other capacitor-start motor. The CSCR motor is used as a belt drive for some small compressors. Once common in air conditioning systems, there are no longer very many CSCR motors used. However, because this type of motor can still be found in some applications, it is important for you to be familiar with it.

THREE-PHASE MOTORS

Up to this point in the Lesson, all of the motors that you have studied have been *single-phase, fractional-horsepower* motors. Recall that motors rated higher than 1 hp are called *integral-horsepower* motors. Some single-phase motors are rated as high as 5 hp, but normally, anything above that will be a *three-phase* motor. Starters (contactors) and overload protection devices used in three-phase motors must also be configured for three-phase operation. Because there are so many different manufacturers of motors, the discussion of three-phase motors that follows will be as generic as possible. At the end of

this Lesson, you will find some NEMA information regarding the frame
dimensions of many specific motors made today.

To start an ac motor from a standstill, there must be some way to shift the phase
relationship between the stator windings. As you know, a single-phase motor
uses a separate winding, or a separate winding and a capacitor. A three-phase
motor uses a different approach.

Three-phase motors operate on three-phase current. This means that
there are three separate circuits in the stator, compared to only one
circuit in the stator of a single-phase motor. Three-phase motors are
wound so that the windings are electrically out of phase by 120°.
Because the three phases follow one another by ⅓ of a cycle, they
produce a rotating field without having to use extra start windings.
Thus, three-phase induction motors are said to be "self-starting."
Figure 8-15 is a schematic diagram of a three-phase motor.

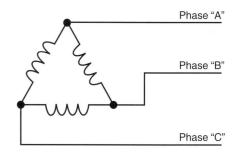

FIGURE 8-15. *Three-phase motor
(delta-connected)*

Three-phase motors come in a wide variety of frame sizes and
horsepower ranges. Voltages range from 208 to 4,800 V. For motors
rated at 10 hp and up, there are three general kinds of winding
connections:

- across-the-line (XL)

- part wind start (PWS)

- wye-delta (sometimes called "soft start").

The "across-the-line start" and "part wind start" connections are
generally used on motors rated at less than 100 hp. The "soft start"
connection is normally used on motors rated at more than 100 hp.
Most motors used in the HVACR field are connected in a "wye"
(or "star") configuration. Figure 8-16 shows a wye-connected motor
(note the "Y" shape). The configuration shown in Figure 8-15 is
called a "delta" configuration, because the shape resembles the
triangular symbol for the Greek letter *delta* (Δ). The delta
configuration is used for very large motors.

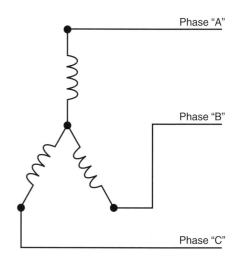

FIGURE 8-16. *Three-phase motor
(wye-connected)*

Figure 8-17 is a schematic representation of a three-phase motor
wired for across-the-line starting. (You may occasionally see the abbreviation
"XL" on a schematic drawing to indicate that the across-the-line starting
method is being used.) Note that there are three sets of contacts, one for
each power line coming into the motor. There are also three separate windings.

When the contactor or starter is energized, all of the contacts close, and each winding is energized at the same time. There *is* a time difference as far as when the *maximum* current passes through each winding. Assuming a normal 60-Hz power supply, the time between each winding's maximum current is 0.0056 seconds. This configuration is commonly used for indoor fan motors, pump motors, condenser fan motors, and small hermetic compressors (5 to 15 hp). Starting voltages are typically, 208, 230, 460, 480, and 575 V (all three-phase). The voltages are usually kept under 1,300 V because of wiring restrictions and codes.

For all three-phase motors, the direction of rotation can be reversed simply by switching any two of the incoming power leads.

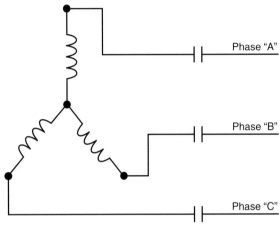

FIGURE 8-17. *Across-the-line starting*

TROUBLESHOOTING THREE-PHASE MOTORS

The majority of three-phase motor failures—perhaps 90 to 95%—are caused by problems with the starting components or the power supply. When you test the windings in an across-the-line three-phase motor with an ohmmeter, the resistance should be the same in each winding (within 3 to 5% of each other). Of course, the resistance will vary greatly from manufacturer to manufacturer, and from horsepower to horsepower. There are standard terminal designations applied to all three-phase motors. Some manufacturers use color codes along with the motor terminal markings.

RESISTANCE TESTING

Single-voltage six-wire and three-wire motors

Figure 8-18 on the next page shows how to check the resistance of a typical 5-hp, 208-V, three-phase motor. This is an open-frame motor operating on 60-Hz power. As you can see, the resistance of each winding is 2 to 4 Ω. (Again, this reading will vary from motor to motor.) This particular motor has six leads brought out through a junction box on the side of the motor. Because *external* overload protection is used, you can test each winding individually. As shown, the terminal designations are T1-T4 for winding A, T2-T5 for winding B, and T3-T6 for winding C. However, it is important to remember that some three-phase motors use *internal* overload protection, and thus have only three wires to test. Their terminal designations will be T1, T2, and T3. As shown in Figure 8-19 on the next page, you are now measuring the resistance across *two* windings, so your readings will be doubled what they were before.

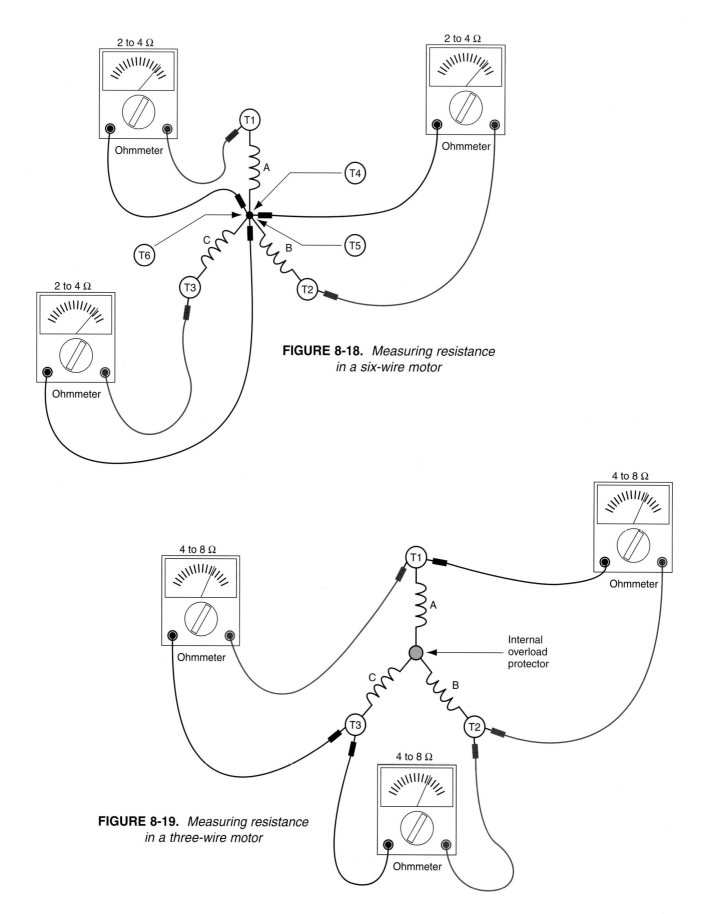

FIGURE 8-18. *Measuring resistance in a six-wire motor*

FIGURE 8-19. *Measuring resistance in a three-wire motor*

Six-wire "part wind start" (PWS) motors

"Part wind start" (PWS) motors are designed with two separate sets of windings built into the stator stack. Electrically they resemble the schematic diagram shown in Figure 8-20. Note the terminal designations. These motors were developed for applications in which it is more economical to use two smaller contactors or starters than to use one large one. When testing a PWS motor with an ohmmeter, you should find that the all windings have the same resistance. PWS motors usually use external protection. They operate on voltages of 208, 230, 460, 480, or 575 V (all three-phase). Their controllers will be covered later in this Lesson.

Dual-voltage six-wire and nine-wire motors

A three-phase motor used for a multiple-voltage application may have either six or nine leads brought out through the connection box, and can be wired in either a wye or a delta configuration. Figure 8-21 on the next page shows the terminal designations for a nine-lead dual-voltage motor. This motor can be connected for either 230-V or 460-V operation. The resistance of the windings in a typical 15-hp motor of this kind will range anywhere from 0.2 Ω to 1.5 Ω, depending on the application. If, for example, the resistance per winding in Figure 8-21 is 0.8 Ω, you could expect the following readings:

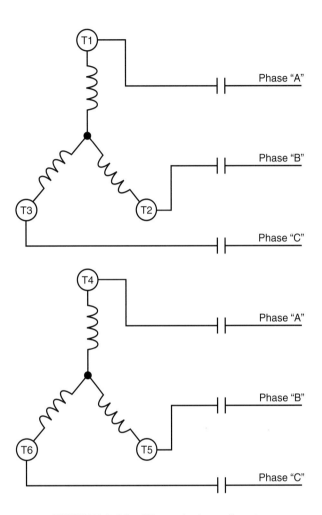

FIGURE 8-20. *"Part wind start" motor*

Terminal numbers	Resistance, Ω
1-4	0.8
2-5	0.8
3-6	0.8
7-8	1.6
7-9	1.6
8-9	1.6

Note: When testing the resistance of the windings of *any* motor, *always* test the windings to ground, or to the frame of the motor. If any resistance is registered on the ohmmeter, replace the motor. (This applies to single-phase motors as well.)

VOLTAGE AND CURRENT TESTING

In order to test the voltage of a motor accurately, you should perform the test at the motor itself, not at the starter or contactor. There are two reasons for this. First, you will get a more accurate reading when the motor is at full load. Second, you will be able to tell if there is a problem with voltage drop across the contactor or starter.

There are several conditions that can cause problems in three-phase motors:

- single phasing

- low voltage

- high voltage

- voltage imbalance

- current imbalance.

Single phasing

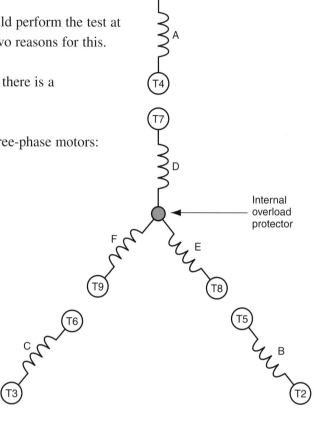

FIGURE 8-21. *Terminal designations for a three-phase dual-voltage motor*

Single phasing occurs when one of the lines is broken between the motor and the supply. In the example shown in Figure 8-22, phase "A" is broken. If this occurs while the motor is running, the motor will continue to operate as a single-phase motor. However, the other two windings will consume more power and the current will increase in each of the other windings to 1½ to 2 times the normal current. The motor will slow down and start drawing excessive current. If the condition is allowed to continue, the motor will begin to overheat. This is because winding A is getting no power, while windings B and C are trying to keep the motor turning.

If one of the three input power connections is open and the motor is *not* running, then when the motor tries to start, the result will be a *locked rotor* condition. Because there are no longer three windings in the circuit, the motor will trip its overload protectors, or the heaters in the starter. Locked rotor problems can also be caused by a bad contactor or starter, or by an open winding. It is even possible for the power company to lose a leg of the incoming power supply.

When you inspect a faulty motor, you can tell that single phasing has occurred if one winding (every third winding) shows no signs of overheating, while the windings adjacent to it, or on either side of it, are burned or show other signs of overheating.

Low voltage

Although very difficult to prove, low voltages probably cause more damage to motors than any other condition. A typical motor will work within a 10% range of its voltage application—that is, within 5% on either side of its nominal rating. For example, a 230-V motor should work within a range of 218.5 to 241.5 V (since ±5% of 230 V is ±11.5 V). The acceptable range for a 208-V motor is different—±5% of 208 V is only ±10.4 V, so the 208-V motor should operate within a range of 197.6 to 228.4 V. A 460-V motor, on the other hand, has a much wider range, and should operate within a range of 437 to 483 V (±5% of 460 V is ±23 V). Remember that any voltage under the minimum will cause high running current. This occurs because the motor is trying to work harder with less energy. The result is added heat in the windings.

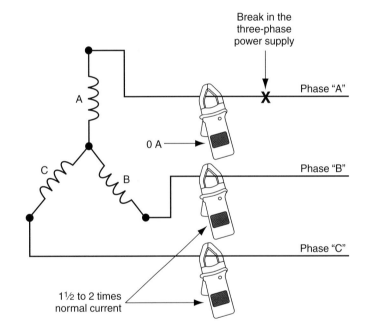

High voltage

As explained in the preceding paragraph, a 230-V motor can function safely up to the top of its operating range at 241.5 V. If an even higher voltage is applied, the motor's windings will overheat. The motor cannot go any faster, because the number of poles and the frequency of the power supply determine its speed. However, the added voltage will cause overheating. Normally, the overloads will trip more quickly in an overvoltage situation than in an undervoltage situation. Both conditions can be hard to diagnose, so if you are in doubt about the voltage, use a recording voltmeter and check the incoming power supply for 24 to 48 hours.

FIGURE 8-22. *Single phasing*

Voltage imbalance

A small imbalance in the input voltage can result in a considerable amount of heat being generated in the motor windings. An imbalance of only 5%, for example, can increase the winding temperature as much as 50% above the safe level. To determine the voltage imbalance in a three-phase system, first measure

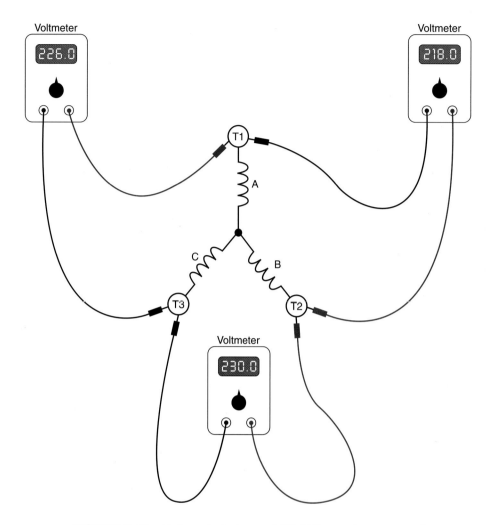

FIGURE 8-23. *Voltage imbalance (230-V three-phase power)*

and record the voltage between T1 and T2, then between T1 and T3, and finally between T2 and T3. In the example shown in Figure 8-23, the readings are 218, 226, and 230 V, respectively. Find the *average* voltage by adding these three figures together and dividing by 3:

Voltage measured between T1 and T2	218 V
Voltage measured between T1 and T3	226 V
Voltage measured between T2 and T3	+ 230 V
Total	674 V

Average voltage = 674 V ÷ 3 = 224.67 V

Determine which reading represents the greatest deviation from the average (in this case it is the 218-V reading). Now you can use the following equation to calculate the voltage imbalance:

$$\% \text{ imbalance} = \frac{\text{maximum deviation from average voltage}}{\text{average voltage}} \times 100$$

$$= \frac{224.67 \text{ V} - 218 \text{ V}}{224.67 \text{ V}} \times 100$$

$$= \frac{6.67 \text{ V}}{224.67 \text{ V}} \times 100$$

$$= 0.0297 \times 100 = 2.97\% = \text{approximately } 3\%$$

Note: The voltage imbalance between any two legs of the supply voltage applied to a three-phase motor must *not* exceed 2%. Any voltage imbalance of more than 2% must be corrected. If a voltage imbalance exceeds 2%, look for an electrical terminal, contact, etc., that is loose or corroded and may be causing a high resistance in that leg. Examine the incoming power supply to the building and the distribution panels for the same things.

Current imbalance

A voltage imbalance always produces a current imbalance, but a current imbalance may occur without a voltage imbalance. A current imbalance can occur when an electrical terminal, contactor, starter, etc. becomes loose or corroded, causing a high resistance in one leg. Since current follows the path of least resistance, the current in the other two legs will increase, causing more heat to be generated in those two windings.

To determine the current imbalance in a three-phase system, first check the motor nameplate for the full-load current (sometimes abbreviated FLA, for full-load amperage). Select the highest range setting (higher than the motor FLA) on your clamp-on ammeter. Turn the power on, and place the clamp-on ammeter around the wire connected to the T1 terminal of the motor. Measure and record the current drawn by the T1 leg. Then, one at a time, measure the current drawn by the remaining two legs. For the example shown in Figure 8-24, the readings are 25, 27, and 26 A.

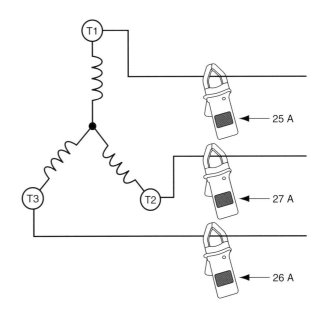

FIGURE 8-24. *Current imbalance*

Again, you can find the *average* current by adding these three figures together and dividing by 3:

Current measured in T1 leg   25 A
Current measured in T2 leg   27 A
Current measured in T3 leg   + 26 A
                        Total   78 A

Average current = 78 A ÷ 3 = 26 A

The readings for legs T1 and T2 (25 and 27 A, respectively) both produce a maximum 1-A deviation from the average of 26 A. Now you can use the following equation to calculate the current imbalance:

$$\% \text{ imbalance} = \frac{\text{maximum deviation from average current}}{\text{average current}} \times 100$$

$$= \frac{1 \text{ A}}{26 \text{ A}} \times 100$$

$$= 0.038 \times 100 = 3.8\%$$

Note: The current imbalance between any two legs of a three-phase system must *not* exceed 10%. If the current imbalance exceeds 10%, look for an electrical terminal, contact, etc., that is loose or corroded and may be causing a high resistance in that leg. Since the imbalance in Figure 8-24 is less than 10%, the current between phases is acceptable.

DUAL-VOLTAGE MOTOR CONNECTIONS

So far, most of the testing examples discussed in this Lesson have pertained to single-voltage motors. It is more economical for manufacturers to make three-phase motors with dual windings. Look back at Figure 8-21, which shows a *dual-voltage* motor. A nine-lead motor of this type can be connected for either 230-V or 460-V operation.

Figure 8-25 shows how a nine-wire dual-voltage motor is connected in a wye configuration. In Figure 8-25A, the leads are connected in *parallel* for 230-V operation. This means that the 230 V of Line 1 will be applied to both windings A and D at the same time. Likewise, the 230 V of Line 2 will be applied to windings B and E at the same time, and the 230 V of Line 3 will be applied to windings C and F at the same time. Therefore, the same voltage will be impressed across each of the windings.

In Figure 8-25B, the leads are connected in *series* for 460-V operation. This means that the 460 V from L1 and L2 will be impressed across windings A, D,

B, and E. The 460 V from L1 and L3 will be impressed across windings A, D, C, and F. The 460 V from L2 and L3 will be impressed across windings B, E, C, and F.

Figure 8-26 on the next page shows how a nine-wire dual-voltage motor is connected in a delta configuration.

The two examples of wye-connected motors shown in Figure 8-25 both use the "across-the-line" (XL) starting method. The nine-lead motor is versatile, however, and can also be wired for "part wind start" (PWS) operation. This option, shown in Figure 8-27 on page 161, is available *only* at the lower (230-V) voltage connection. Starting is accomplished in steps, with a time delay between steps. Contactor C1 is energized first, and contactor C2 is energized after a delay of ¾ to 1½ seconds. (If the time delay is any longer, there is a possibility of the first winding overheating.)

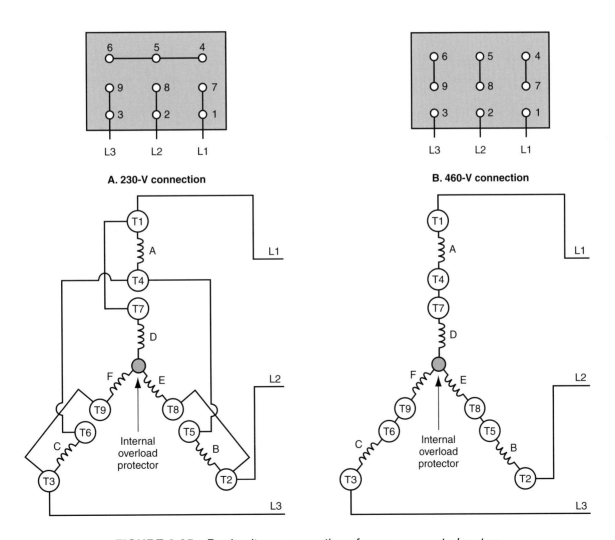

FIGURE 8-25. *Dual-voltage connections for wye-connected motors*

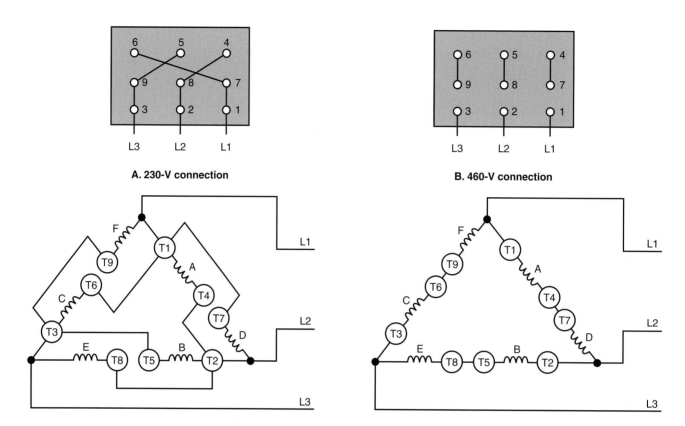

FIGURE 8-26. *Dual-voltage connections for delta-connected motors*

This configuration allows the 230 V of Line 1 to be applied to winding A, the 230 V of Line 2 to be applied to winding B, and the 230 V of Line 3 to be applied to winding C. This first step is accomplished through contacts C1a, C1b, and C1c. After the time delay, the second contactor is energized, allowing the 230 V of Line 1 to be applied to winding D, the 230 V of Line 2 to be applied to winding E, and the 230 V of Line 3 to be applied to winding F. This second step is accomplished through contacts C2a, C2b, and C2c.

Cross phasing

It is important to remember that the windings of a PWS motor must be "in phase." In Figure 8-27, for example, winding D must be powered with the same line as winding A. The same holds true for windings E and B, and for windings F and C. If for some reason the connections have been changed or the motor has been wired incorrectly, a problem called *cross phasing* can occur. Assume, for example, that the connections to windings E and F are reversed by mistake. Then, when the second contactor C2 is energized, windings E and F are no longer rotating in the same direction as their counterparts B and C. As a result, one set of windings will be trying to go in one direction while the other set of windings will be trying to go in the opposite direction, in effect cancelling each other out. Normally this will cause the motor to overheat and trip its protectors. In some cases, it can cause the motor to burn out. Always make sure that a three-phase PWS motor is wired correctly.

VARIABLE-SPEED MOTORS

More and more multispeed and variable-speed motors are being incorporated into HVACR systems to increase the efficiency of the equipment. *Variable-speed* motors go by several names. You may hear a variable-speed motor referred to as a "brushless permanent magnet" (BPM) device, as an "electronic commutated motor" (ECM), or as an "integrated controlled motor" (ICM). All of these motors work on the same basic principle. Changes in a variable— air flow or static pressure, for example—are monitored by a sensor. By responding to changes in the variable, the motor has the ability to adjust the speed of a blower or fan, and thus maintain a predetermined setpoint. The motor's electronic controls can be pre-programmed, and are contained in a package or module mounted on the rear of the motor housing. Figure 8-28 on the next page shows the difference between a "standard" 56 frame and a BPM 56 frame motor.

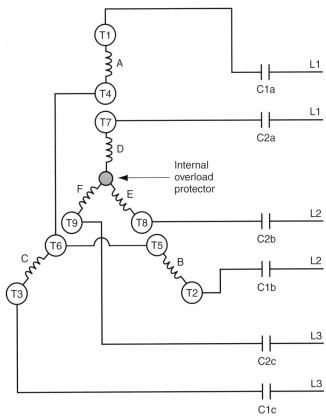

FIGURE 8-27. *Typical "part wind start" connection*

TROUBLESHOOTING VARIABLE-SPEED MOTORS

Diagnosing problems in conventional electric motors usually involves using an ohmmeter to check for open, shorted, or grounded windings. You *cannot* use an ohmmeter to check variable-speed motor windings, because of the variety of electronic components built into the motor. If you were to place an ohmmeter across the leads of a variable-speed motor, the readings would make little sense. Instead, you must check for correct inputs and outputs. *Always* confirm that the input signals and voltages supplied to an ECM are correct before condemning the motor.

When troubleshooting an ECM, think of the motor as a "black box," as you would when troubleshooting a circuit with an electronic control. Most manufacturers use some type of error code display. This may take the form of a flashing LED or an LCD readout. First check the equipment for any fault codes that may be indicated by the built-in self-diagnostic function (if so equipped).

It is always a good idea to consult the manufacturer's troubleshooting guide as well. Then check the input and output voltages or signals. If they are correct and if the motor does not run, the motor is probably defective. If input voltages are present but they are the wrong value, there is a good chance that the problem is not in the motor, but somewhere else.

Table 8-5 shows what a typical input/output voltage chart looks like. The information and the style in which it is presented will vary from manufacturer to manufacturer.

COMMON MAINTENANCE PROCEDURES

The following paragraphs discuss some common problems that you may encounter when working with ECMs, and the corrective steps to take.

Board fuse keeps blowing

When the low-voltage fuse blows, it is likely that the transformer would have blown too, had the low-voltage fuse not been in the circuit to protect it. The fuse usually blows when there is a high current drawn on the transformer, a high voltage applied to the low-voltage circuit, or a direct secondary short. When a high current is drawn on the transformer, it is usually because the transformer has been shorted, or because the system is drawing more volt-amperes than the transformer rating allows. When a fuse blows because of high voltage, the system has mixed high- and low-voltage signals.

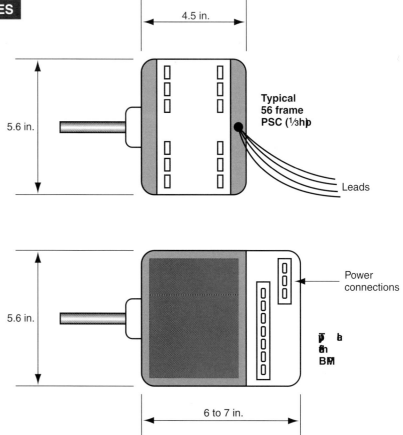

FIGURE 8-28. *Conventional and BPM motor frames*

Perform the following checks:

1. Check the transformer, thermostat, and control box wiring.

2. Check to be sure that all low-voltage and high-voltage wires are connected to the proper terminals.

Location*	Normal reading	Purpose
Input voltages		
L1 & L2	115 V ac	Main power supply to furnace
PL8-4 & 5	115 V ac	Power to ICM
PR1 & PR2	115 V ac	Power to transformer primary
SEC1 & SEC2	24 V ac	Power to transformer secondary
R & Com	24 V ac	Power from transformer secondary
W/W1 & Com	24 V ac	Call for heat signal from room thermostat
Y/Y2 & Com	24 V ac	Call for cooling signal from room thermostat
G & Com	24 V ac	Call for continuous fan signal from room thermostat
PL1-3 & Com	24 V ac	Present if fuse, rollout switch, and limit switch are closed
PL1-5 & Com	24 V ac	Present on call for heat (indicates closed LPS, DSS, and ALS)
Output voltages		
PL3-2 & 3	115 V ac	Power to inducer (low-stage heat)
PL3-1 & 3	115 V ac	Power to inducer (high-stage heat)
PL6-1 & 2	115 V ac	Power to HSI
EAC-1 & EAC-2	115 V ac	Power to electronic air cleaner whenever blower operates
PL1-1 & Com	24 V ac	Energizes low-stage heat gas valve solenoid
PL1-4 & Com	24 V ac	Energizes high-stage heat gas valve solenoid
HUM & Com	24 V ac	Energizes humidifier when gas valve energizes

*Place meter probes at locations shown on manufacturer's diagram. Use a digital meter for best results.

TABLE 8-5. *Typical ECM input/output voltages*

3. Check the VA draw on the transformer. If the VA draw is more than the VA rating of the transformer, the fuse will blow. The transformer must be replaced with one that has a higher VA rating.

Motor does not run

Perform the following checks:

1. Check all of the plugs and receptacles on the ECM circuit board and motor for bad connections. Be sure that all plugs are fully inserted.

2. Verify that the voltage at the terminals of the contactor is approximately 230 V. If it is not, determine whether high voltage is entering the unit.

3. Verify that there is a low-voltage control signal to the motor. The motor receives control signals through the motor plug. The voltage output of each pin in the plug will be different, depending on the mode of operation.

What if all of the values for any one of the operating modes check out, and the motor still fails to run? Then the motor is probably defective, and will need to be replaced.

Motor shaft does not rotate smoothly

The motor shaft normally does not run smoothly. This is due to steps in rotation, called motor *cogging*. The cogging is caused by permanent magnets passing each pole in the motor. However, excessive force should not be required to turn the shaft. If the shaft is very difficult to turn, either the motor control or the bearings have failed, and the motor must be replaced.

Motor does not run smoothly

If the motor does not run smoothly, check the blower wheel for damage. Determine whether the blower wheel is out of balance. If it is not defective, the motor will probably need to be replaced.

Motor does not stop running

Perform the following checks:

1. Check for proper grounding between the motor ground lead, the transformer common lead, and the control board. If this does not stop the motor, continue to Step 2.

2. Remove all of the thermostat wiring. If this makes the motor stop, it means that the circuit board is faulty and must be replaced. If the motor does not stop, continue to Step 3.

3. Remove the control plug. If the motor continues to run, replace the motor.

STEPPER MOTORS

Stepper motors are similar to ECMs in that they are electronically controlled and cannot be tested with conventional meters. They are usually smaller, however, and require a different kind of controlling system. Most stepper motors are used to control the action of valves and damper assemblies in variable-air systems.

The stepper motor is a dc motor. It derives its name from the fact that its motion consists of discrete *steps* of uniform magnitude, instead of continuous rotation.

Whatever the application, the manufacturer is the best source of information when it comes to troubleshooting stepper motors. For more basic information about stepper motor operation, refer to Lesson 6 of Unit 2 in this Course.

GENERAL INFORMATION FOR REPLACING ELECTRIC MOTORS

This Lesson has provided a good deal of information about troubleshooting electric motors, but "on-the-job" experience is also valuable. Always learn as much as you can, in the field and in the classroom, and remember to practice "safety first." The following items of general information are further reminders that you may find helpful when repairing and replacing motors:

- *Never* carry a motor by its leads. Leads are not designed to serve as handles. Carrying a motor by the leads can have serious results—perhaps an open where the leads are joined to the stator, or cracks in the insulation that will allow moisture to enter and cause a short.

- Always replace a 6-pole motor with another 6-pole motor, a 4-pole motor with a 4 pole motor, and so on. There are two reasons for this. First, replacing a 4-pole motor (that runs at 1,400 to 1,600 rpm) with a slower 6-pole motor (900 to 1,150 rpm) results in reduced air delivery and greatly reduced efficiency in an air conditioning system. The reduced air flow may be significant enough to ice up the evaporator and shut down the system automatically. Second, if the situation is reversed and you replace a 6-pole motor with a 4-pole motor, the replacement motor will be seriously overloaded. The 4-pole motor will overheat, causing cycling on the overload protector. Keep in mind that horsepower requirements vary as the cube of the speed. In other words, doubling the speed ($\times 2$) means that 8 times as much power ($2^3 = 8$) will be needed! If you replace a 6-pole motor with a 4-pole motor, the 4-pole motor will require more than 3 times as much horsepower.

- Cycling on the overload protector indicates that a motor is overheating, and probably misapplied. It is rare for the overload protector itself to be defective. To check for overload, check the current draw using a clamp-on ammeter. If the current draw of a replacement motor is 20% greater than its nameplate value, it is overloaded. The solution is to use a more powerful motor. This is the most common reason for cycling on the overload. A second reason may be that the original motor was better ventilated. Try to use a motor with as much ventilation as the original (include a rain shield if moisture is a problem). Cycling on overload also may occur if the motor is *too* powerful and is drawing 25% less current than its nameplate value. Finally, the overload could be tripping due to incorrect rotation—that is, the motor is drawing hot air over itself instead of away from itself.

■ If the stator of a multispeed motor has voltage applied to two or more speeds at once, the stator will burn out within a very short time (too quickly for the overload protector to cut off power to the stator). When wiring multispeed motors, first connect the motor's common lead (normally white, but not always) directly to the power. The leads for the various speeds go to the switch. At any one time, there should be only two power leads connected—the common and one other. Green is usually the ground wire. Always check the wiring diagrams supplied by the manufacturer.

■ Before replacing a start-capacitor motor, always check first to see if the capacitor is bad. To do so, substitute a new capacitor of the same value. If the motor still does not operate correctly, replace the motor. Be aware, though, that a motor with a shorted capacitor may still start and run. It will not run at full speed, but instead will operate as if it is overloaded (that is, it will draw high current and trip the overload protector).

■ Although sleeve bearings are less costly, quieter, and last longer under normal operating conditions than ball bearings, ball bearings should be used when high ambient temperatures or unbalanced loads are present.

MOTOR NAMEPLATE DATA

Much of the information that you need to know when servicing or replacing a motor can be found on the motor nameplate. Make yourself a quick checklist of necessary information. This information may include, but is not limited to, the following:

■ *Manufacturer's name* and any identifying codes or serial numbers.

■ *Frame size* as defined by the National Electrical Manufacturers Association (NEMA). You also may want to know the diameter and length of the stator stack, and the diameter and length of the shaft. (Shaft bushings are available to increase the shaft diameter.)

■ *Motor type* (split-phase, shaded-pole, capacitor-start, etc.).

■ *Type of power* on which the motor is designed to operate (single-phase ac, three-phase ac, dc).

- *Voltage* at which the motor may be operated (115 V, 208 V, 230 V, 277 V, etc.).

- *Current* (in amperes) that the motor draws at its rated load, voltage, and frequency.

- *Speed* (in rpm) at which the motor will operate at its rated horsepower, voltage, and frequency.

- *Frequency* at which the motor is to be operated (usually 60 Hz).

- *Horsepower* the motor will produce at its rated speed. This may not be the best way to match a fractional-horsepower motor. Matching the current draw is usually more accurate, especially for motors of less than ¼ hp. In small motors, the hp rating is often on the high side or low side, since NEMA standards do not include smaller than 48 frame motors. The nameplate current of the replacement motor should be at least equal to the original, and may be up to 25% higher. In general, an "under-powered" replacement is more apt to cause problems than an "over-powered" one.

- *Duty rating* (the period of time, in hours, for which the motor may be operated continuously without overheating).

- *Type of protection* installed in the motor.

OPERATING TEMPERATURES

The amount by which a motor's temperature will increase over the *ambient* (surrounding) air temperature when operating at its rated load and speed is known as temperature *rise*. Temperature rise is usually measured in degrees Celsius. For most open motors, a 75°C rise is acceptable. An 80°C rise is acceptable for closed motors. The *total* temperature of the motor at these levels may be over 100°C, so the motor will be uncomfortable to the touch (hotter than boiling water). This does not necessarily mean that the motor is *too* hot. But if the overload trips and you see or smell burning varnish, it is too hot.

STATIC PRESSURE

Static pressure can have an effect on fans and blowers. Static pressure on the blades of a propeller-type fan is increased when a coil is placed in front of the fan, or when a filter becomes dirty (thereby restricting the flow of air). The effect is to increase the load on the motor and slow down the speed of the fan.

The effect of increasing static pressure on a blower is exactly the opposite. Motor speed is lowest when the blower is operating in a "free air" condition. As static pressure is increased—by putting an obstacle in front of the outlet or intake of the blower, for example—the load on the motor is reduced and motor speed increases.

The speed of a furnace blower increases as the filter becomes clogged with dirt from extended usage. If you test a blower in the shop or in a "free air" situation, be aware that the load on the motor is greater than it would be in the air conditioner or furnace. To obtain a more accurate measure of the running current of the motor, install the motor in the unit and make sure that all access panels, filters, and plates are in place.

THE EFFECTS OF "OVERMOTORING"

Some people think that if a $\frac{1}{3}$-hp motor works well in a given application, then a $\frac{1}{2}$-hp motor will work even better. This is not necessarily true. The following paragraphs explain some of the reasons why you should not intentionally "overmotor," and what can happen if you do.

For purposes of comparison, let's say that you are going to replace an original equipment $\frac{1}{3}$-hp condenser fan motor that has failed. The old fan motor had a nameplate rating of 3.9 A at 1,075 rpm. Technically, this motor was designed to turn the original equipment condenser fan blade at 1,015 rpm, with an acceptable temperature rise.

The replacement that you select is a $\frac{1}{2}$-hp motor, also rated at 3.9 A at 1,075 rpm. You install the replacement motor, but when you check the speed of the condenser fan with a strobe light or tachometer, you get a reading of 1,130 rpm. The increased speed is due to the extra horsepower. At 1,130 rpm, the motor is turning near its idle (no-load) speed, and therefore is operating very inefficiently. The efficiency of the motor increases as the speed approaches the nameplate rpm rating. For this motor, the point of maximum efficiency would roughly correspond to 1,075 rpm. Additional loading reduces the rpm further, and efficiency drops off rapidly. This inefficiency results in wasted electrical energy, energy that manifests itself in the form of potentially wire-damaging heat instead of the mechanical energy needed to supply torque to the motor.

Although the fan is turning faster and is probably causing more air to circulate around the motor, it normally will not be enough to offset the extra temperature generated. It is true that increased speed will result in increased cfm, but only up to a point. There is a maximum cfm value that can be achieved by any blower or fan.

Even if the motor does not get hot enough to cut out on an internal overload, any increase in winding temperature has a detrimental effect on the life of the bearings and windings. Every 10°C (18°F) increase in temperature will reduce the life of many motor materials by more than ⅓, and some by as much as ½.

Another factor that is frequently overlooked in cases of overmotoring is the capacitor voltage. For example, a motor designed to run at or near a nameplate speed of 1,015 rpm has a capacitor rating of 7.5 μF at 370 V ac. At 1,015 rpm, the voltage across the capacitor is only 357 V. However, at 1,091 rpm, the maximum capacitor voltage of 370 V would be exceeded, and could result in capacitor failure and possible motor failure.

Some newer, energy-efficient motors seem to withstand overmotoring much better than their older, less efficient counterparts. However, the old rule that recommends a maximum overmotoring limit of ±10% is still a good one.

NEMA LISTINGS

Standard dimensions of electric motors according to frame numbers have been adopted by the National Electrical Manufacturers Association (NEMA). Standard NEMA frame sizes for fractional-horsepower and integral-horsepower motors, along with their principal mounting dimensions, are shown in Table 8-6 on the next two pages.

Frame	D	E	2F	H	U	BA	N-W
48	3.0	2.12	2.75	0.34	0.5	2.5	1.5
56	3.5	2.44	3.0	0.34	0.625	2.75	1.88
143	3.5	2.75	4.0	0.34	0.75	2.25	2.0
143T	3.5	2.75	4.0	0.34	0.875	2.25	2.25
145	3.5	2.75	5.0	0.34	0.75	2.25	2.0
182	4.5	3.75	4.5	0.41	0.875	2.75	2.25
182T	4.5	3.75	4.5	0.41	1.125	2.75	2.75
184	4.5	3.75	5.5	0.41	0.875	2.75	2.25
184T	4.5	3.75	5.5	0.41	1.125	2.75	2.75
203	5.0	4.0	5.5	0.41	0.75	3.12	2.25
204	5.0	4.0	6.5	0.41	0.75	3.12	2.25
213	5.25	4.25	5.5	0.41	1.125	3.5	3.0
213T	5.25	4.25	5.5	0.41	1.375	3.5	3.38
215	5.25	4.25	7.0	0.41	1.125	3.5	3.0
215T	5.25	4.25	7.0	0.41	1.375	3.5	3.38
145T	3.5	2.75	5.0	0.34	0.875	2.25	2.25
224	5.5	4.5	6.75	0.41	1.0	3.5	3.0
225	5.5	4.5	7.5	0.41	1.0	3.5	3.0
254	6.25	5.0	8.25	0.53	1.125	4.25	3.37
254U	6.25	5.0	8.25	0.53	1.375	4.25	3.75
254T	6.25	5.0	8.25	0.53	1.625	4.25	4.0
256U	6.25	5.0	10.0	0.53	1.375	4.25	3.75
256T	6.25	5.0	10.0	0.53	1.625	4.25	4.0
284	7.0	5.5	9.5	0.53	1.25	4.75	3.75
284U	7.0	5.5	9.5	0.53	1.625	4.75	4.88
284T	7.0	5.5	9.5	0.53	1.875	4.75	4.62
284TS	7.0	5.5	9.5	0.53	1.625	4.75	3.25
286U	7.0	5.5	11.0	0.53	1.625	4.75	4.88
286T	7.0	5.5	11.0	0.53	1.875	4.75	4.62
286TS	7.0	5.5	11.0	0.53	1.625	4.75	3.25
324	8.0	6.25	10.5	0.66	1.625	5.25	4.87
324U	8.0	6.25	10.5	0.66	1.875	5.25	5.62
324S	8.0	6.25	10.5	0.66	1.625	5.25	3.25
324T	8.0	6.25	10.5	0.66	2.125	5.25	5.25
324TS	8.0	6.25	10.5	0.66	1.875	5.25	3.75
326	8.0	6.25	12.0	0.66	1.625	5.25	4.87
326U	8.0	6.25	12.0	0.66	1.875	5.25	5.62
326S	8.0	6.25	12.0	0.66	1.625	5.25	3.25
326T	8.0	6.25	12.0	0.66	2.125	5.25	5.25
326TS	8.0	6.25	12.0	0.66	1.875	5.25	3.75
364	9.0	7.0	11.25	0.66	1.875	5.88	5.62
364S	9.0	7.0	11.25	0.66	1.625	5.88	3.25
364U	9.0	7.0	11.25	0.66	2.125	5.88	6.37
364US	9.0	7.0	11.25	0.66	1.875	5.88	3.75
364T	9.0	7.0	11.25	0.66	2.375	5.88	5.88
364TS	9.0	7.0	11.25	0.66	1.875	5.88	3.75
365	9.0	7.0	12.25	0.66	1.875	5.88	5.62
365S	9.0	7.0	12.25	0.66	1.625	5.88	3.25

TABLE 8-6. *NEMA frame dimensions for ac motors (in inches)*

Frame	D	E	2F	H	U	BA	N-W
365U	9.0	7.0	12.25	0.66	2.125	5.88	6.37
365US	9.0	7.0	12.25	0.66	1.875	5.88	3.75
365T	9.0	7.0	12.25	0.66	2.375	5.88	5.88
365TS	9.0	7.0	12.25	0.66	1.875	5.88	3.75
404	10.0	8.0	12.25	0.81	2.125	6.62	6.37
404S	10.0	8.0	12.25	0.81	1.875	6.62	3.75
404U	10.0	8.0	12.25	0.81	2.375	6.62	7.12
404US	10.0	8.0	12.25	0.81	2.125	6.62	4.25
404T	10.0	8.0	12.25	0.81	2.875	6.62	7.25
404TS	10.0	8.0	12.25	0.81	2.125	6.62	4.25
405	10.0	8.0	13.75	0.81	2.125	6.62	6.37
405S	10.0	8.0	13.75	0.81	1.875	6.62	3.75
405U	10.0	8.0	13.75	0.81	2.375	6.62	7.12
405US	10.0	8.0	13.75	0.81	2.125	6.62	4.25
405T	10.0	8.0	13.75	0.81	2.875	6.62	7.25
405TS	10.0	8.0	13.75	0.81	2.125	6.62	4.25
444	11.0	9.0	14.5	0.81	2.375	7.5	7.12
444S	11.0	9.0	14.5	0.81	2.125	7.5	4.25
444U	11.0	9.0	14.5	0.81	2.875	7.5	8.62
444US	11.0	9.0	14.5	0.81	2.125	7.5	4.25
444T	11.0	9.0	14.5	0.81	3.375	7.5	8.5
444TS	11.0	9.0	14.5	0.81	2.375	7.5	4.75
445	11.0	9.0	16.5	0.81	2.375	7.5	7.12
445S	11.0	9.0	16.5	0.81	2.125	7.5	4.25
445U	11.0	9.0	16.5	0.81	2.875	7.5	8.62
445US	11.0	9.0	16.5	0.81	2.125	7.5	4.25
445T	11.0	9.0	16.5	0.81	3.375	7.5	8.5
445TS	11.0	9.0	16.5	0.81	2.375	7.5	4.75
447TS	11.0	9.0	20.0	Dimensions vary with manufacturer			
449TS	11.0	9.0	25.0	Dimensions vary with manufacturer			
504U	12.5	10.0	16.0	0.94	2.875	8.5	8.62
505	12.5	10.0	18.0	0.94	2.875	8.5	8.62
505S	12.5	10.0	18.0	0.94	2.12	8.5	4.25

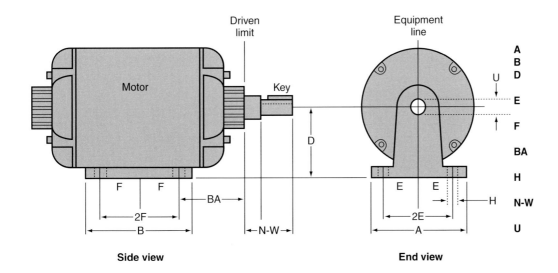

A	Maximum base width
B	Maximum base length
D	Lower edge of base to shaft center
E	Mounting hole center to shaft center
F	Mounting hole center to frame center
BA	Mounting hole center to shaft collar at end plate
H	Diameter of (4) holes in mounting base
N-W	Overall shaft length minus shaft collar width
U	Shaft diameter

Side view   End view

171

1. How does NEMA define the difference between *integral-horsepower* motors and *fractional-horsepower* motors?

2. What is a *universal* motor?

3. How can you determine the direction of rotor rotation in a shaded-pole motor?

4. How can you determine the synchronous speed of a motor?

5. How do permanent split-capacitor motor starting currents compare with shaded-pole motor starting currents?

6. In what respects are PSC motors more versatile than shaded-pole motors?

7. If a PSC motor will not start, or draws excessive current when running, what is the most likely cause?

8. When you replace a PSC motor, should you also replace the capacitor? Why or why not?

9. What is the best way to determine the direction of rotation of a PSC motor?

10. What is the function of the centrifugal switch attached to the shaft of a split-phase motor?

11. Capacitor-start motors are used in applications that require a relatively high _____ load, but a relatively low _____ load.

12.   How does a "start" capacitor differ from a "run" capacitor?

13.   What are the three types of winding connections generally used in three-phase motors?

14.   How do you reverse the direction of rotation in a three-phase motor?

15.   The resistance in the individual windings of a three-phase motor should be within _____% of each other.

16.   What should you do if you obtain a measurable ohmmeter reading when testing the resistance of the windings of any motor to ground?

17.   When does *single phasing* occur in a three-phase motor?

18.   A typical motor is designed to operate within a(n) _____% range of its rated voltage.

19.   What is the result of even a small imbalance in input voltage?

20.   The voltage imbalance between any two legs of the supply voltage applied to a three-phase motor must not exceed _____%.

21.   If the *average* current through the windings of a three-phase motor is 25 A, and the current measured through one of the individual windings is 28 A, is the maximum allowable current imbalance being exceeded?

22.   Dual-voltage motors are connected in _____ for low-voltage operation, and in _____ for high-voltage operation.

23.   After the first contactor in a PWS motor is energized, there is a time delay of _____ before the second contactor is energized.

24.   What is *cross phasing*?

25.   Can you use an ohmmeter to check the resistance in variable-speed motor windings?

26.   When you must replace a motor rated at ¼ hp or less, is it more accurate to match horsepower or current draw?

27.   What is temperature *rise*?

28.   What is an acceptable temperature rise for an open-frame motor?

29.   When does "overmotoring" occur?

Hermetic Compressors

TYPES OF COMPRESSORS

There are many different types of compressors used in the HVACR field, including reciprocating, rotary, scroll, screw, and centrifugal compressors. All of these names refer to the method used to compress the refrigerant vapor. However, compressors can also be classified according to how the motor or "prime mover" is connected to the compressor. From this point of view, there are just three basic types of compressors used in the HVACR industry—open, semi-hermetic, and hermetic.

An *open* compressor has a drive shaft protruding from the compressor. An electric motor or some other external power source is connected to the shaft, and a shaft seal prevents the refrigerant and system oil from escaping. Open compressors may be either direct-driven or belt-driven. A *semi-hermetic* compressor has no shaft openings. The motor is completely enclosed in one section of the assembly, and the compressor is in another section. The two sections are gasketed and bolted together.

This Lesson is about *hermetic* compressors. In a hermetic compressor, the drive motor is completely sealed inside the same housing with the compressor.

The motor is directly connected to the compressor, so no shaft seal is required. Figure 9-1 shows a small hermetic compressor. Note the capacitor and terminal cover. Because the housing of a hermetic compressor is welded closed, all testing and troubleshooting must be done externally.

There are a number of manufacturers, both domestic and foreign, that build full hermetic compressors. It is well beyond the scope of this Lesson to cover all of them in detail. The discussion of hermetic compressors in this Lesson will be "generic" by necessity. In general, hermetic compressors used for refrigeration service range from $\frac{1}{20}$ hp to 15 hp. Those used for air conditioning service range from $\frac{1}{2}$ hp to 15 hp. Table 9-1 lists some common characteristics of hermetic compressors.

FIGURE 9-1. *Typical hermetic compressor*

SINGLE-PHASE COMPRESSORS

Because both motor and compressor are contained within the same sealed housing, most people refer to the whole unit simply as a hermetic "compressor." However, most of the information in this Lesson actually pertains to the *motor*, so be aware that the terminology associated with hermetic compressors can be somewhat "loose." In fact, a good deal of the material that follows will be a review of material covered in the previous Lesson on motors.

All *single-phase* compressors have two distinct windings. When a compressor starts, it requires a large amount of torque, because the motor has to start from a stopped position and may have refrigerant in the cylinders. The windings are called the *start* and the *run* windings. They are wound onto a laminated steel core called the *stator*. Depending on the application and starting requirements, all single-phase compressors use some form of start relay and/or start capacitor.

The drawing at the top of the next page illustrates how the start and run windings are wired in a single-phase hermetic compressor. The terminals are marked "C" (common), "S" (start), and "R" (run). The "common"

AIR CONDITIONING SERVICE		
Horsepower range	**Voltage**	**Number of phases**
$\frac{1}{2}$ to 1	115 V	1
1 to 5	230 V	1
3 to 15	208 V	3
3 to 15	460 V	3
REFRIGERATION SERVICE		
Horsepower range	**Voltage**	**Number of phases**
$\frac{1}{20}$ to 1	115 V	1
$\frac{1}{2}$ to 5	230 V	1
1 to 5	230 V	1
3 to 15	208 V	3
3 to 15	460 V	3

TABLE 9-1. *Characteristics of hermetic compressors*

terminal is the point where the run and start windings are electrically joined together. Although not normally shown in this manner in a schematic diagram, note in the illustration below that the run winding is made with heavier wire and has fewer turns than the start winding. The reason for this is that more inductance is required to *start* the compressor than to keep it running. Finer wire and more turns in the start winding create a greater magnetic field— therefore, the compressor will start more easily.

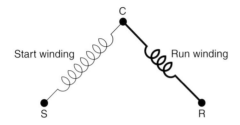

SINGLE-PHASE COMPRESSOR STARTING METHODS

Permanent split-capacitor (PSC) method

There are three basic starting systems used for single-phase compressors. *Permanent split-capacitor* (PSC) compressors, like the PSC motors studied in the previous Lesson, have high starting torques. PSC compressors are commonly used in residential air conditioning equipment because of cost considerations. A PSC compressor has a run capacitor in the start winding circuit at all times. The start and run windings, which are placed in slots in the stator frame, are approximately 90° apart. The run capacitor introduces the phase shift necessary for the compressor to start when power is applied, even under adverse load conditions. Figure 9-2 shows how a PSC compressor is wired. The run capacitor is external, so remember to test it first when you encounter trouble with a PSC compressor. The capacitor is probably the greatest cause of compressor failures.

Potential relay method

As you learned in Lesson 5 of this Unit, "start" relays may be either potential relays or current relays. *Potential* relays are used with single-phase compressors when there are very difficult starting conditions—when there is low voltage in an air conditioning system, for example, or when the expansion valves in a commercial refrigeration system are hard to shut off. The *capacitor-start, capacitor-run* (CSCR) compressor uses an

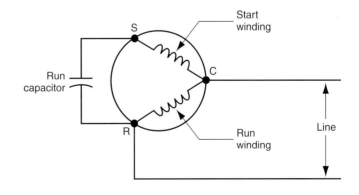

FIGURE 9-2. *PSC starting method*

177

external potential (or voltage)
relay to control the action of
a start capacitor. The coil of
the potential relay is wired
in parallel with the start winding
of the compressor, as illustrated
in Figure 9-3. When you are
troubleshooting, remember that
a potential relay is a normally
closed switch. If you must
replace a potential relay, always
replace the start capacitor as
well. The CSCR compressor
combines a high starting torque
and a fair running efficiency,
but is susceptible to the same
problems as any other capacitor-
start motor.

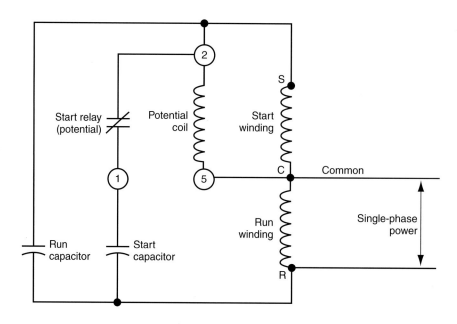

FIGURE 9-3. *Potential relay starting method*

Current relay method

In smaller domestic refrigerators, beverage coolers,
ice machines, and de-humidifiers, the simplest form
of starting a compressor is the *current* relay. A current
relay may be used with or without a start capacitor.
Figure 9-4 is a typical schematic of a single-phase
compressor that uses a current relay. Remember that
a current relay is a normally open switch, with the
coil wired in series with the run winding. Refer to
Lesson 2 of this Unit for more information about
testing relays.

SINGLE-PHASE COMPRESSOR OVERLOADS

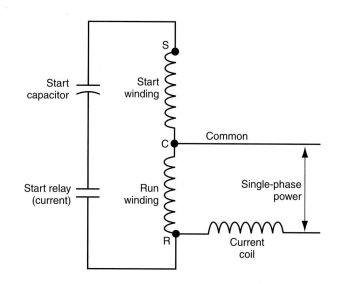

FIGURE 9-4. *Current relay starting method*

The typical hermetic compressor is equipped with some type of overload
protection device. Small single-phase compressors have an *external* overload
mounted next to the terminal block, in order to facilitate wiring the overload
device to the compressor's terminals. This is illustrated in Figure 9-5. Most
external overloads will respond to extremes of temperature and/or current.

Many newer hermetic compressors have some type of *internal* overload.
Single-phase compressors have internal overloads called *line breaks*. A line
break overload, pictured in Figure 9-6, senses both motor current and winding

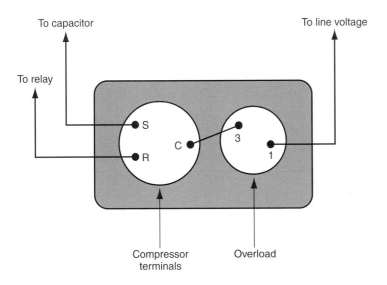

FIGURE 9-5. *External overload*

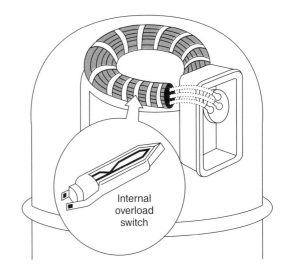

FIGURE 9-6. *Internal overload*

temperature. If the overload opens, it breaks the current path and shuts down the motor. This is shown schematically in Figure 9-7.

Generally speaking, if a line break overload or internal thermostat fails in the open position, the compressor must be replaced. However, *always make sure that the compressor has cooled down enough to allow any internal overload device to reset before replacing a compressor because of an open winding or internal overload*. It may require more than an hour for the overload to reset. Normally, the motor temperature must be below 115°F before you check the continuity of the motor windings through an internal overload device. A great number of compressors have been diagnosed incorrectly and replaced because of an open internal line break overload.

Some single-phase and three-phase hermetic compressors have an internal thermostat that senses winding temperature only. This type of thermostat is wired in series with other components

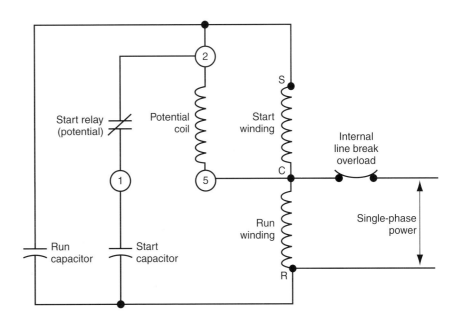

FIGURE 9-7. *How a line break overload works*

in the low-voltage control circuit, and will open if temperature limits are exceeded. This action, in turn, opens the control circuit, de-energizing the compressor contactor. A single-phase compressor with an internal thermostat is shown schematically in Figure 9-8.

One way to ensure that sufficient cool-down time has elapsed is to advise the customer to turn the indoor thermostat switch to OFF immediately. The time between the customer's call and the service call visit is usually long enough for the motor to cool down. (This pertains to residential air conditioning equipment.)

TERMINAL IDENTIFICATION

There are numerous manufacturers of hermetic compressors, both domestic and foreign. It would clearly be impossible to list every single terminal identification format. The terminals on most single-phase hermetic compressors, however, are arranged in triangular, circular, or straight-line patterns, as shown in the illustration below. All use the same terminology (C = common, S = start, and R = run).

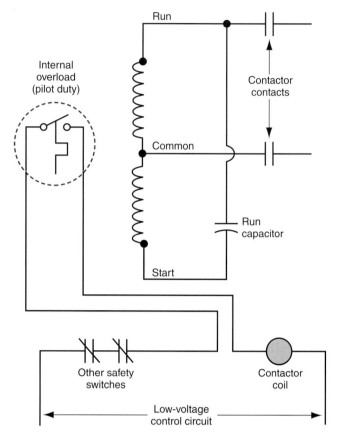

FIGURE 9-8. *Internal thermostat*

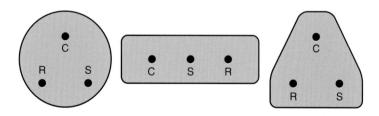

Compressors may have push-on terminals, spade (quick-connect) terminals, or screw terminals. Whatever type is used, it is important for the terminals to be tight. Any loose terminal can cause high resistance and overheating.

RESISTANCE TESTING OF SINGLE-PHASE COMPRESSORS

 WARNING: Before making any resistance measurements, turn off all power to the circuit being tested and disconnect the compressor from the power supply.

Testing single-phase compressors for continuity

Figure 9-9 shows how to use an ohmmeter to test for continuity. First place one lead of the ohmmeter on the common (C) terminal. Then place the other lead on the start (S) and run (R) terminals in succession. If you get a resistance reading, go on to the next test for grounds.

Note: A reading of infinite resistance across any two of the terminals indicates an open winding, and the compressor must be replaced.

Testing single-phase compressors for grounds

Figure 9-10 shows how to test the compressor for grounds to the shell. Set the ohmmeter's range scale to R × 10,000 and connect one test lead to a clean spot on the compressor shell. Remember that a coat of paint or dirt may give you an inaccurate reading. Connect the other test lead to each of the compressor terminals in turn.

 WARNING: Compressor terminals must not be moved if the system is pressurized. A damaged terminal could blow out, causing injury. Do not remove or place anything on the terminals until the system pressure has been reduced to 0 psig.

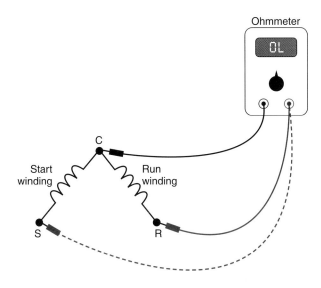

FIGURE 9-9. *Testing a single-phase compressor for continuity*

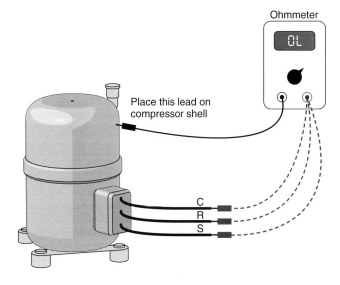

FIGURE 9-10. *Testing a single-phase compressor for grounds*

To determine whether or not the windings are grounded to the compressor shell, you can use the "1,000 ohms per volt" rule of thumb—that is, if you are testing a 230-V compressor, the resistance reading should not be less than 230,000 Ω (230 V × 1,000 Ω/V). This very high resistance indicates that the windings are *not* grounded or shorted to the compressor shell. A reading of *no* resistance would indicate that the winding *is* grounded or shorted to the compressors shell.

Caution: You may obtain erroneous ground readings if oil and refrigerant are present in the compressor. Reclaim the refrigerant and re-test the compressor. If the reading is still less than 1,000 Ω, replace the compressor.

Testing single-phase compressors for shorted or open windings

As previously stated, all single-phase compressors have two windings, the start winding and the run winding. The resistance of the windings varies from manufacturer to manufacturer. Obviously, this Lesson cannot cover the specifications of every compressor made. However, there are certain guidelines that you can use to help identify unmarked compressor terminals.

The resistance values of compressor windings are very low. They may be measured in tenths of an ohm. Therefore, you should use an accurate digital ohmmeter. The average resistance of a *start* winding ranges from 0.1 Ω to 2 Ω, depending on the manufacturer and the horsepower of the motor inside the compressor. The average resistance of a *run* winding may be as low as 1 Ω and as high as 5 to 10 Ω, again depending on the manufacturer and the horsepower of the motor.

The example below illustrates a simple rule of thumb: The resistance of the start winding (measured across C and S) should equal three to six times the resistance of the run winding (measured across C and R).

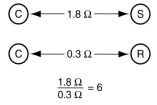

Figure 9-11 shows how to measure winding resistance in a single-phase PSC compressor. The steps used in this procedure are:

1. Start by testing across the common (C) and run (R) terminals, as shown in Figure 9-11A. The reading in this example is 1 Ω. Make a note of this resistance for future reference.

2. Next, test across the common (C) and start (S) terminals, as shown in Figure 9-11B. The reading in this example is 6 Ω. Again, make a note of this resistance.

3. Finally, test across the start (S) and run (R) terminals, as shown in Figure 9-11C. The reading in this example is 7 Ω. (This gives you the *total* resistance of the start winding plus the run winding.)

4. Now, by applying the previously stated rule of thumb to your readings, you find that the resistance of the start winding (C to S = 6 Ω) equals six times the resistance of the run winding (C to R = 1 Ω). This compressor is OK according to the above readings.

Shorted winding example. Using the same type of compressor and testing method as shown in Figure 9-11, suppose that the reading across the common (C) and start (S) terminals is 0.13 Ω, instead of 6 Ω. Suppose, also, that there is a very low resistance (0.00 Ω) across the common (C) and run (R) terminals. In this case, you can assume that the compressor has a *shorted* winding between the R and C terminals, and also between the C and S terminals. The compressor must be replaced.

Open winding example. Again using the same type of compressor and the same testing method, suppose that the reading across the common (C) and start (S) terminals is *infinity* (∞) or "OL" ("out of limits"). In this case, you can assume that the compressor has an *open* winding between the C and S terminals. The compressor must be replaced.

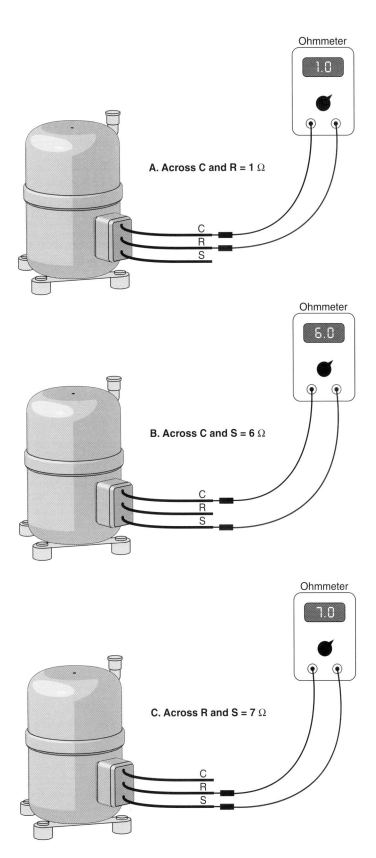

A. Across C and R = 1 Ω

B. Across C and S = 6 Ω

C. Across R and S = 7 Ω

FIGURE 9-11. *Testing a single-phase compressor for shorted or open windings*

Testing single-phase compressors with unmarked terminals

Diagnosing compressor problems is not a difficult job with the proper instruments and a little know-how. However, before diagnosis can begin, the terminals on the compressor must be identified. Most of the time, the terminals are clearly marked with the three letters "C," "S," and "R." However, some compressor terminals are *not* marked and are difficult to identify, even with a wiring diagram. There is an easy three-step method of identifying these terminals with a digital ohmmeter:

1. Find the two terminals across which the greatest resistance occurs. The third or remaining terminal is the common (C) terminal.

2. Put one lead of the ohmmeter on this common terminal and find which of the remaining two terminals produces the highest resistance reading on the meter. This will be the start (S) terminal.

3. The remaining terminal is, of course, the run (R) terminal.

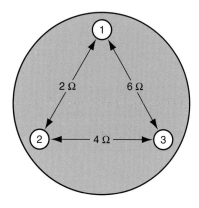

FIGURE 9-12. *Identifying unmarked terminals*

Look at the example shown in Figure 9-12. First number the terminals 1, 2, and 3. Then use an ohmmeter to measure between the terminals, as shown. The highest reading is 6 Ω, between terminals 1 and 3. Therefore, terminal 2 is the common (C) terminal. The reading between terminals 2 and 3 is 4 Ω, which is higher than the reading between terminals 2 and 1. Therefore, terminal 3 is the start (S) terminal and, by process of elimination, terminal 1 is the run (R) terminal.

VOLTAGE TESTING OF SINGLE-PHASE COMPRESSORS

Figure 9-13 illustrates in schematic form the windings of a PSC compressor at a line voltage of 220 V. If you set your voltmeter to the highest scale and measure the voltage between the common and run windings, your reading should be within ±5% of the line voltage. The reading shown in the example in Figure 9-13 is 221 V ac, and therefore falls within this range. Voltage readings should be taken when the compressor is running. It is impractical to try to measure the CEMF of a compressor. It has no real value to the service technician, but be aware that the CEMF may be double or more the line voltage.

CURRENT TESTING OF SINGLE-PHASE COMPRESSORS

Figure 9-14 shows the same compressor as Figure 9-13, at the same line voltage. A typical 3-hp, single-phase, 220-V PSC compressor will draw approximately 20 RLA (rated load amperes). Place your ammeter on the

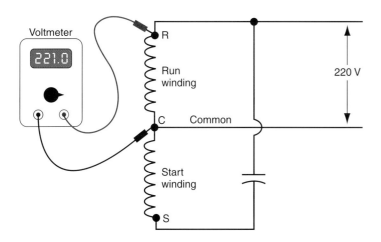

FIGURE 9-13. *Testing voltage in a single-phase compressor*

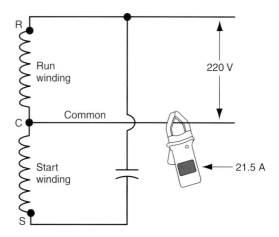

FIGURE 9-14. *Testing current in a single-phase compressor*

common lead of the compressor to get an accurate reading. Your reading should be within ±2% of the nameplate rating. If it is not (the reading shown in the example in Figure 9-14 is out of range), look for a problem in the power supply, or possibly in the compressor itself.

THREE-PHASE COMPRESSORS

Large hermetic compressors used in industrial and commercial applications are usually driven by three-phase motors. The building in which the compressor is to be installed must be wired for three-phase service. Very few residences have three-phase electrical power. Three-phase compressors have several advantages over single-phase compressors, including:

- better operating efficiency

- lower operating costs

- lower installation costs.

In addition, three-phase compressors require no starting relays or start capacitors.

THREE-PHASE COMPRESSOR TERMINAL IDENTIFICATION

There are many different terminal designations used in three-phase hermetic compressors. Usually, instead of the letters C, S, and R, the designations "T1," "T2," and "T3" are used. The arrangement of the terminals is somewhat different than it is for single-phase compressors. Three typical arrangements are shown in the illustration below. Note that the one in the center includes the terminals for an internal overload switch.

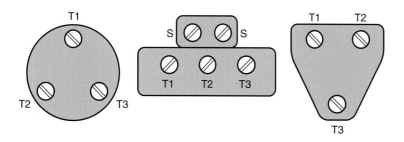

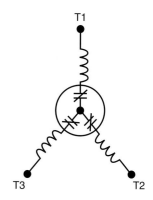

FIGURE 9-15. *Internal line break overload*

THREE-PHASE COMPRESSOR OVERLOADS

Many three-phase compressors use internal line break overload protectors. This type of overload device is *not* repairable or replaceable in the field. Figure 9-15 shows a typical schematic of an internal line break overload used for a three-phase compressor. Note that the overload breaks all three lines at the same time. This prevents any possibility of *single phasing*.

The internal overload may also be a thermostat that operates a pilot switch in the control circuit of the compressor. This form of protection is similar to the internal thermostat used in the single-phase compressor. However, there are usually three of them wired in series. These are then brought out to terminals on the outside of the compressor, as shown in Figure 9-16.

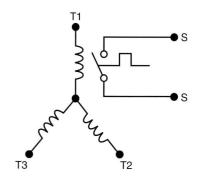

FIGURE 9-16. *Internal thermostat*

RESISTANCE TESTING OF THREE-PHASE COMPRESSORS

Testing three-phase compressors for grounds

Testing a three-phase compressor for grounds to the shell is very similar to testing a single-phase compressor. Set the ohmmeter's range scale to the R × 10,000 setting and connect one test lead to a clean spot on the compressor shell, as shown in Figure 9-17. Make sure that you select a spot where the surface is metallic or conductive, and remember that a coat of paint or dirt may give you an inaccurate reading. Connect the other test lead to each of the compressor terminals in turn.

To determine whether or not the windings are grounded to the compressor shell, you can use the "1,000 ohms per volt" rule of thumb again.

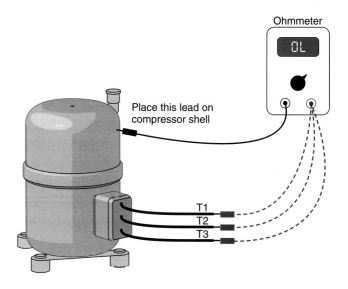

FIGURE 9-17. *Testing a three-phase compressor for grounds*

For a 208-V compressor, therefore, the resistance reading should not be less than 208,000 Ω (208 V × 1,000 Ω/V). This very high resistance indicates that the windings are *not* grounded or shorted to the compressor shell. A reading of *no* resistance would indicate that the winding *is* grounded or shorted to the compressors shell.

Testing three-phase compressors for shorted or open windings

The windings in a three-phase compressor should all have the same (or very close to the same) resistance. Figure 9-18 shows how to measure winding resistance in a three-phase compressor. Again, the procedure is very similar to testing a single-phase compressor. Use your ohmmeter to test across each pair of leads in turn, making a note of each reading for purposes of comparison. In Figure 9-18A, the reading across T1 and T2 is 4.48 Ω. In Figure 9-18B, the reading across T1 and T3 is 4.5 Ω. In Figure 9-18C, the reading across T2 and T3 is 4.59 Ω. These three resistance readings are well within the manufacturer's guidelines for windings with "identical" resistance values. This compressor is considered to be a good compressor.

Shorted winding example. Using the same compressor and testing method, suppose that the reading across T2 and T3 is 0.5 Ω, instead of 4.59 Ω. Suppose, further, that the reading across T1 and T3 is also 0.5 Ω. In this case, you can assume that the compressor has a *shorted* winding between T1 and T3, and also between T2 and T3. The compressor must be replaced.

Open winding example. Again using the same compressor and testing method, suppose that the reading across T2 and T3 remains 4.59 Ω, but the reading across T1 and T2 is "OL." In this case, you can assume that the compressor has an *open* winding between T1 and T2. The compressor must be replaced.

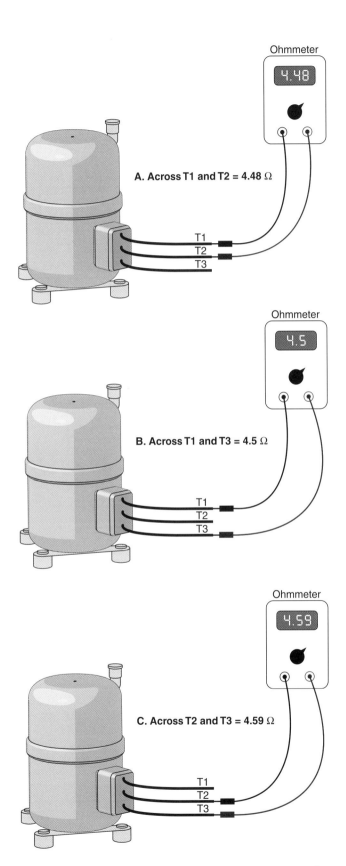

FIGURE 9-18. *Testing a three-phase compressor for shorted or open windings*

VOLTAGE TESTING OF THREE-PHASE COMPRESSORS

In order to get an accurate reading of the voltage at the terminals of a three-phase hermetic compressor, always take your voltage measurements while the compressor is running. The voltage variation between any two lines must not exceed 2%.

Voltage imbalance

A small imbalance in the input voltage can result in a considerable amount of heat being generated in the motor windings. An imbalance of only 5%, for example, can increase the winding temperature as much as 50% above the safe level. To determine the voltage imbalance in a three-phase system, first measure and record the voltage between T1 and T2, then between T1 and T3, and finally between T2 and T3. In the example shown in Figure 9-19, the readings are 440, 460, and 465 V, respectively. Find the *average* voltage by adding these three figures together and dividing by 3:

Voltage measured between T1 and T2	440 V
Voltage measured between T1 and T3	460 V
Voltage measured between T2 and T3	+ 465 V
Total	1,365 V

Average voltage = 1,365 V ÷ 3 = 455 V

Determine which reading represents the greatest deviation from the average (in this case it is the 440-V reading). Now you can use the following equation to calculate the voltage imbalance:

$$\% \text{ imbalance} = \frac{\text{maximum deviation from average voltage}}{\text{average voltage}} \times 100$$

$$= \frac{455 \text{ V} - 440 \text{ V}}{455 \text{ V}} \times 100$$

$$= \frac{15 \text{ V}}{455 \text{ V}} \times 100$$

$$= 0.03297 \times 100 = 3.297\% = \text{approximately } 3.3\%$$

Note: The voltage imbalance between any two legs of the supply voltage applied to a three-phase compressor must not exceed 2%. Any voltage imbalance of more than 2% must be corrected. If a voltage imbalance exceeds 2%, look for

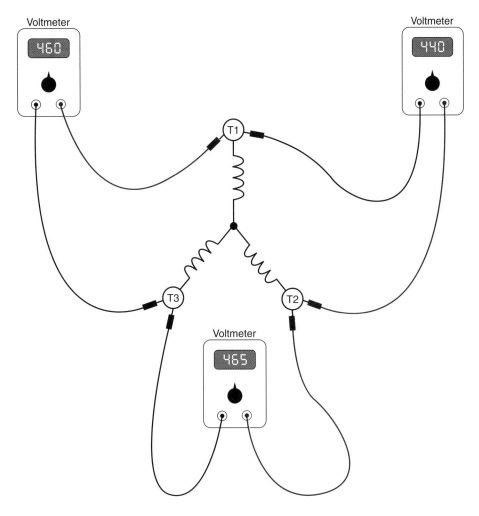

FIGURE 9-19. *Voltage imbalance (460-V three-phase power)*

an electrical terminal, contact, etc., that is loose or corroded and may be causing a high resistance in that leg. Examine the incoming power supply to the building and the distribution panels. Since the compressor in this example has a voltage imbalance of 3.3%, the problem must be corrected.

CURRENT TESTING OF THREE-PHASE COMPRESSORS

In order to obtain accurate current readings for a three-phase hermetic compressor, take your measurements at the compressor, *not* at the contactor. The wires and contactor could be the cause of a false reading.

Current imbalance

A voltage imbalance always produces a current imbalance, but a current imbalance may occur without a voltage imbalance. A current imbalance can occur when an electrical terminal, contactor, starter, etc. becomes loose or corroded, causing a high resistance in one leg. Since current follows the path of least resistance, the current in the other two legs will increase, causing more heat to be generated in those two windings.

To determine the current imbalance in a three-phase compressor, first check the nameplate for the full-load current (sometimes abbreviated FLA, for full-load amperage). Select the highest range setting (higher than the motor FLA) on your clamp-on ammeter. Turn the power on, and place the clamp-on ammeter around the wire connected to the T1 terminal. Measure and record the current drawn by the T1 leg. Then, one at a time, measure the current drawn by the remaining two legs. For the example shown in Figure 9-20, the readings are 24, 27, and 27 A.

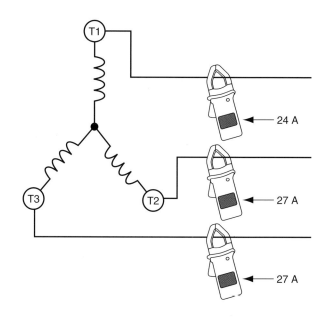

FIGURE 9-20. *Current imbalance*

Again, you can find the *average* current by adding these three figures together and dividing by 3:

Current measured in T1 leg	24 A
Current measured in T2 leg	27 A
Current measured in T3 leg	+ 27 A
Total	78 A

Average current = 78 A ÷ 3 = 26 A

The T1 reading represents a maximum 2-A deviation from the average of 26 A. Now you can use the following equation to calculate the current imbalance:

$$\% \text{ imbalance } = \frac{\text{maximum deviation from average current}}{\text{average current}} \times 100$$

$$= \frac{2 \text{ A}}{26 \text{ A}} \times 100$$

$$= 0.07692 \times 100 = 7.692\% = \text{approximately } 7.7\%$$

Note: The current imbalance between any two legs of a three-phase compressor must not exceed 10%. If the current imbalance exceeds 10%, look for an electrical terminal, contact, etc., that is loose or corroded and may be causing a high resistance in that leg. Since the imbalance in this example is less than 10%, the current between phases is acceptable.

SINGLE PHASING

Single phasing occurs when one of the lines is broken between a three-phase compressor and the power supply. In the example shown in Figure 9-21, phase "A" is broken. If this occurs while the compressor is running, the compressor motor will continue to operate as a single-phase motor. However, the other two windings will consume more power and the current will increase in each of the other windings to 1½ to 2 times the normal current. The compressor motor will slow down and start drawing excessive current. If the condition is allowed to continue, the motor will begin to overheat. This is because winding A is getting no power, while windings B and C are trying to keep the motor turning.

If one of the three input power connections is open and the compressor is *not* running, then when the compressor motor tries to start, the result will be a *locked rotor* condition. Because there are no longer three windings in the circuit, the motor will trip its overload protectors, or the heaters in the starter. Locked rotor problems can also be caused by a bad contactor or starter, or by an open winding. It is even possible for the power company to lose a leg of the incoming power supply.

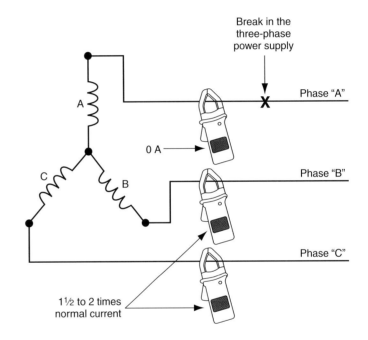

FIGURE 9-21. *Single phasing*

Although ohmmeter readings may indicate that one winding has a measurably higher resistance than another, you will not be able to inspect the motor for visual evidence of overheating, since it is not accessible in a hermetic compressor.

SCROLL COMPRESSORS

Scroll compressors are relatively new to the HVACR industry. A scroll compressor is a hermetic compressor, and utilizes the same type of motor as other hermetic compressors. However, the scroll compressor does present a problem when three-phase power is applied. A scroll compressor is designed to operate in one direction only. If, by chance, the compressor is wired so that it runs in the opposite direction when a three-phase voltage is applied, it will not develop any pressures. You will be able to tell if this happens, because the compressor will be very noisy. To correct this problem, all you need to do is change or reverse two of the three phase leads. This is illustrated in Figure 9-22, in which L1 and L3 are reversed.

TROUBLESHOOTING COMPRESSOR PROTECTION MODULES

A number of newer hermetic compressors use solid-state motor protection to prevent burnouts and other compressor failures. Such failures may be related to overheating, or to conditions of overvoltage and undervoltage. Solid-state compressor protection modules may be checked in or out of the circuitry. However, they cannot be repaired or adjusted. If inoperative, they must be replaced. Internal compressor sensors are always checked as part of the procedure. If the sensors are determined to be faulty, then the compressor must be replaced.

Figure 9-23 depicts a typical solid-state motor protection module used with hermetic compressors. The module is a single-channel device that connects internally to three positive temperature coefficient (PTC) thermistor sensors in series with the compressor. The three sensors are mounted directly in the motor windings. The module's output is connected in series with the compressor contactor control circuit. If one or more high-resistance sensors reach their trip temperature, the module automatically resets after the minimum OFF delay has timed out, and the sensor temperature has decreased to below its low-resistance reset point. The module also protects against shorted sensor input by de-energizing its output if the sensor resistance approaches 0 Ω.

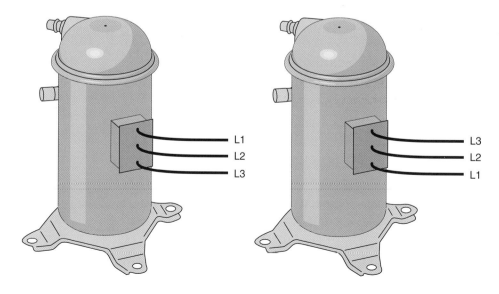

FIGURE 9-22. *Reversing the leads in a scroll compressor*

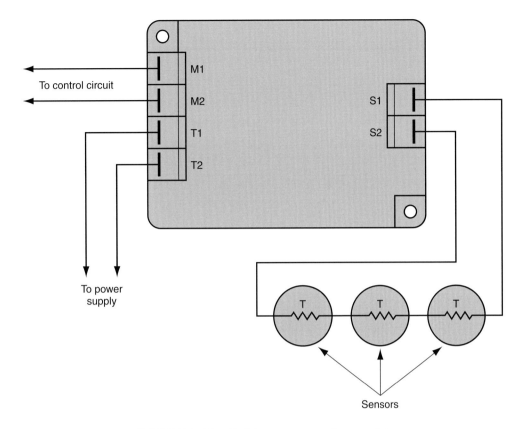

FIGURE 9-23. *Solid-state protection module*

The average module incorporates a minimum OFF time delay of 1 to 4 minutes. This delay can be actuated only by an interruption of the supply power to the unit, or by a temperature trip. The delay is *not* actuated during normal cycling of the compressor contactor circuit.

Power supply check

To check the power supply, check for control power across terminals T1 and T2. Check the unit wiring, as well as fuses and transformers, if used.

Sensor resistance check

If the compressor has been operating and has been stopped by the module because of a temperature trip, allow the compressor to cool at least one hour and/or make the following check to determine sensor condition. Disconnect the sensor leads from terminals S1 and S2 and check the resistance with an ohmmeter. If the resistance across S1 and S2 is less than 7.5 kΩ but greater than 500 Ω, the sensors are within acceptable limits. If (following sufficient time for the compressor to cool completely) the sensor resistance approaches infinity, a break in the sensor circuit is indicated.

The module senses this as an over-temperature condition and prevents the compressor from operating. If the sensor resistance approaches 0 Ω, a short is indicated. Again, the module will prevent the compressor from operating. *Shorted or open sensors require the replacement of the compressor.*

Shorted module. A *shorted* module will not de-energize the compressor control circuit if excessive temperatures are sensed. To verify the ability of the module to de-energize the compressor circuit, initiate a cooling demand to run the compressor. With the compressor running, disconnect any one of the sensor leads. The compressor will stop running. If the compressor continues to run, replace the module.

Open module. If the compressor does not operate, first check the unit controls. Verify a cooling demand and see that power is provided to terminal M1 of the protection module. Also verify that the low-pressure and high-pressure switches and the discharge thermostat in the contactor circuit are closed. If the compressor contactor does not energize, disconnect the module and jump across the leads M1 and M2.

Caution: In systems that use 230 V ac, the module must be replaced if the contactor energizes. If the contactor does not energize, the problem is not within the module. Recheck the other controls in the circuit and the contactor coil.

1.	Why does the start winding in a single-phase compressor have more turns and finer wire than the run winding?

2.	What should you check first when you encounter trouble with a PSC compressor, and why?

3.	A potential relay a normally _____ switch.

4.	If you replace a potential relay, what else should you replace?

5.	A current relay is a normally _____ switch.

6.	What is the purpose of an *overload* in a hermetic compressor?

7.	Before replacing a compressor because of an internal line break overload, what should you do and why?

8.	What must you do before performing any resistance tests on a compressor?

9.	What should you do if you obtain an infinite resistance reading between any two of the three terminals of a single-phase compressor?

10.	Before placing a test lead on a compressor terminal, you should make sure that the system pressure has been reduced to _____ psig.

11.	If you are testing to see whether or not the windings of a 115-V compressor are grounded or shorted to the compressor shell, what would be a favorable resistance reading?

12. Why is it best to use a very accurate digital ohmmeter when testing the resistance of compressor windings?

13. The resistance of the start winding should equal _____ times the resistance of the run winding.

14. How can you identify the terminals of a single-phase compressor if they are unmarked?

15. Is it best to read the line voltage of a compressor when it is running or not running?

16. The current draw of a single-phase hermetic compressor should be within _____% of the nameplate rating.

17. What advantages do three-phase compressors have over single-phase compressors?

18. In a three-phase compressor, why is a line break overload designed to break all three lines at the same time?

19. Why must the voltage imbalance between any two legs of the supply voltage applied to a three-phase compressor *not* exceed 2%?

20. The applied voltages between successive terminals of a three-phase compressor are 435, 440, and 442 V. What is the voltage imbalance (calculated as a percentage)?

21. What is *single phasing*?

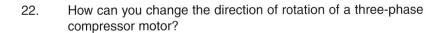

22.   How can you change the direction of rotation of a three-phase
        compressor motor?

23.   How long should you wait before checking the sensors of a solid-state
        compressor protection module after a temperature trip?

Semi-Hermetic Compressors

SEMI-HERMETIC COMPRESSORS

This Lesson is about the electrical troubleshooting of *semi-hermetic* compressors. Much of the information will be similar to that contained in the previous Lesson, which covered hermetic compressors. But remember that the shell of a semi-hermetic compressor is bolted together, rather than welded together. This means that the semi-hermetic compressor can be disassembled and serviced in the field. Certain mechanical components, especially, such as the valve plates or an oil pump, can be repaired or replaced. However, this Lesson pertains only to the electrical aspects of the semi-hermetic compressor. Although semi-hermetic compressors have the advantage of being accessible for service, a semi-hermetic compressor is proportionately more expensive than a sealed hermetic compressor of equal capacity.

Figure 10-1 shows a typical semi-hermetic compressor. In general, semi-hermetic compressors used for air conditioning and

TECUMSEH/BITZER

FIGURE 10-1. *Semi-hermetic compressor*

199

refrigeration service range in size from ¼ hp all the way up to 125 hp. Table 10-1 lists common characteristics of semi-hermetic compressors.

SINGLE-PHASE COMPRESSORS

Recall that all single-phase compressors have two distinct windings, the *start* and *run* windings, wound onto a laminated steel core called the *stator*. The start winding is made with finer wire and has more turns than the run winding. The reason for this is that more inductance is required to *start* the compressor than to keep it running. All single-phase semi-hermetic compressors use some form of start relay and/or start capacitor.

Horsepower range	Voltage	Number of phases
¼ to 1	115 V	1
¼ to 1	230 V	1
1 to 5	208 to 230 V	1
1 to 125	208 to 230 V	3
1 to 125	460 V	3
1 to 125	575 V	3

TABLE 10-1. *Characteristics of semi-hermetic compressors*

The terminals on single-phase semi-hermetic compressors of up to 5 hp are configured in triangular, circular, or straight-line patterns, as shown below. All use the same terminology as hermetic compressors (C = common, S = start, and R = run).

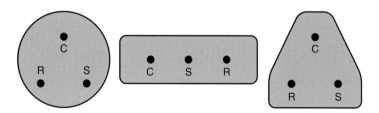

Semi-hermetic compressors normally use screw terminals. It is very important for them to be tight. Any loose terminal can cause high resistance and overheating.

SINGLE-PHASE COMPRESSOR STARTING METHODS

Permanent split-capacitor (PSC) method

Relatively few semi-hermetic compressors use the *permanent split-capacitor* (PSC) starting method. Like their hermetic counterparts studied in the previous Lesson, they have high starting torques. PSC compressors are commonly used in residential air conditioning equipment because of cost considerations. A PSC compressor has a run capacitor in the start winding circuit at all times. The start and run windings, which are placed in slots in the stator frame, are approximately 90° apart. The run capacitor introduces the phase shift necessary for the compressor to start when power is applied, even under adverse load conditions. Figure 10-2 shows how a PSC compressor is wired. Remember to test the run capacitor first when you encounter trouble with a PSC compressor. The capacitor is probably the most common cause of compressor failures.

Potential relay method

The *potential relay* starting method is used with single-phase compressors when there are very difficult starting conditions—when there is low voltage in an air conditioning system, for example, or when the expansion valves in a commercial refrigeration system are hard to shut off. The *capacitor-start, capacitor-run* (CSCR) compressor uses an external potential (or voltage) relay to control the action of a start capacitor. The coil of the potential relay is wired in parallel with the start winding of the compressor, as illustrated in Figure 10-3. Remember that a potential relay is a normally closed switch. The CSCR compressor combines a high starting torque and a fair running efficiency, but is susceptible to the same problems as any other capacitor-start motor.

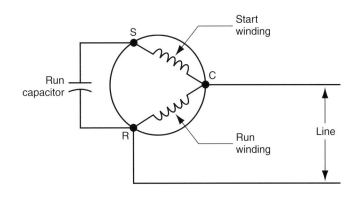

FIGURE 10-2. *PSC starting method*

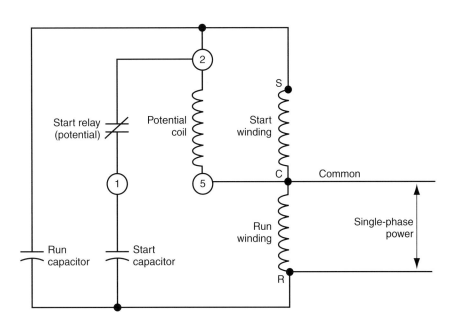

FIGURE 10-3. *Potential relay starting method*

Because start and run capacitors have high capacitance values, some manufacturers use two of each, placed in parallel in the starting circuit. It is important to test each capacitor. If you must replace a potential relay, always replace the capacitor(s) as well.

RESISTANCE TESTING OF SINGLE-PHASE COMPRESSORS

WARNING: Before making any resistance measurements, turn off all power to the circuit being tested and disconnect the compressor from the power supply.

Testing single-phase compressors for continuity

Figure 10-4 shows how to use an ohmmeter to test for continuity. First place one lead of the ohmmeter on the common (C) terminal. Then place the other lead on the start (S) and run (R) terminals in succession. If you get a resistance reading, go on to the next test for grounds. *Note*: A reading of infinite resistance across any two of the terminals indicates an open winding, and the compressor must be replaced.

Testing single-phase compressors for grounds

Figure 10-5 shows how to test the compressor for grounds to the shell. Set the ohmmeter's range scale to R × 10,000 and connect one test lead to a clean spot on the compressor shell. Remember that a coat of paint or dirt may give you an inaccurate reading. Connect the other test lead to each of the compressor terminals in turn.

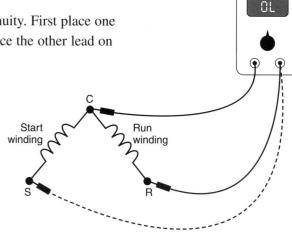

FIGURE 10-4. *Testing a single-phase compressor for continuity*

WARNING: Compressor terminals must not be moved if the system is pressurized. A damaged terminal could blow out, causing injury. Do not remove or place anything on the terminals until the system pressure has been reduced to 0 psig.

To determine whether or not the windings are grounded to the compressor shell, you can use the "1,000 ohms per volt" rule of thumb—that is, if you are testing a 230-V compressor, the resistance reading should not be less than 230,000 Ω (230 V × 1,000 Ω/V). This very high resistance indicates that the windings are *not* grounded or shorted to the compressor shell. A reading of *no* resistance would indicate that the winding *is* grounded or shorted to the compressors shell.

Caution: You may obtain erroneous ground readings if oil and refrigerant are present in the compressor. Reclaim the refrigerant and re-test the compressor. If the reading is still less than 1,000 Ω, replace the compressor.

Testing single-phase compressors for shorted or open windings

As previously stated, all single-phase compressors have two windings, the start winding and the run winding. The resistance of the windings varies from manufacturer to manufacturer. Obviously, this Lesson cannot cover the specifications of every compressor made. However, there are certain guidelines that you can use to help identify unmarked compressor terminals.

The resistance values of compressor windings are very low. They may be measured in tenths of an ohm. Therefore, you should use an accurate digital ohmmeter. The average resistance of a *start* winding ranges from 0.1 Ω to 2 Ω, depending on the manufacturer and the horsepower of the motor inside the compressor. The average resistance of a *run* winding may be as low as 1 Ω and as high as 5 to 10 Ω, again depending on the manufacturer and the horsepower of the motor.

The example below illustrates a simple rule of thumb: The resistance of the start winding (measured across C and S) should equal three to six times the resistance of the run winding (measured across C and R).

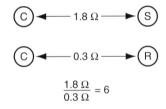

$$\frac{1.8\ \Omega}{0.3\ \Omega} = 6$$

Figure 10-6 on the next page shows how to measure winding resistance in a single-phase semi-hermetic compressor. The steps used in this procedure are:

1. Start by testing across the common (C) and run (R) terminals, as shown in Figure 10-6A. The reading in this example is 1 Ω. Make a note of this resistance for future reference.

2. Next, test across the common (C) and start (S) terminals, as shown in Figure 10-6B. The reading in this example is 6 Ω. Again, make a note of this resistance.

3. Finally, test across the start (S) and run (R) terminals, as shown in Figure 10-6C. The reading in this example is 7 Ω. (This gives you the *total* resistance of the start winding plus the run winding.)

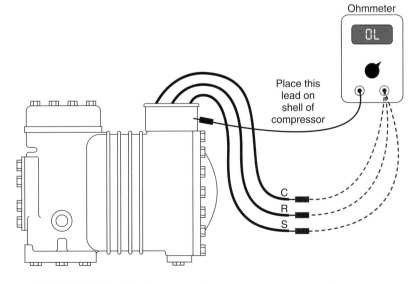

FIGURE 10-5. *Testing a single-phase compressor for grounds*

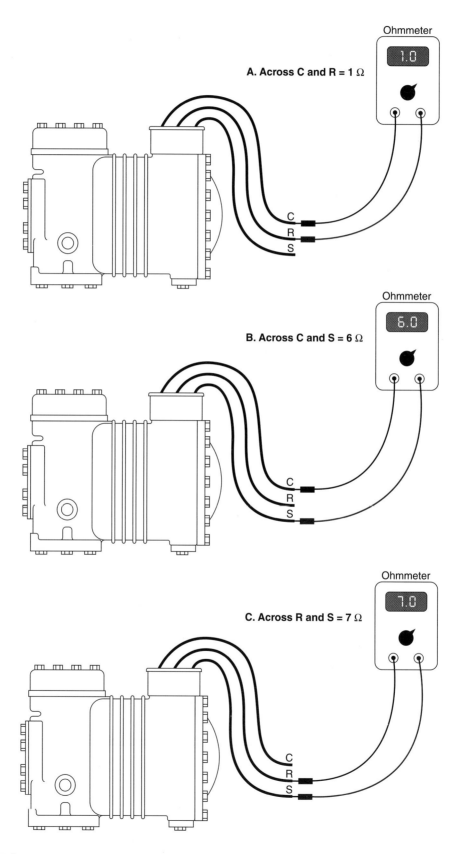

Ohmmeter

1.0

A. Across C and R = 1 Ω

C
R
S

Ohmmeter

6.0

B. Across C and S = 6 Ω

C
R
S

Ohmmeter

7.0

C. Across R and S = 7 Ω

C
R
S

FIGURE 10-6. *Testing a single-phase compressor for shorted or open windings*

4. Now, by applying the previously stated rule of thumb to your readings, you find that the resistance of the start winding (C to S = 6 Ω) equals six times the resistance of the run winding (C to R = 1 Ω). This compressor is OK according to the above readings.

Shorted winding example. Using the same compressor and testing method as shown in Figure 10-6, suppose that the reading across the common (C) and start (S) terminals is 0.13 Ω, instead of 6 Ω. Suppose, also, that there is *no* resistance (0.00 Ω) across the common (C) and run (R) terminals. In this case, you can assume that the compressor has a *shorted* winding between the R and C terminals, and also between the C and S terminals. The compressor must be replaced.

Open winding example. Again using the same compressor and testing method, suppose that the reading across the common (C) and start (S) terminals is "OL," and that there is *no* resistance (0.00 Ω) across the common (C) and run (R) terminals. In this case, you can assume that the compressor has an *open* winding between the R and S terminals. The compressor must be replaced.

Testing single-phase compressors with unmarked terminals

Diagnosing compressor problems is not a difficult job with the proper instruments and a little know-how. However, before diagnosis can begin, the terminals on the compressor must be identified. Most of the time, the terminals are clearly marked with the three letters "C," "S," and "R." However, some compressor terminals are *not* marked and are difficult to identify, even with a wiring diagram. There is an easy three-step method of identifying these terminals with a digital ohmmeter:

1. Find the two terminals across which the greatest resistance occurs. The third or remaining terminal is the common (C) terminal.

2. Put one lead of the ohmmeter on this common terminal and find which of the remaining two terminals produces the highest resistance reading on the meter. This will be the start (S) terminal.

3. The remaining terminal is, of course, the run (R) terminal.

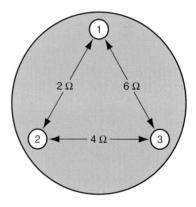

FIGURE 10-7. *Identifying unmarked terminals*

Look at the example shown in Figure 10-7. First number the terminals 1, 2, and 3. Then use an ohmmeter to measure between the terminals, as shown. The highest reading is 6 Ω, between terminals 1 and 3. Therefore, terminal 2 is the common (C) terminal. The reading between terminals 2 and 3 is 4 Ω, which is higher than the reading between terminals 2 and 1. Therefore, terminal 3 is the start (S) terminal and, by process of elimination, terminal 1 is the run (R) terminal.

THREE-PHASE COMPRESSORS

Some three-phase semi-hermetic compressors used for refrigeration duty are fractional-horsepower (e.g., ¼ hp, ½ hp, ¾ hp) units. The terminals of these compressors, as well as those of nominal 1 through 15-hp three-phase semi-hermetic compressors, are designated as shown in the illustration below. As you can see, these "three-lead" compressors, as they are called, use two basic identification schemes, the "circle" and the "T." The insulating barriers are also shown.

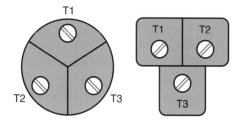

For semi-hermetic compressors of 20 hp and greater, the terminal designations are quite different. Such compressors can be used for multiple voltages, and employ different starting systems.

The windings of a three-lead, three-phase semi-hermetic compressor should all have the same (or very close to the same) resistance.

RESISTANCE TESTING OF THREE-PHASE COMPRESSORS

Testing three-phase compressors for grounds

Testing a three-phase compressor for grounds to the shell is very similar to testing a single-phase compressor. Set the ohmmeter's range scale to the R × 10,000 setting and connect one test lead to a clean spot on the compressor shell, as shown in Figure 10-8. Make sure that you select a spot where the surface is metallic or conductive, and remember that a coat of paint or dirt may give you an inaccurate reading. Connect the other test lead to each of the compressor terminals in turn.

To determine whether or not the windings are grounded to the compressor shell, you can use the "1,000 ohms per volt" rule of thumb again. For a 208-V compressor, therefore, the resistance reading should not be less than 208,000 Ω (208 V × 1,000 Ω/V). This very high resistance indicates that the windings are

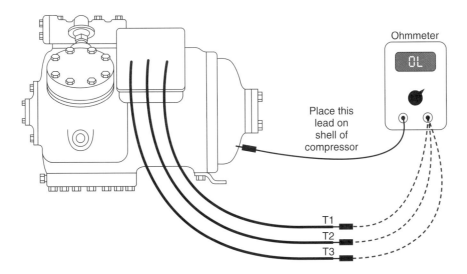

FIGURE 10-8. *Testing a three-phase compressor for grounds*

not grounded or shorted to the compressor shell. A reading of *no* resistance would indicate that the winding *is* grounded or shorted to the compressors shell.

Note: When you are performing resistance tests on *any* compressor, it is imperative that you test the windings to ground, or to the frame of the compressor. If any resistance under 500 Ω is registered on the ohmmeter, replace the compressor. This applies to *all* single-phase and three-phase compressors.

Six-wire "across-the-line" and "part wind start" compressors

Six-wire "across-the-line" (XL) and "part wind start" (PWS) motors, discussed in Lesson 8 of this Unit, are designed with two separate sets of windings built into the stator stack. Electrically, they resemble the diagram in Figure 10-9. Note the terminal designations. These compressors are used when a single starter is more costly than two smaller starters or contactors. When resistance testing this motor, you should find that the windings all have the same resistance.

In order to perform resistance tests on this type of compressor, make sure that all of the leads are disconnected from the contactors or starters. Each winding must be tested separately. The average winding resistance for a 460-V, three-phase, six-wire compressor ranges from 0.6 Ω to 1.0 Ω.

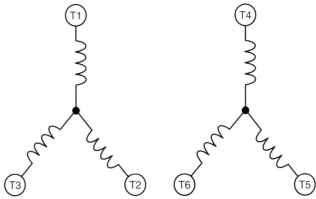

FIGURE 10-9. *Single-voltage six-wire compressor motor*

207

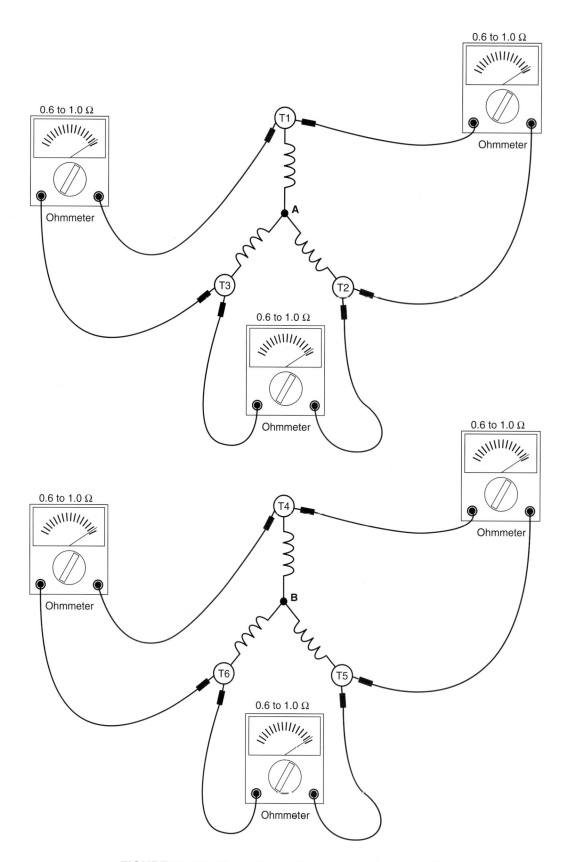

FIGURE 10-10. *Measuring resistance in a six-wire motor*

Figure 10-10 shows how to check the resistance of this type of compressor. First test one set of windings, as shown in Figure 10-10A, and then the other set, as shown in Figure 10-10B. Their controllers will be covered later in this Lesson. Compressors of this type usually have some form of internal or external protection, which also will be discussed later in this Lesson. The resistances of the individual windings should always be within 2 to 5% of each other. These compressors are supplied with either 208, 230, 460, 480, or 575-V three-phase power.

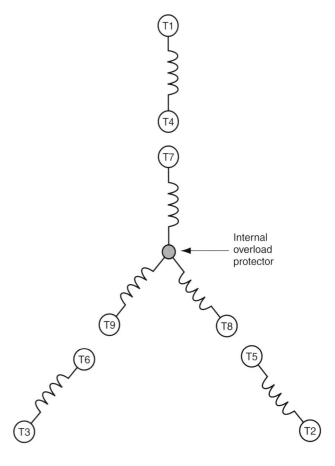

FIGURE 10-11. *Terminal designations for a three-phase dual-voltage motor*

Dual-voltage six-wire and nine-wire compressors

A three-phase motor used for a multiple-voltage application may have either six or nine leads brought out through the connection box, and can be wired in either a wye or a delta configuration. Figure 10-11 shows the terminal designations for a nine-lead dual-voltage motor. This motor can be connected for either 230-V or 460-V operation. The resistance of the windings in a typical 15-hp motor of this kind will range anywhere from 0.2 Ω to 1.5 Ω, depending on the application. If, for example, the resistance per winding in Figure 10-11 is 0.8 Ω, you could expect the following readings:

Terminal numbers	Resistance, Ω
1-4	0.8
2-5	0.8
3-6	0.8
7-8	1.6
7-9	1.6
8-9	1.6

VOLTAGE AND CURRENT TESTING

In order to test the voltage of a motor accurately, you should perform the test at the motor itself, not at the starter or contactor. There are two reasons for this. First, you will get a more accurate reading when the motor is at full load.

Second, you will be able to tell if there is a problem with voltage drop across the contactor or starter.

There are several conditions that can cause problems in three-phase motors:

- single phasing

- low voltage

- high voltage

- voltage imbalance

- current imbalance.

Single phasing

Single phasing occurs when one of the lines is broken between the motor and the supply. In the example shown in Figure 10-12, phase "A" is broken. If this occurs while the motor is running, the motor will continue to operate as a single-phase motor. However, the other two windings will consume more power and the current will increase in each of the other windings to 1½ to 2 times the normal current. The motor will slow down and start drawing excessive current. If the condition is allowed to continue, the motor will begin to overheat. This is because winding A is getting no power, while windings B and C are trying to keep the motor turning.

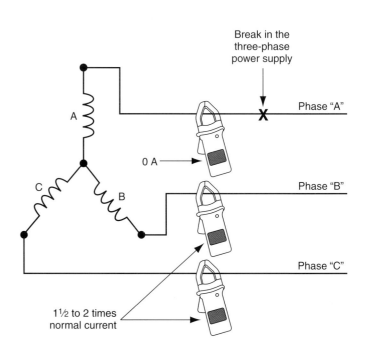

FIGURE 10-12. *Single phasing*

If one of the three input power connections is open and the motor is *not* running, then when the motor tries to start, the result will be a *locked rotor* condition. Because there are no longer three windings in the circuit, the motor will trip its overload protectors, or the heaters in the starter. Locked rotor problems can also be caused by a bad contactor or starter, or by an open winding. It is even possible for the power company to lose a leg of the incoming power supply.

When you inspect a faulty motor, you can tell that single phasing has occurred if one winding (every third winding) shows no signs of overheating, while the windings adjacent to it, or on either side of it, are burned or show other signs of overheating.

Low voltage

Although very difficult to prove, low voltages probably cause more damage to motors than any other condition. A typical motor will work within a 10% range of its voltage application—that is, within 5% on either side of its nominal rating. For example, a 230-V motor should work within a range of 218.5 to 241.5 V (since ±5% of 230 V is ±11.5 V). The acceptable range for a 208-V motor is different—±5% of 208 V is only ±10.4 V, so the 208-V motor should operate within a range of 197.6 to 228.4 V. A 460-V motor, on the other hand, has a much wider range, and should operate within a range of 437 to 483 V (±5% of 460 V is ±23 V). Remember that any voltage under the minimum will cause high running current. This occurs because the motor is trying to work harder with less energy. The result is added heat in the windings.

High voltage

As explained in the preceding paragraph, a 230-V motor can function safely up to the top of its operating range at 241.5 V. If an even higher voltage is applied, the motor's windings will overheat. The motor cannot go any faster, because the number of poles and the frequency of the power supply determine its speed. However, the added voltage will cause overheating. Normally, the overloads will trip more quickly in an overvoltage situation than in an undervoltage situation. Both conditions can be hard to diagnose, so if you are in doubt about the voltage, use a recording voltmeter and check the incoming power supply for 24 to 48 hours.

Voltage imbalance

A small imbalance in the input voltage can result in a considerable amount of heat being generated in the motor windings. An imbalance of only 5%, for example, can increase the winding temperature as much as 50% above the safe level. To determine the voltage imbalance in a three-phase system, first measure and record the voltage between T1 and T2, then between T1 and T3, and finally between T2 and T3. In the example shown in Figure 10-13 on the next page, the readings are 218, 226, and 230 V, respectively. Find the *average* voltage by adding these three figures together and dividing by 3:

Voltage measured between T1 and T2	218 V
Voltage measured between T1 and T3	226 V
Voltage measured between T2 and T3	+ 230 V
Total	674 V

Average voltage = 674 V ÷ 3 = 224.67 V

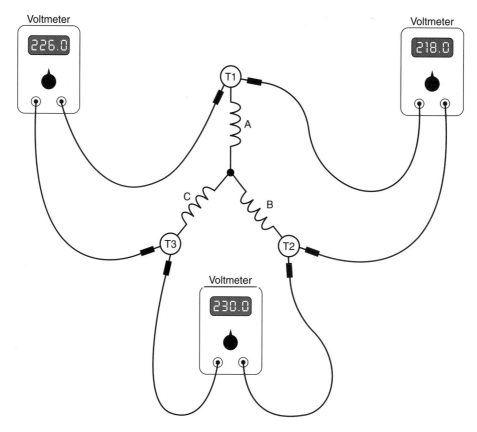

FIGURE 10-13. *Voltage imbalance (230-V three-phase power)*

Determine which reading represents the greatest deviation from the average (in this case it is the 218-V reading). Now you can use the following equation to calculate the voltage imbalance:

$$\% \text{ imbalance} = \frac{\text{maximum deviation from average voltage}}{\text{average voltage}} \times 100$$

$$= \frac{224.67 \text{ V} - 218 \text{ V}}{224.67 \text{ V}} \times 100$$

$$= \frac{6.67 \text{ V}}{224.67 \text{ V}} \times 100$$

$$= 0.0297 \times 100 = 2.97\% = \text{approximately } 3\%$$

Note: The voltage imbalance between any two legs of the supply voltage applied to a three-phase compressor must *not* exceed 2%. Any voltage imbalance of more than 2% must be corrected. The compressor in Figure 10-13 has an imbalance of almost 3%. The problem must be corrected.

Current imbalance

A voltage imbalance always produces a current imbalance, but a current imbalance may occur without a voltage imbalance. A current imbalance can occur when an electrical terminal, contactor, starter, etc. becomes loose or corroded, causing a high resistance in one leg. Since current follows the path of least resistance, the current in the other two legs will increase, causing more heat to be generated in those two windings.

To determine the current imbalance in a three-phase system, first check the motor nameplate for the full-load current (sometimes abbreviated FLA, for full-load amperage). Select the highest range setting (higher than the motor FLA) on your clamp-on ammeter. Turn the power on, and place the clamp-on ammeter around the wire connected to the T1 terminal of the motor. Measure and record the current drawn by the T1 leg. Then, one at a time, measure the current drawn by the remaining two legs. For the example shown in Figure 10-14, the readings are 25, 27, and 26 A.

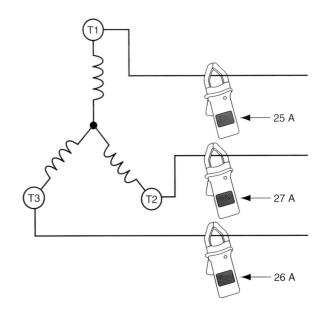

FIGURE 10-14. *Current imbalance*

Again, you can find the *average* current by adding these three figures together and dividing by 3:

Current measured in T1 leg	25 A
Current measured in T2 leg	27 A
Current measured in T3 leg	+ 26 A
Total	78 A

Average current = 78 A ÷ 3 = 26 A

The readings for legs T1 and T2 (25 and 27 A, respectively) both produce a maximum 1-A deviation from the average of 26 A. Now you can use the following equation to calculate the current imbalance:

$$\% \text{ imbalance } = \frac{\text{maximum deviation from average current}}{\text{average current}} \times 100$$

$$= \frac{1 \text{ A}}{26 \text{ A}} \times 100$$

$$= 0.038 \times 100 = 3.8\%$$

Note: The current imbalance between any two legs of a three-phase compressor must *not* exceed 10%. If the current imbalance exceeds 10%, look for an electrical terminal, contact, etc., that is loose or corroded and may be causing a high resistance in that leg. Since the imbalance in Figure 10-14 is less than 10%, the current between phases is acceptable.

DUAL-VOLTAGE MOTOR CONNECTIONS

So far, all of the testing examples discussed in this Lesson have pertained to single-voltage compressors. It is more economical for manufacturers to make semi-hermetic compressors that have dual windings. Look back at Figure 10-11, which shows a dual-voltage compressor motor. A nine-lead motor of this type can be connected for either 230-V or 460-V operation.

Figure 10-15 shows how a nine-wire dual-voltage motor is connected in a wye configuration. In Figure 10-15A, the leads are connected in *parallel* for 230-V operation. This means that the 230 V of Line 1 will be applied to both windings A and D at the same time. Likewise, the 230 V of Line 2 will be applied to windings B and E at the same time, and the 230 V of Line 3 will be applied to windings C and F at the same time. Therefore, the same voltage will be impressed across each of the windings. (The numbers and letters are used for illustration purposes only. Normally the windings are not identified with letters.)

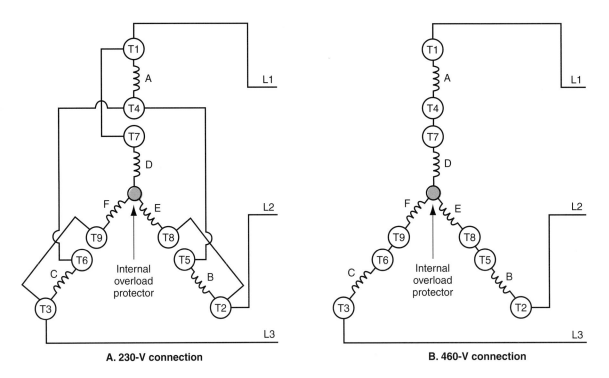

FIGURE 10-15. *Dual-voltage configurations for wye-connected motors*

In Figure 10-15B, the leads are connected in *series* for 460-V operation. This means that the 460 V from L1 and L2 will be impressed across windings A, D, B, and E. The 460 V from L1 and L3 will be impressed across windings A, D, C, and F. The 460 V from L2 and L3 will be impressed across windings B, E, C, and F.

Note that he two examples of wye-connected motors shown in Figure 10-15 both use the "across-the-line" (XL) starting method. However, the nine-lead motor is versatile, and also can be wired for "part wind start" (PWS) operation. This option, shown in Figure 10-16, is available *only* at the lower (230-V) voltage connection. Starting is accomplished in steps, with a time delay between steps. Contactor C1 is energized first, and contactor C2 is energized after a time delay of ¾ to 1½ seconds. (If the time delay is any longer, there is a possibility of the first winding overheating.)

This configuration allows the 230 V of Line 1 to be applied to winding A, the 230 V of Line 2 to be applied to winding B, and the 230 V of Line 3 to be applied to winding C. This first step is accomplished through contacts C1a, C1b, and C1c. After the time delay, the second contactor is energized, allowing the 230 V of Line 1 to be applied to winding D, the 230 V of Line 2 to be applied to winding E, and the 230 V of Line 3 to be applied to winding F. This second step is accomplished through contacts C2a, C2b, and C2c.

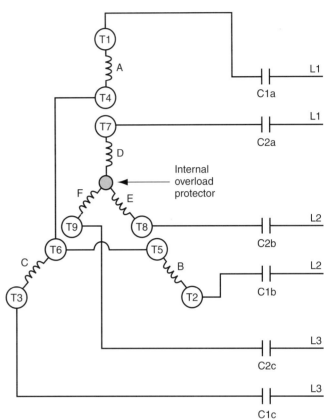

FIGURE 10-16. *Typical PWS connection*

The starting components used in a PWS arrangement are smaller and less expensive than those used in across-the-line configurations. Finer wire can be used, which also cuts down on the cost.

Figure 10-17 shows a very basic control circuit for a PWS compressor. It includes control relay contacts CR1 and CR2, a time-delay relay (TDR), and the contactor coils C1 and C2. In operation, when the control relay is energized, it causes both contactor C1 and the time-delay relay (TDR) to energize at the same time. After a time period of *no longer* than 1 second, contactor C2 is energized.

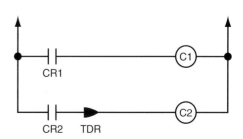

FIGURE 10-17. *Typical control circuit for PWS compressor*

SOLID-STATE OVERLOAD PROTECTION

Since the introduction of electronics into the HVACR industry, compressor manufacturers have tried to find better ways of protecting compressors from overheating, and of preventing motor windings from being destroyed due to current and voltage imbalances. Eventually, a solid-state device was developed that senses the temperature of the windings directly. This type of motor protector uses a special sensor to sense and monitor the temperature of the motor windings. This information is sent to a control module designed to open a control circuit and take the compressor off-line when the temperature exceeds the safe limit.

Sensors

The sensors used in the windings of motor compressors are called *thermistors*. Thermistors are temperature-sensitive solid-state devices. They are imbedded in the motor windings and are wired in a parallel arrangement. A thermistor's resistance changes with changes in temperature. There are two types of thermistors made today. They are:

- *Positive temperature coefficient* (PTC) thermistors—as the temperature increases, so does the resistance of the thermistor.

- *Negative temperature coefficient* (NTC) thermistors—as the temperature increases, the resistance of the thermistor decreases.

The sensors used in today's compressors are positive temperature coefficient (PTC) thermistors. There are two basic styles used. "Round-style" thermistors are made by Texas Instruments Inc., and have a nominal resistance of 2,200 Ω at 72°F. "Rectangular-style" thermistors are made by Robertshaw Controls Co., and have a nominal resistance of 82 Ω at 72°F.

Thermistors respond quickly to changes in temperature (rates of 50°F per second are possible). The resistance of the thermistor changes by 3% for every degree of temperature change. Both the Texas Instruments and the Robertshaw thermistors work on the same principle, but the higher resistances are being used by most compressor manufacturers today.

Modules

The original modules made by Robertshaw (MP13 series), and Texas Instruments (Klixon 3AA series) incorporated a mechanical relay that interfaced with the compressor control circuit. These devices were prone to the same problems that plague any mechanical device—i.e., dirt, moisture, and vibration. Newer solid-state modules incorporate a combination of a transistorized amplifier and a modified Wheatstone bridge. The changing resistance of a thermistor can cause the bridge to become unbalanced and open a relay, or gate a silicon-controlled rectifier (SCR). Figure 10-18 illustrates the newer modules. The use of silicon-controlled rectifiers and triacs have made the modules more sophisticated and reliable, although they can be difficult to troubleshoot when something does go wrong.

Module connections

The manufacturers of solid-state modules have maintained a standard terminal nomenclature. Listed below are the terminal designations and their functions:

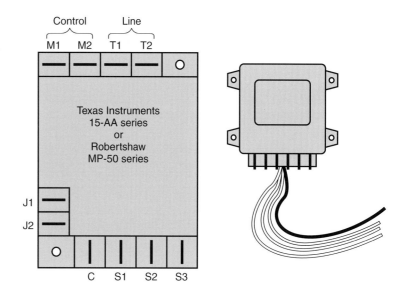

FIGURE 10-18. *Solid-state module*

- *M1* and *M2* are the control circuit connections. They should be placed in series with the compressor contactor coil. Remember that this is a switch circuit and should be used for pilot duty only.

- *T1* and *T2* are the power supply connections. They should be connected to the correct supply voltage at all times.

- *S1*, *S2*, *S3*, and *C* are the "sensor" and "common" connections, respectively. However, some manufacturers use wire leads for these connections. They are color-coded. The "sensor" wires are orange, and the "common" wire is black (sometimes black with an orange tracer).

- *J1* and *J2* are the remote reset connections. These terminals are not found on all modules. They are used to make the module a manual reset or remote reset type. If these terminals are not present, then the module you are working with is an automatic reset type.

Compressor connections

The thermistors that are imbedded in the motor windings of the compressor are brought out of the compressor to separate terminals in the compressor's terminal

box ("C" for the common, and "S1," "S2," and "S3" for the sensors).
Make certain that the module is connected to the sensors correctly.
If it is not, the module will sense a false resistance and keep the
machine from running.

The sensors usually are wired as shown in Figure 10-19. They have a
common tie point and are brought out individually. Not all are wired
identically—always consult the manufacturer's literature to be sure.

Troubleshooting

If you suspect a module or sensor to be defective, use the following
procedures to locate the fault:

1. If the unit is not running, check the voltage at T1 and T2
   (the module should indicate 115-V and 220-V terminal
   locations). If there is voltage present, go on to Step 2. If not,
   correct the problem (blown fuse, loose or broken wire, etc.).

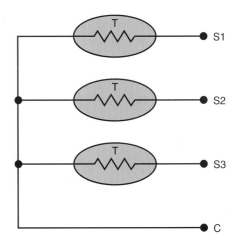

FIGURE 10-19. *Solid-state module connections*

2. In order to determine whether the module is responsible for keeping the
   unit off-line:

   a. Turn off the power.

   b. Disconnect M1 and M2 from the module.

   c. Connect a jumper wire between
      M1 and M2 (*not* the module).
      If you do *not* disconnect the
      module and you bridge M1 and
      M2, you will destroy the module!

   d. Turn the power back on. If the
      unit starts, then the fault is in
      the module or the sensors.

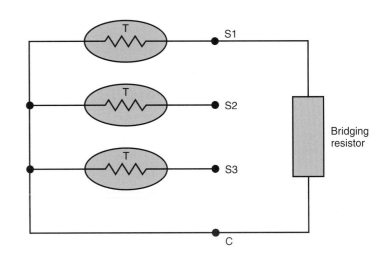

FIGURE 10-20. *Bridging an internal thermistor*

3. To check the sensors, you will need
   an ohmmeter with less than 3 V for
   its power supply (one or two penlight
   cells). If you use more than 3 V in
   measuring the sensors, you will stand
   the chance of destroying a good
   sensor. Follow these steps:

a. Allow the compressor enough time to cool down. If you do not, you will be testing a hot thermistor and possibly get an incorrect reading.

b. Disconnect all of the sensor leads, including the common lead.

c. With an appropriate ohmmeter, measure the resistance of the thermistor from the common lead to S1, S2, and S3 in turn. Thermistors in a Robertshaw module should have a resistance of 82 Ω at 72°F. Thermistors in a Texas Instruments module should have a resistance of 2,200 Ω at 72°F.

d. If one or two of the sensors are open, you can "bridge" the sensor with a resistor to get the compressor back on-line. Use a resistor with a value that corresponds to that of the thermistor. For both Robertshaw and Texas Instruments modules, the resistor should have a power rating of 2 W and a tolerance of 10%. *Note*: The efficiency of the module will be reduced by doing this. However, it is less expensive than buying a new compressor. Figure 10-20 shows the correct way to bridge an internal thermistor.

The newer families of modules have a built-in time delay of 120 seconds (2 minutes). If for any reason the power to the module is interrupted, the time delay will postpone the start of the machine by 2 minutes. This is also true if there is a change in one of the thermistors. The time delay prevents the compressor from short cycling and allows time for it to cool down.

A wiring diagram for a typical solid-state module is illustrated in Figure 10-21 on the next page. Remember that whenever the power is interrupted to T1 and T2, there will be a 2-minute delay. Electronic devices like these are being used more and more. They are reliable and efficient. They protect the compressor from excessive heat, voltage imbalance, low voltage, and power loss. There are new families of controls that incorporate oil failure protection, single-phase protection, and low voltage protection, all in one.

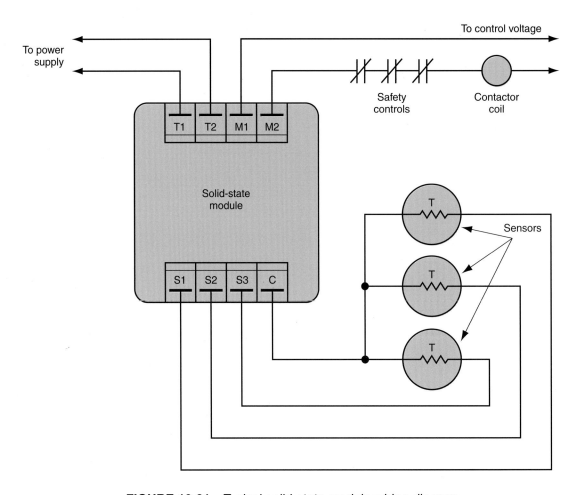

FIGURE 10-21. *Typical solid-state module wiring diagram*

WIRING DIAGRAMS

On pages 221 to 226, you will find wiring diagrams that show terminal
connections for a variety of multi-voltage and "part wind start" semi-hermetic
compressors. *Note*: The wiring diagrams on the following pages are to be used
for *representative* purposes only. The original equipment manufacturers produce
several different orientations in both single-voltage and multi-voltage versions.
It is essential for you to identify particular terminals and numbers for specific
compressors, and wire accordingly.

CARRIER (6L-6G SERIES)

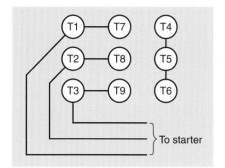

9-lead across-the-line
220 V

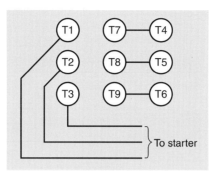

9-lead across-the-line
440 V

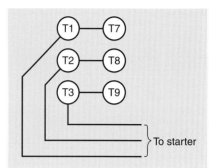

6-lead across-the-line
single-voltage 220 V

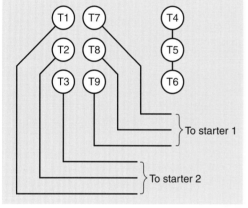

9-lead "part wind start"
220 V

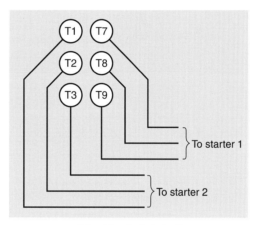

6-lead "part wind start"
single-voltage 220 V or 440 V

CARRIER (06D)

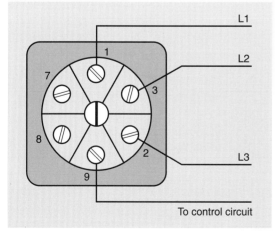

3-lead across-the-line
single-voltage 220 V or 440 V

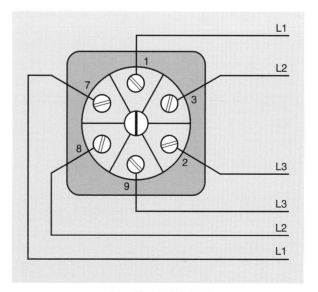

6-lead "part wind start"
single-voltage 220 V or 440 V

CARRIER (06E)

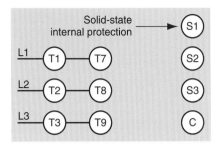

6-lead 3-wire across-the-line
220 V or 440 V three-phase

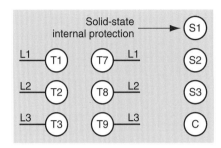

6-lead "part wind start"
220 V or 440 V three-phase

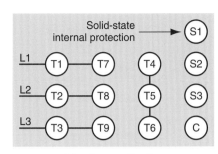

9-lead across-the-line
208/220 V three-phase

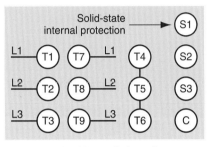

9-lead "part wind start"
208/220 V (only) three-phase

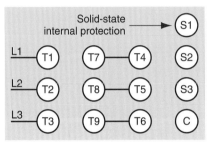

9-lead across-the-line
440/460 V three-phase

COPELAND

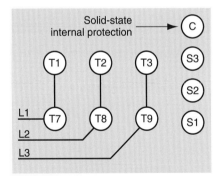

6-lead 3-wire across-the-line
single-voltage 220 V or 440 V
three-phase

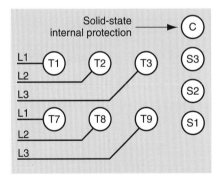

6-lead "part wind start"
single-voltage 220 V or 440 V
three-phase

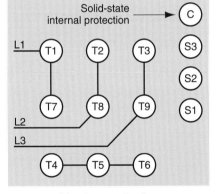

9-lead across-the-line
208/220 V three-phase

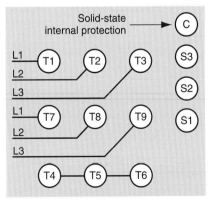

9-lead "part wind start"
208/220 V (only) three-phase

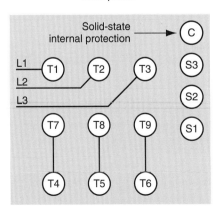

9-lead across-the-line
440/460 V three-phase

DUNHAM-BUSH (BRUNNER) (D-B-METICS)

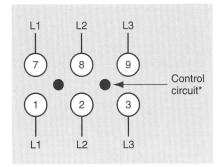

**6-lead "part wind start" three-phase
2-contactor single-voltage 208/220 V

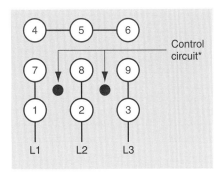

**9-lead "part wind start" three-phase
2-contactor single-voltage 208/220 V

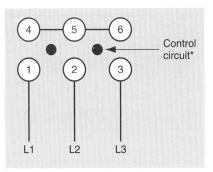

6-lead across-the-line three-phase
1-contactor single-voltage 208/220 V

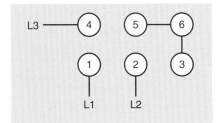

6-lead across-the-line three-phase
1-contactor single-voltage 208/220 V
(no control circuit) "L7 wiring"

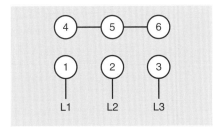

6-lead across-the-line three-phase
1-contactor single-voltage 208/220 V
(no control circuit)

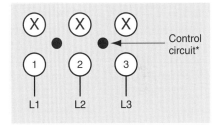

3-lead across-the-line three-phase
1-contactor single-voltage

DUNHAM-BUSH (BRUNNER) ("BIG FOUR")

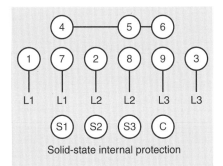

**9-lead "part wind start" three-phase
2-contactor multi-voltage 208/220 V

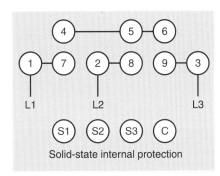

9-lead across-the-line three-phase
1-contactor multi-voltage 208/220 V

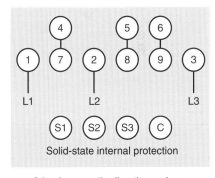

9-lead across-the-line three-phase
1-contactor multi-voltage 440/460 V

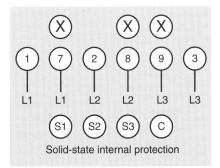

**6-lead "part wind start" three-phase
2-contactor single-voltage 220/460 V

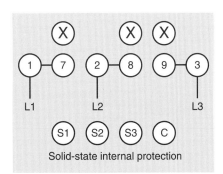

9-lead across-the-line three-phase
1-contactor multi-voltage 208/220 V

* Pilot-duty only control thermostat

** 1 and 7, 2 and 8, 3 and 9 each must
be the same phase

 Dummy terminal

*Always check line voltage against
nameplate voltage.*

TRANE (E AND F SERIES)

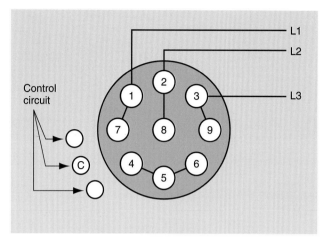

3-wire across-the-line three-phase
1-contactor 208/220 V

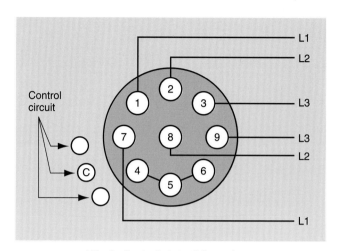

**6-wire "part wind start" three-phase
2-contactor 208/220 V

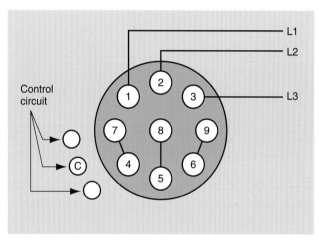

3-wire across-the-line three-phase
1-contactor 440/460 V

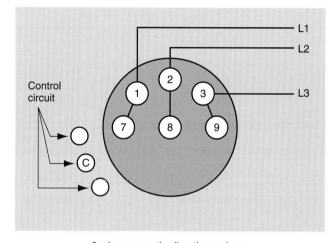

3-wire across-the-line three-phase
1-contactor 440/460 V

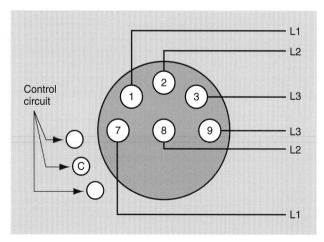

**6-wire "part wind start" three-phase
2-contactor 440/460 V

** 1 and 7, 2 and 8, 3 and 9 each must be the same phase

TRANE (M AND R SERIES)

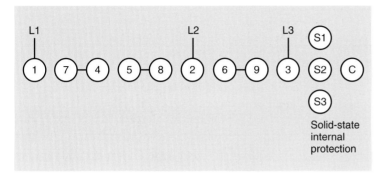

9-lead 3-wire three-phase
dual-voltage high (460 V)

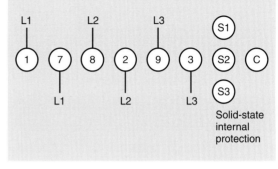

**6-lead "part wind start" three-phase
2-contactor single-voltage 220/460 V

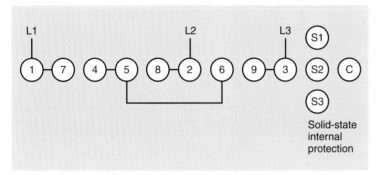

9-lead 3-wire full winding start three-phase
dual-voltage low (220 V)

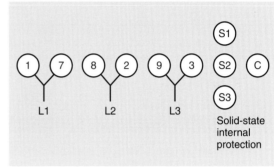

*6-lead 6-wire full winding start three-phase
single-voltage

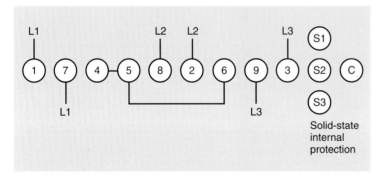

**9-lead 3-wire "part wind start" three-phase
dual-voltage low (220 V)

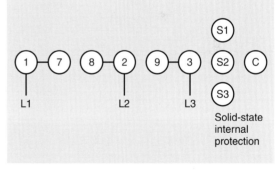

6-lead 3-wire full winding start
single-voltage

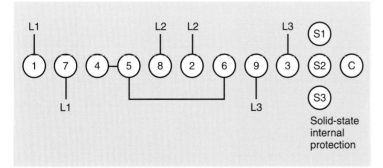

*9-lead 6-wire full winding start three-phase
dual-voltage low (220 V)

* Use in place of 3-wire to avoid
excessive wire size

** 1 and 7, 2 and 8, 3 and 9 each must
be the same phase

*Always check line voltage against
nameplate voltage.*

WORTHINGTON ("JJ")

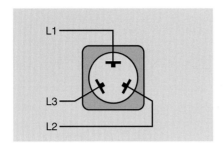

3-lead single-voltage

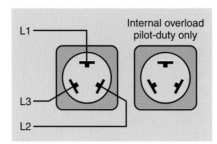

3-lead single-voltage (internal protection)

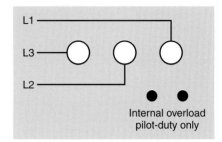

3-lead single-voltage (internal protection)

WORTHINGTON (2VH AND 3VH)

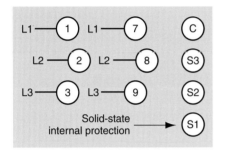

6-lead "part wind start"
single-voltage 220 V or 440 V

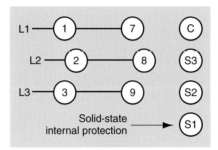

6-lead across-the-line
single-voltage 220 V or 440 V

WESTINGHOUSE

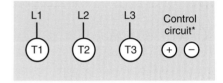

"CB" compressors

YORK

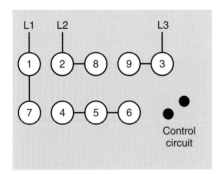

9-lead across-the-line three-phase
1-contactor multi-voltage 208/220 V

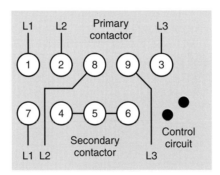

**9-lead "part wind start" three-phase
2-contactor multi-voltage 208/220 V

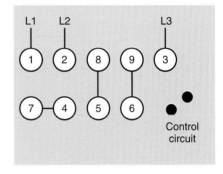

9-lead across-the-line three-phase
1-contactor multi-voltage 440/460 V

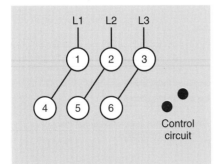

6-lead across-the-line three-phase
1-contactor single-voltage 208/220 V

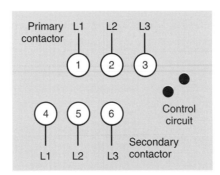

**6-lead "part wind start" three-phase
2-contactor single-voltage 208/220 V

* Always note polarity of control circuit
because of internal diode. "In" is
always positive.

** 1 and 7, 2 and 8, 3 and 9 each must
be the same phase

*Always check line voltage against
nameplate voltage.*

1.   What advantage does a semi-hermetic compressor have over a hermetic compressor as far as maintenance is concerned?

2.   The start winding in a semi-hermetic compressor motor is made with _____ wire and has _____ turns than the run winding.

3.   What problems can result if a semi-hermetic compressor's screw terminals are too loose?

4.   What is probably the greatest cause of compressor failures?

5.   In a capacitor-start, capacitor-run compressor, the start capacitor is controlled by a(n) _____.

6.   When you test a single-phase semi-hermetic compressor for a grounded winding, the ohmmeter range switch should be set to the _____ scale.

7.   When you measure the resistance between a compressor's shell and one of its leads, what is the significance of a *zero* reading?

8.   The following ohmmeter readings are taken from a single-phase semi-hermetic compressor with unmarked terminals: between terminals 1 and 2 = 2 Ω, between terminals 1 and 3 = 6 Ω, between terminals 2 and 3 = 4 Ω. Identify the terminals.

9.   The resistance values of the individual windings in a three-lead, three-phase semi-hermetic compressor motor should all be _____.

10.   You want to determine whether or not the windings of a three-phase semi-hermetic compressor are grounded to the compressor shell. If you are checking a 208-V compressor, what would be a satisfactory resistance reading?

11. What resistance reading would indicate that the compressor should be replaced?

12. What are the two reasons for testing the voltage applied to a motor at the motor itself rather than at its starter or contactor?

13. What happens if one of the power lines is broken between a three-phase compressor and the supply?

14. As a general rule, a motor will operate satisfactorily within a(n) _____ % range of its designed voltage application.

15. The voltage imbalance between any two legs of the supply voltage applied to a three-phase compressor must not exceed _____%.

16. What is the relationship between voltage imbalance and current imbalance?

17. The current imbalance between any two legs of a three-phase compressor must not exceed _____%.

18. A typical nine-lead dual-voltage compressor motor can be wired for either 230-V or 460-V operation. If such a motor is configured for "across-the-line" low-voltage operation, the leads are connected in _____. If it is configured for "across-the-line" high-voltage operation, the leads are connected in _____.

19. A nine-lead dual-voltage compressor motor can be wired for "part wind start" (PWS) operation only if the _____ of the two possible voltages is applied.

20. What type of thermistors are used as sensors in overload protection devices?

21. In solid-state overload protection modules, the *T1* and *T2* terminals indicate the _____ connections.

22. If a solid-state overload protection module has color-coded wire leads, what color is the "common" wire?

23. When you check the internal sensors of a solid-state overload protection module with an ohmmeter, the meter's battery should be _____ V or less.

24. Newer protection modules have a built-in time delay of _____.

Electronic Components

TESTING DIODES

Troubleshooting the electronic components in HVACR systems is normally a matter of finding and replacing faulty components, rather than repairing them. The primary goal of this Lesson, therefore, is to familiarize the service technician with the testing and application of a few basic electronic components and some of their associated circuits. You may wish to review the relevant portions of Unit 3 in this Course if you feel the need to "brush up" on the fundamentals of solid-state theory.

As you know from studying Lesson 3 in Unit 3, a *diode* conducts current in one direction only. Figure 11-1 shows the schematic symbol for a semiconductor diode as it appears in electrical diagrams. The arrowhead stands for the *anode*, or positive electrode.
It represents the P-type material toward which the electrons flow. The vertical bar stands for the *cathode*, or negative electrode. It represents the N-type material, the source of the electrons. In some schematic diagrams, letters are used to designate the parts of the diode ("A" for anode and "K" for cathode).

Solid-state diodes come in a variety of shapes and sizes. Figure 11-2 shows some typical diodes. There are markings on all diodes to distinguish the cathode

Anode (+) ▶|— Cathode (−)
A   K

FIGURE 11-1. *Schematic symbol for a semiconductor diode*

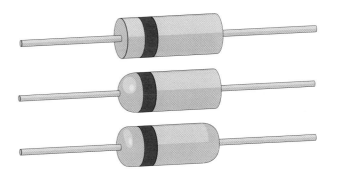

FIGURE 11-2. *Typical diodes*

end from the anode end. The banded (and/or sometimes rounded) end designates the cathode end of the diode.

> ⚠ **WARNING: Before making any resistance measurements, turn off all power to the circuit being tested and disconnect the power supply.**

A faulty diode—one that is not conducting correctly—may be either open or shorted. An *open* diode will not pass or conduct current in either direction. If you are using an analog ohmmeter, the reading for an open diode will be infinity (∞). If you are using a digital ohmmeter, the reading for an open diode will be "OL." A zero reading indicates a *shorted* diode. Some digital ohmmeters have a special diode test function that checks the diode automatically. The diode to be tested must have at least one end removed from the circuit, and the power to the circuit must be turned off.

Testing with an analog meter

In order to determine the polarity of a diode, you first must determine the polarity of the battery in your ohmmeter. As you know, most meters have two jacks, one marked "negative" and one marked "positive." But this does not always mean that the negative terminal of the internal battery is connected through the meter's negative jack. You can use a known good diode to find the polarity of your meter's battery. Set the ohmmeter's range scale to R × 1,000 and plug the test probes into the meter jacks. Connect the black probe to the common (COM) or minus (−) jack, and the red probe to the plus (+) or V-Ω jack.

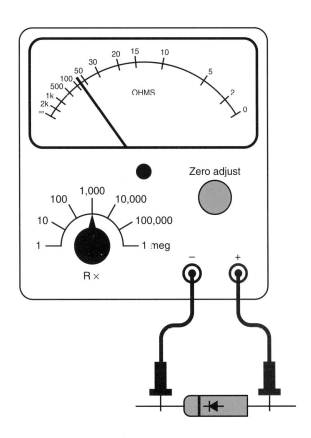

Place the diode across the leads as shown in Figure 11-3, with the negative lead on the cathode end of the diode and the positive lead on the anode end. If the battery's negative terminal is connected through the meter's negative jack, the meter should read anywhere from 50 to 100 Ω, depending on the diode. This indicates that the diode is *forward-biased*, and will allow current to pass.

If the meter reads between 50,000 and 100,000 Ω, reverse the leads (so that the lead formerly in contact with the cathode end of the diode is now in contact with the anode end, and vice versa). Such a high reading indicates that the

FIGURE 11-3. *Testing a diode with an analog ohmmeter*

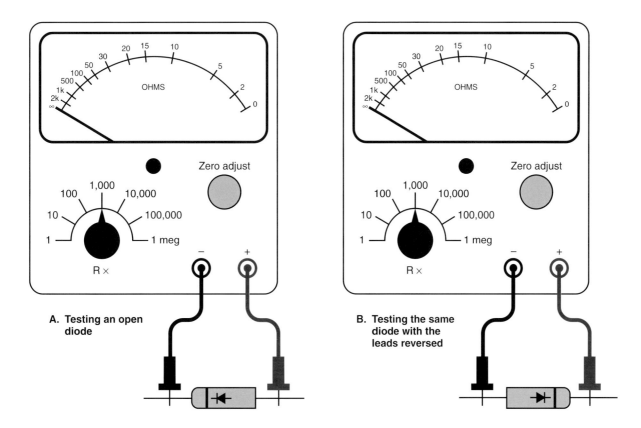

FIGURE 11-4. *Testing a suspected open diode*

diode is *reverse-biased*, which means that very little or no current will
be allowed to pass. Remember that a "good" diode will conduct current in
one direction, but not the other. Once you obtain a low resistance reading
(50 to 100 Ω), you will know that the lead touching the cathode end of the
diode is connected to the negative terminal of the meter's internal battery.
If necessary, you can mark your meter jacks accordingly for future reference.

Open diode example. An *open* diode acts like a "broken" circuit or an open
switch—it does not allow any current to pass at all. Figure 11-4A shows an
ohmmeter connected across an open diode. The meter reads infinity (∞), so
you know that no current is present. Even when the leads are reversed, as shown
in Figure 11-4 B, the reading will be the same. An open diode cannot be used.
In a practical circuit, an open diode is very similar to an open fuse, preventing
power from being applied to any of the components.

Shorted diode example. A *shorted* diode has just the opposite effect. No matter
what scale is used on the ohmmeter, a shorted diode results in a zero (or very
low) resistance reading. Figure 11-5A at the top of the next page shows an
ohmmeter set to the R × 1,000 scale connected across a shorted diode. Note
that even when the leads are reversed and/or a different scale setting is selected,

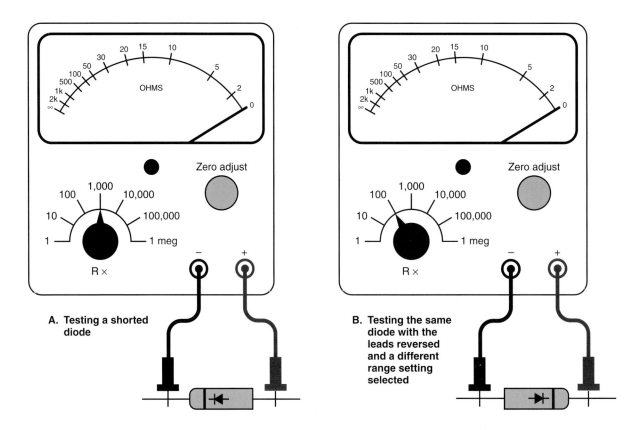

FIGURE 11-5. *Testing a suspected shorted diode*

as shown in Figure 11-5B, the same reading (0 Ω) is obtained. If this diode were an integral part of a power supply, the fuses or other components could be open or possibly destroyed. A shorted diode must be replaced. However, it is important to remember that a diode may have been shorted due to some external cause.

Testing with a digital meter

Due to the fact that there are so many digital instruments on the market today, this portion of the Lesson must be generic in nature. Always make sure to read the instructions that come with your particular meter or test instrument and follow the manufacturer's recommended operating procedures.

Most digital ohmmeters have a special diode test function that allows accurate measurements of forward voltage drops across diode and transistor junctions. This test function is marked on the ohmmeter range switch with the diode symbol, as illustrated in Figure 11-6. When the test function is used, a constant current (usually 2 mA) is applied to the semiconductor under test. As a result, the meter readout displays a voltage drop. Normally you can use the diode test function to check a diode while it is in the circuit. The limited current produced by most instruments when the test function is used reduces the possibility of damage to low-power diodes and transistors, a common problem caused by many analog meters.

To perform diode test measurements, use the following procedure:

1. Connect the red test lead to the "V-Ω" input and the black test lead to the "COM" input.

2. Set the range switch to the diode test position (shown at the far right of the dial in Figure 11-6).

3. If the diode being tested is connected to a circuit, turn off all power to the circuit and discharge all capacitors.

4. Connect the test leads to the diode as shown in Figure 11-7.

5. Read the forward voltage drop displayed on the digital readout.

6. If the display reads "OL," reverse the leads. The placement of the leads when the forward voltage drop is displayed (normally 600 to 900 mV) indicates the bias of the diode. Make sure that the red lead is connected to the anode end of the diode and the black lead to the cathode end. If "OL" is displayed regardless of how the leads are connected, the diode is open.

7. If the reading is very low (less than 1 V), and the same low reading is obtained even when the leads are reversed, the diode is shorted internally—or, if tested in a circuit, shunted by a resistance of less than 500 Ω. In the latter case, the diode must be disconnected from the circuit in order to determine its condition.

Testing unknown diodes

In order to test an unknown diode, you first must establish the polarity of the battery in your ohmmeter,

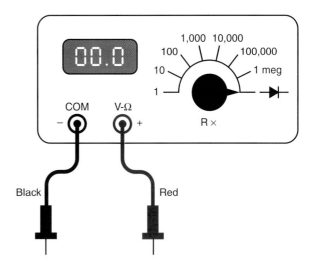

FIGURE 11-6. *Digital ohmmeter with special diode test function*

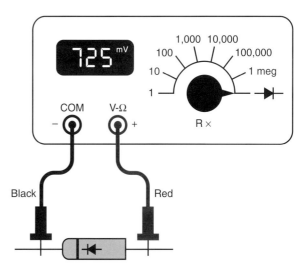

FIGURE 11-7. *Testing a diode with a digital ohmmeter*

as described earlier in this Lesson. Measure the resistance of the diode, then reverse the leads and measure the resistance again. This simple test can provide information about a diode's characteristics and placement in a power supply. Remember that a high resistance reading indicates a reverse bias, and a low resistance reading indicates a forward bias. The resistance measured when the diode is connected with a reverse bias should be no less than 10 times the resistance measured when it is connected with a forward bias. More typically, the reverse-biased reading will be between 100 and 1,000 times the forward-biased reading.

Diodes can be made of either germanium or silicon. A germanium diode starts to conduct current when a minimum voltage of 0.25 V is applied across it. A silicon diode requires a minimum voltage of 0.6 V in order to conduct current. You can use a voltmeter and an ohmmeter, connected as shown in Figure 11-8, to determine whether a diode is made of germanium or silicon. Measure the voltage drop across the diode with the voltmeter while reading the forward-biased resistance with the ohmmeter. Use an analog ohmmeter with a low range setting.

TESTING TRANSISTORS

Recall from Lesson 5 of Unit 3 that a simple *transistor* is a two-junction, three-electrode semiconductor device. The three electrodes used in a two-junction transistor are the *emitter*, the *base*, and the *collector*. One junction is between the emitter and the base, and the other is between the base and the collector. Like the diode, a transistor contains both P-type material and N-type material. Transistors are classified as either *NPN* or *PNP* transistors. An NPN transistor has a thin region of P-type material between two regions of N-type material. A PNP transistor has a thin region of N-type material between two regions of P-type material. Figure 11-9 shows the schematic symbols for both.

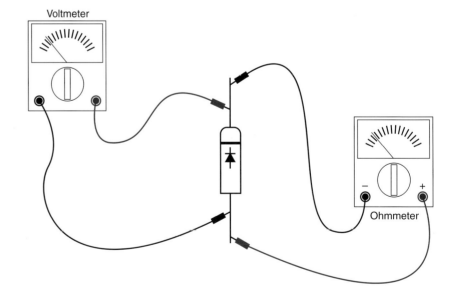

FIGURE 11-8. *Testing an unknown diode*

Testing transistors is similar to testing diodes. Resistance measurements can be made across both junctions—that is, between the base and the emitter and between the base and the collector. You can also take an ohmmeter reading between the emitter and the collector to determine whether a short or a leak exists. It is important to remember that a transistor must be removed from the circuit in order for you to test it correctly. There are some special test instruments on the market that will test transistors "in circuit," but these devices are for laboratory work, not field service.

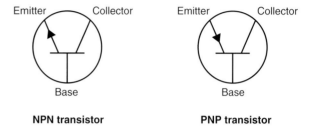

FIGURE 11-9. *Schematic symbols for transistors*

When testing transistors, use an analog ohmmeter with a low-voltage battery. (A battery of 3 to 9 V is acceptable. Anything more than 9 V could damage the transistor under test.) As discussed earlier in this Lesson, it is imperative for the ohmmeter's leads to be identified correctly.

For the examples that follow, two generic NPN transistors and two generic PNP transistors have been selected. One of each type is a standard audio or "low-power" transistor, and the other is a "high-power" transistor. These devices can be purchased in any electronics wholesale house or general electronics parts store.

NPN low-power transistors

An NPN transistor is similar in construction to two diodes that are connected by their anodes (positive ends), as shown below.

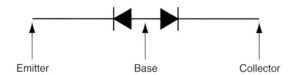

To measure the resistance between the base and the emitter of a *low-power* NPN transistor, start with the ohmmeter's range switch set to the R × 1,000 scale. Connect the positive lead of the ohmmeter to the base of the transistor and the negative lead to the emitter, as shown in Figure 11-10A on the next page. You can measure the resistance between the base and the collector in the same way, as illustrated in Figure 11-10B. In both cases, a *low* meter reading (50 to 500 Ω) indicates that the portion of the transistor under test is "good."

Now reverse the test leads, so that the negative lead of the ohmmeter is connected to the base of the transistor and the positive lead to the emitter,

A. Low resistance reading between base (positive) and emitter (negative)

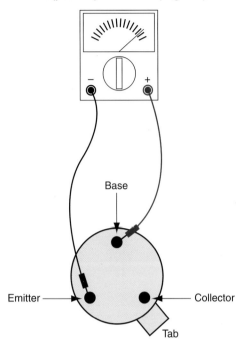

B. Low resistance reading between base (positive) and collector (negative)

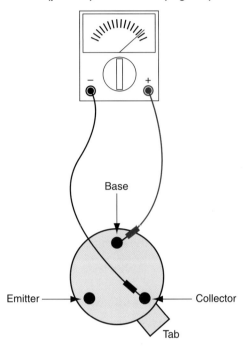

C. High resistance reading between base (negative) and emitter (positive)

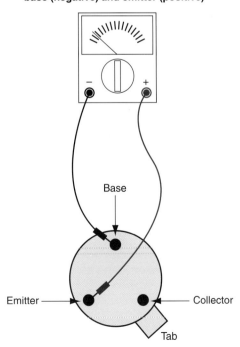

D. High resistance reading between base (negative) and collector (positive)

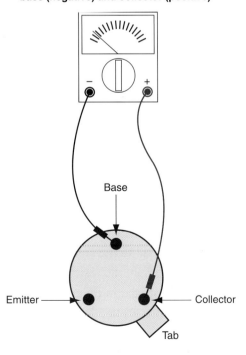

FIGURE 11-10. *Testing an NPN low-power transistor*

as shown in Figure 11-10C. Start with the ohmmeter's range switch set to the R × 100,000 scale. This time a *high* meter reading (50,000 to 100,000 Ω) indicates that the portion of the transistor under test is "good." Again, you can measure the resistance between the base and the collector in the same way, as illustrated in Figure 11-10D.

It is always a good practice to measure the resistance between the emitter and the collector of a transistor as a separate test. A "breakdown" between the emitter and the collector can lead to the possible destruction of other components in associated circuits. Figure 11-11A illustrates this test for an NPN low-power transistor. Figure 11-11B shows the same test with the leads reversed. A "good" transistor will exhibit very high resistance, usually in the 1 to 2-MΩ range, in either direction. (Accordingly, you will have to utilize an appropriate meter range.)

NPN high-power transistors

To measure the resistance across the junctions of a *high-power* NPN transistor, follow the same procedures that you used for low-power transistors. Start with the ohmmeter's range switch set to the R × 1,000 scale. Connect the positive lead of the ohmmeter to the base of the transistor and the negative lead to the

A. Very high resistance reading between emitter (negative) and collector (positive)

B. Very high resistance reading between collector (negative) and emitter (positive)

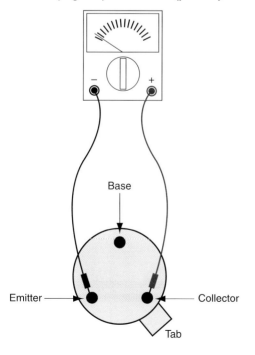
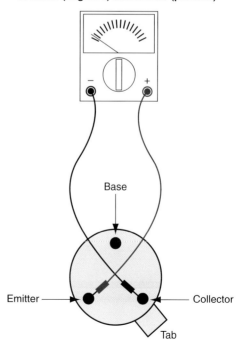

FIGURE 11-11. *Measuring resistance between the emitter and the collector of an NPN low-power transistor*

A. Low resistance reading between base (positive) and emitter (negative)

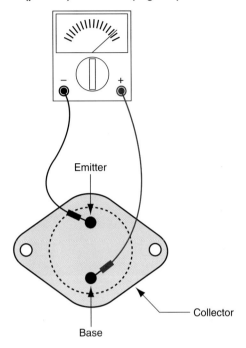

Emitter

Collector

Base

B. Low resistance reading between base (positive) and collector (negative)

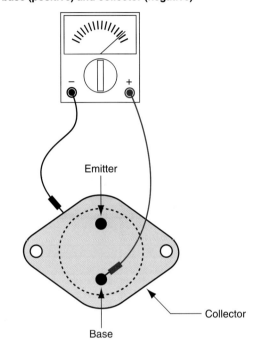

Emitter

Collector

Base

C. High resistance reading between base (negative) and emitter (positive)

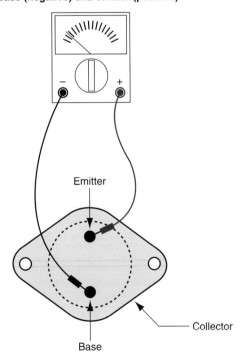

Emitter

Collector

Base

D. High resistance reading between base (negative) and collector (positive)

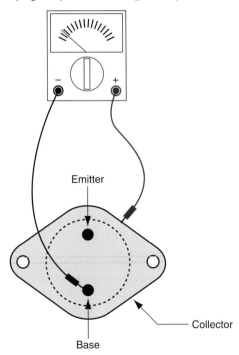

Emitter

Collector

Base

FIGURE 11-12. *Testing an NPN high-power transistor*

emitter, as shown in Figure 11-12A. You can measure the resistance across the other junction—that is, between the base and the collector—in the same way, as illustrated in Figure 11-12B. In both cases, a *low* meter reading (usually in the 50 to 500-Ω range) indicates that the portion of the transistor under test is "good."

Now reverse the test leads, so that the negative lead of the ohmmeter is connected to the base of the transistor and the positive lead to the emitter, as shown in Figure 11-12C. Start with the ohmmeter's range switch set to the R × 100,000 scale. This time a *high* meter reading (25,000 to 75,000 Ω) indicates that the portion of the transistor under test is "good." Again, you can measure the resistance between the base and the collector in the same way, as illustrated in Figure 11-12D.

As stated previously, it is a good idea to measure the resistance between the emitter and the collector as a separate test. Figure 11-13A illustrates this test for an NPN high-power transistor. Figure 11-13B shows the same test with the leads reversed. A "good" transistor will exhibit very high resistance, usually in the 1 to 2-MΩ range, in either direction. (Accordingly, you will have to utilize an appropriate meter range.)

A. Very high resistance reading between emitter (negative) and collector (positive)

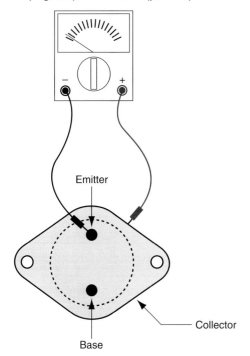

B. Very high resistance reading between collector (negative) and emitter (positive)

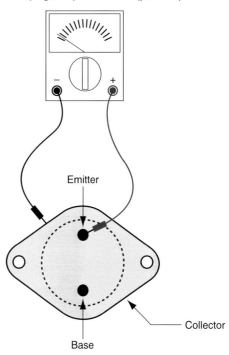

FIGURE 11-13. *Measuring resistance between the emitter and the collector of an NPN high-power transistor*

A. High resistance reading between base (positive) and emitter (negative)

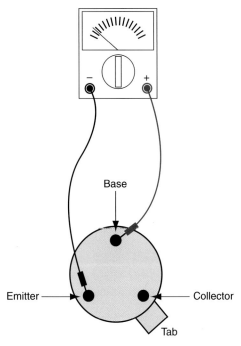

B. High resistance reading between base (positive) and collector (negative)

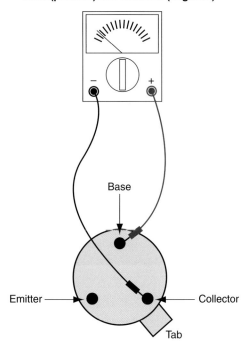

C. Low resistance reading between base (negative) and emitter (positive)

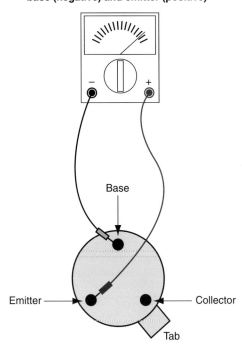

D. Low resistance reading between base (negative) and collector (positive)

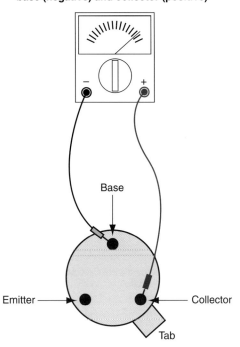

FIGURE 11-14. *Testing a PNP low-power transistor*

PNP low-power transistors

A PNP transistor is similar in construction to two diodes that are connected by their cathodes (negative ends), as shown below.

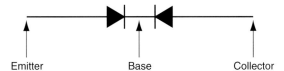

To measure the resistance between the base and the emitter of a *low-power* PNP transistor, start with the ohmmeter's range switch set to the R × 100,000 scale. Connect the positive lead of the ohmmeter to the base of the transistor and the negative lead to the emitter, as shown in Figure 11-14A. You can measure the resistance between the base and the collector in the same way, as illustrated in Figure 11-14B. In both cases, a *high* meter reading (50,000 to 100,000 Ω) indicates that the portion of the transistor under test is "good."

Now reverse the test leads, so that the negative lead of the ohmmeter is connected to the base of the transistor and the positive lead to the emitter, as shown in Figure 11-14C. Start with the ohmmeter's range switch set to

A. Very high resistance reading between emitter (negative) and collector (positive)

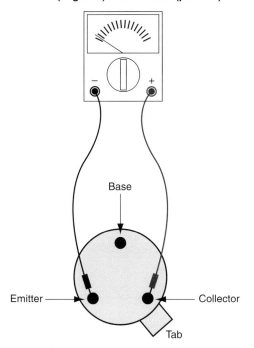

B. Very high resistance reading between collector (negative) and emitter (positive)

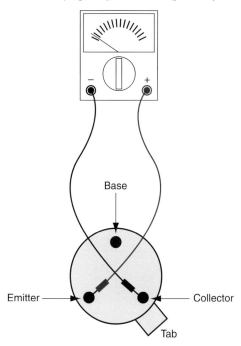

FIGURE 11-15. *Measuring resistance between the emitter and the collector of a PNP low-power transistor*

243

A. High resistance reading between base (positive) and emitter (negative)

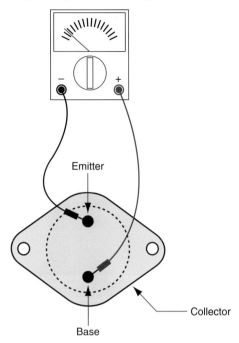

B. High resistance reading between base (positive) and collector (negative)

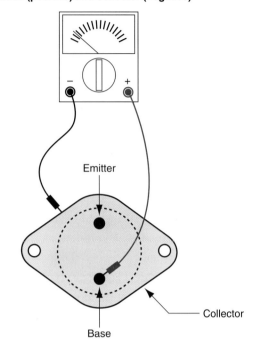

C. Low resistance reading between base (negative) and emitter (positive)

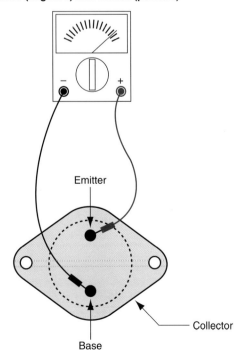

D. Low resistance reading between base (negative) and collector (positive)

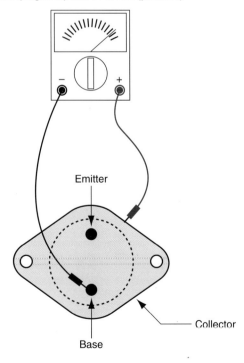

FIGURE 11-16. *Testing a PNP high-power transistor*

the R × 1,000 scale. This time a *low* meter reading (50 to 500 Ω) indicates that the portion of the transistor under test is "good." Again, you can measure the resistance between the base and the collector in the same way, as illustrated in Figure 11-14D.

The next step is to measure the resistance between the emitter and the collector. Figure 11-15A on the previous page illustrates this test for a PNP low-power transistor. Figure 11-15B shows the same test with the leads reversed. As with the NPN transistors, a "good" PNP transistor will exhibit very high resistance, usually in the 1 to 2-MΩ range, in either direction. (Accordingly, you will have to utilize an appropriate meter range.)

PNP high-power transistors

To measure the resistance between the base and the emitter of a *high-power* PNP transistor, start with the ohmmeter's range switch set to the R × 100,000 scale. Connect the positive lead of the ohmmeter to the base of the transistor and the negative lead to the emitter, as shown in Figure 11-16A. You can measure the resistance between the base and the collector in the same way, as illustrated in Figure 11-16B. In both cases, a *high* meter reading (in the

A. Very high resistance reading between emitter (negative) and collector (positive)

B. Very high resistance reading between collector (negative) and emitter (positive)

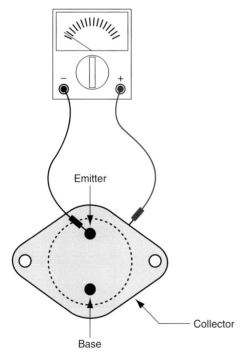

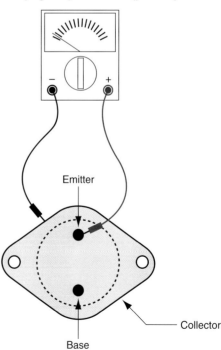

FIGURE 11-17. *Measuring resistance between the emitter and the collector of a PNP high-power transistor*

25,000 to 75,000-Ω range) indicates that the portion of the transistor under test is "good."

Now reverse the test leads, so that the negative lead of the ohmmeter is connected to the base of the transistor and the positive lead to the emitter, as shown in Figure 11-16C. Start with the ohmmeter's range switch set to the R × 1,000 scale. This time a *low* meter reading (50 to 500 Ω) indicates that the portion of the transistor under test is "good." Again, you can measure the resistance between the base and the collector in the same way, as illustrated in Figure 11-16D.

The next step is to measure the resistance between the emitter and the collector. Figure 11-17A on the previous page illustrates this test for a PNP high-power transistor. Figure 11-17B shows the same test with the leads reversed. Again, a "good" PNP transistor will exhibit very high resistance, usually in the 1 to 2-MΩ range, in either direction. (Accordingly, you will have to utilize an appropriate meter range.)

Transistor summary

Table 11-1 can be used as a quick guide in testing transistors. The information contained in Table 11-1, which applies to both low-power and high-power transistors, can be summarized as follows: If the negative lead of the ohmmeter is connected to the base of the transistor and the positive lead is connected to either the emitter or the collector, a high resistance reading indicates that the device under test is a "good" NPN transistor. If you obtain a low resistance reading, reverse the leads so that the positive lead of the ohmmeter is connected to the base of the transistor. Now when the negative lead is connected to either the emitter or the collector, a high resistance reading indicates that the device under test is a "good" PNP transistor. Of course, if you get a low resistance reading in *both* directions, then the transistor is *shorted*. If there is no continuity (indicated by a very high resistance reading regardless of the bias), the transistor is probably *open*.

	PNP	NPN
Negative base		
B to E	Low	High
B to C	Low	High
Positive base		
B to E	High	Low
B to C	High	Low
Positive collector		
C to E	Very high	Very high
Positive emitter		
C to E	Very high	Very high

B = base, C = collector, E = emitter

TABLE 11-1. *Transistor junction resistances*

Your instructor may provide some transistors for the class to experiment with. The following "generic" transistors should be relatively easy to procure:

NPN	PNP
2N2222 (low-power)	2N3904 (low-power)
2N3055 (high-power)	2N1702 (high-power)

TESTING SILICON-CONTROLLED RECTIFIERS

As you learned in Lesson 6 of Unit 3, a *silicon-controlled rectifier* (SCR) is a multi-layer semiconductor device that acts as a switch. An SCR is controlled by a small amount of current through the gate circuit. The schematic symbol for a typical SCR is pictured in Figure 11-18. (The circle is not always shown.)

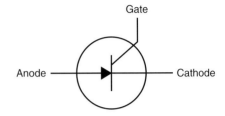

FIGURE 11-18. *Schematic symbol for an SCR*

Checking an SCR with an ohmmeter is similar to checking a diode. Connect the positive lead of the ohmmeter to the anode and the negative lead to the cathode. A high resistance should be read (even if you have the leads reversed), because the SCR does not conduct until the gate is forward-biased. Now take a jumper wire and connect the anode to the gate, as shown in Figure 11-19.

With the SCR connected in this way, the ohmmeter's pointer should instantly drop to a low resistance reading and stay there, even if the jumper to the gate is removed. The SCR will continue to conduct as long as the ohmmeter is connected. In order for an SCR to turn off a circuit, it must be disconnected electrically. (In this case, one of the ohmmeter leads would have to be removed.)

When testing an SCR with an ohmmeter, start at a high range setting. If the current is too low to make the SCR conduct, try successively lower settings. Be aware, however, that the current produced at the R × 1 range setting might be too *high* for some SCRs, and could damage the gate circuit of the solid-state device.

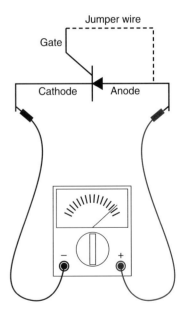

FIGURE 11-19. *Testing an SCR*

A very simple tester can be constructed to demonstrate the operation of an SCR. As shown in Figure 11-20 on the next page, a 100-Ω resistor protects the gate circuit from too much current. The normally open (NO) pushbutton switch applies the gate current, and the normally closed (NC) pushbutton switch is used to break the circuit. When the gate circuit is closed, the light bulb will light. The bulb will continue to burn even if the gate circuit is opened. When the NC pushbutton switch is pressed, the current passing through the SCR is interrupted and the light goes out. Make sure that the positive terminal of the battery is connected to the anode of the SCR, and the negative terminal to the cathode. If the wiring is reversed, the SCR will not conduct.

SCR devices are used to regulate current draw during the start-up of ac motors and electric resistance heaters.

TESTING TRIACS

A *triac* essentially consists of two SCRs connected in parallel. Figure 11-21 is a schematic representation of two SCRs forming a triac. (Again, the circle is optional.) Note that the terms "anode" and "cathode" are not used for triacs. Instead, the lead on the same side as the gate is called "main terminal 1" (MT-1) and the lead opposite the gate is called "main terminal 2" (MT-2). Either terminal can receive an input. The third terminal, of course, is the common gate. Unlike the SCR, the triac is a *bidirectional* device—that is, it allows for conduction in both directions in an ac circuit. Either positive or negative gate signals may be used to trigger (or "gate") the triac into conduction. Figure 11-22 shows a variety of styles of rectifiers and triacs that are on the market today (not drawn to scale).

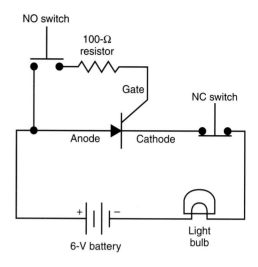

FIGURE 11-20. *SCR operation*

Checking a triac with an ohmmeter is similar to checking an SCR. Connect the negative lead of the ohmmeter to MT-1 and the positive lead to MT-2. You should read a high resistance. Now place a jumper wire across the gate and MT-2, as shown in Figure 11-23A. The ohmmeter's pointer should instantly drop to a low resistance reading and stay there, even with the jumper removed.

You can check the other half of the triac by reversing the ohmmeter leads, as shown in Figure 11-23B. Now the positive lead is connected to MT-1 and the negative lead to MT-2. You should read a high resistance. Again, when you place a jumper wire across the gate and MT-2, the resistance should drop to a low reading.

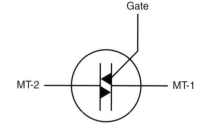

FIGURE 11-21. *Schematic symbol for a triac*

When testing a triac with an ohmmeter, start at a high range setting, just as you did with the SCR. If the current is too low to make the triac conduct, try successively lower settings. Be aware, however, that the current produced at the R × 1 range setting might be too *high* for some triacs, and could damage the gate of the solid-state device.

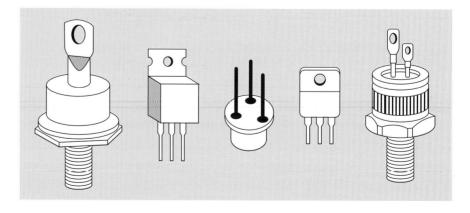

FIGURE 11-22. *Assortment of typical rectifiers and triacs*

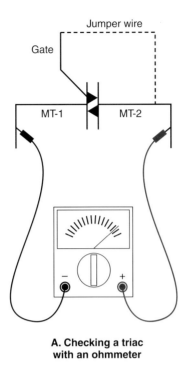

A. Checking a triac with an ohmmeter

FIGURE 11-23. *Testing a triac*

As illustrated in Figure 11-24, the same type of simple tester used to demonstrate the operation of an SCR can be used to show how a triac conducts. The only difference is that the connections between the battery terminals and the triac terminals *can* be reversed. Even when wired "backwards," the triac will conduct. This is because a triac conducts during both the positive *and* negative half-cycles of the ac waveform.

You may wish to experiment with the following "generic" SCRs and triacs:

SCRs	Triacs
2N4188	MAC3030-4

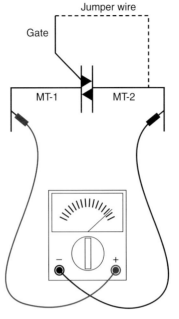

FIGURE 11-24. *Triac operation*

ELECTROSTATIC DISCHARGE

Electrostatic discharge (ESD) can destroy or damage many electronic components, including integrated circuits and discrete semiconductor devices. Static electricity is caused by the transfer of electrons from one substance to another. One substance then becomes positively charged and the other becomes negatively charged. When either of these charged substances comes in contact with a conductor, an electric current flows until that substance is at the same electrical potential as ground.

You must be aware of static electricity discharges when you are servicing the electronic components in any HVACR system, whether it is a residential furnace or a large commercial rooftop unit. Electrostatic discharges may be the result of lightning, but they can also be caused by the technician working on the equipment. Some devices are more susceptible to ESD damage than others. The most affected components are generally the microprocessors or "chips" on printed circuit (PC) boards. Many manufacturers post some form of warning notice on the equipment stating that the contents are subject to damage by static electricity, and reminding technicians that static-sensitive devices require special handling. The warning may include a symbol like the one below.

 CAUTION: The components in this equipment are susceptible to electrostatic discharge voltages! Standard precautions must be observed.

Damage to electronic components by static discharge is caused by the penetration of the silicon layers within the integrated circuit (IC) itself. Figure 11-25A shows a simplified cross section of a "chip," made up of layers of silicon with various openings and connecting channels cut between the layers. An electrostatic discharge or "spike" that enters the IC through the leads causes a short circuit between the layers of semiconductor materials, as depicted in Figure 11-25B. A static spike may also cause an open circuit between the semiconductor material and the attached lead, as shown in Figure 11-25C. An IC that has suffered ESD damage must be replaced. If replacement of the individual component is not feasible, then the whole printed circuited board must be replaced.

There are certain precautions that you can take when working on electronic circuits:

- Request replacement components to be shipped in anti-static plastic bags. Keep the parts in the bags until they are to be used.

- Use a wrist grounding strap when working on specialized electronic equipment.

- Make sure that the power is turned off before making any component or printed circuit board replacement.

■ Do not turn the power back on until the component or PC board is firmly in place and you have double-checked your wiring.

DIAGNOSING PRINTED CIRCUIT BOARDS

Before looking at printed circuit boards, let's review some important safety information. Whenever possible, shut off all power before you begin working on electrical equipment. Be extremely careful when working around energized electrical equipment—remember to remove watches and rings to minimize shock hazards. Since electronic controls are subject to damage from ESD, make it a habit to ground yourself momentarily before handling any electronic component. Finally, always read and follow the instructions in the manufacturer's literature before performing service on any specific electronic control or control system. The information that follows is general in nature.

A *printed circuit*, as its name implies, is "printed" on a board. Instead of wires, a type of photographic process is used to construct the circuit. A thin layer of copper is bonded to a board. A light-sensitive material is added on top of the copper. An image of the circuit is then projected onto the board. When the light-sensitive material is exposed to light, its chemical composition is changed. As a result, when the board is "developed," excess copper is etched away and the copper that remains forms the desired circuit. Components are then soldered to the board, completing the circuit.

There are several advantages to designing a circuit in this way. Printed circuits are very compact, and can be manufactured easily and inexpensively. They are also very reliable, because the method of construction greatly reduces the possibility of wiring errors.

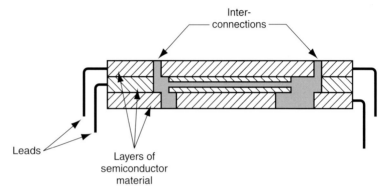

A. Construction of a microprocessor chip

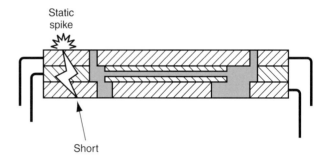

B. Short circuit between layers of semiconductor material

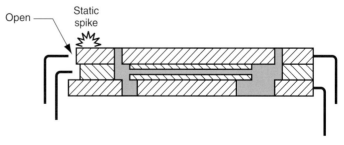

C. Open circuit between semiconductor material and leads

FIGURE 11-25. *How ESD damage affects a microprocessor chip*

Figure 11-26A illustrates the bottom side of a generic PC board for a furnace controller. Figure 11-26B depicts the top side of the same furnace control board, showing all the components conveniently and neatly mounted and easily accessible. This circuit board serves as a convenient location for electrical connections, as well as a place to mount electronic components. Note that the heating and cooling fan relays are mounted on the board, as is the low-voltage terminal strip. Convenient connection points for the transformer are also provided. On this board, electronic components such as resistors, capacitors, and ICs are used to make up a simple fan delay circuit.

Let's examine one operation of this particular board as a fan controller. The function of the ICs on the board is to can determine the speed at which the fan should operate. Most fan centers operate at high speed on a "continuous fan" call for either heating or cooling. The flow chart shown below depicts the operation of "telling" the board that low speed is wanted for heating. This is a very simple and generic representation, of course, but most microprocessors operate in the same manner.

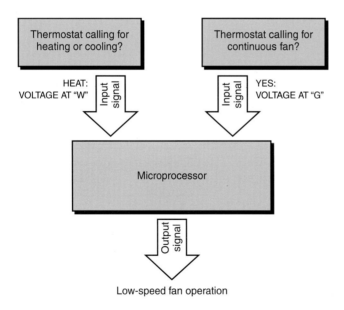

TROUBLESHOOTING PRINTED CIRCUIT BOARDS

There are so many different PC boards used in the HVACR industry that any discussion of troubleshooting must be as generic as possible. However, there are some basic steps that you can follow in locating a problem with a PC board:

- Do not *assume* that the board is bad. First make sure that you have determined the source of the problem. Failure to do so leads to many PC board replacements that are not necessary.

- Read the manufacturer's literature on the particular piece of equipment that requires service. It is very important that you know the proper sequence of operation.

- If there is a self-diagnostic test, go through each of the steps outlined. More than 90% of the time the board will "tell" you if there is a problem. The message may be in the form of flashing LEDs, or even a liquid crystal display that actually identifies the error.

- No special test equipment is required to check out most boards. If necessary, the manufacturer can tell you what specialized test equipment to use. In general, a good DVM will suffice for most service calls.

- You will not be expected to replace the components on the board, but you should be able to check the input and output voltages.

- Look for visual signs of problems with the board—for example, a component that has been burned or a part of the board that has a crack in it. Any of these symptoms means that the board must be replaced.

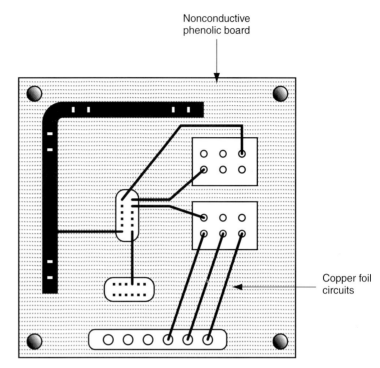

A. Bottom side

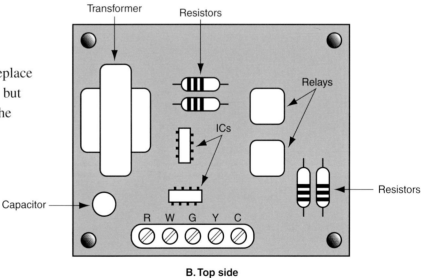

B. Top side

FIGURE 11-26. *Typical PC board for furnace controller*

Simulated service call

Suppose that you have received a call to service a warm air furnace in which the fan has stopped running. When you arrive at the customer's house, you find that

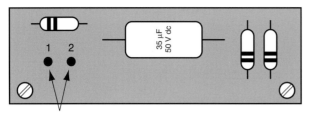

Jumper pins 1 and 2
for self-diagnostic test

1. The red LED #1 on solid means that the board has failed, and must be replaced.
2. The red LED #2 on solid means that the blower motor is not running.
3. The green LED on solid means that the furnace is operating in high heat mode.
4. The yellow LED on solid means that the furnace is operating in low heat mode.
5. The green and yellow flashing LEDs indicate the faults. (See example below.)

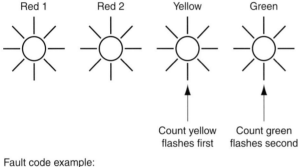

Fault code example:
    Yellow—3 flashes
    Green—2 flashes

Fault: CODE 32 (INDUCER MOTOR OUT OF SPEED RANGE)

FIGURE 11-27. *Self-diagnostic test*

Code	Status
11	No codes listed
12	Blower on after power is applied (burner normally runs for 90 seconds)
13	Limit switch lockout (see #33 for reset)
14	Flame roll-out lockout (see #33 for reset)
15	Ignition lockout (see #34 for reset)
21	Gas heating lockout (cannot be reset)
22	Abnormal flame-proving signal (flame is proved while gas valve is de-energized)
23	Gas pressure switch did not open
24	Secondary voltage fuse is open
25	Draft lockout (if off longer than 3 minutes, unit shuts off—see #33 for reset)
32	Inducer motor not running
33	Limit, flame roll-out, or draft lockout switch is open for more than 3 minutes or three tries (code changes to #13)
34	Ignition-proving failure control has tried three times to start, then locks out (code changes to #14)

TABLE 11-2. *LED status codes*

the furnace has a PC board with a self-diagnostic test function. Figure 11-27 depicts both the PC board and the instruction for the self-diagnostic test. Table 11-2 shows a typical LED status chart for this furnace.

You find that the red LED #2 is on constantly, telling you that the blower motor is not running. You test the voltage at the motor and find it to be correct, so you test the motor's windings with an ohmmeter. You find an open winding, and replace the motor. Without this self-diagnostic test, many technicians would condemn the board, since it contains the relays and controls for the motor.

Troubleshooting summary

Follow these general procedures when troubleshooting PC boards:

1. Make a visual inspection of the PC board.

2. Check the power supply.

3. Perform the self-diagnostic test (if there is one).

4. Test the output voltages.

5. Test the output switch sequence.

When you are troubleshooting *any* component or piece of equipment, a logical approach is the only way to find the problem. There are several common-sense steps that you can take to ensure a logical approach:

- Become as familiar as you can with the equipment on which you are working.

- Make sure that you know the power supply voltage.

- Read the manufacturer's literature.

- Ask the customer questions regarding the problem and its symptoms.

- Look for obvious problems first, by making a visual inspection.

- Test the sequence of operation.

- Keep a record of your findings.

- Most of all, be safety conscious!

1. The positive electrode of a diode is called the _____, and the negative electrode is called the _____.

2. A zero ohmmeter reading indicates a(n) _____ diode.

3. The resistance of a good diode connected with a forward bias usually ranges from _____ to _____ Ω.

4. What should you do before using a digital meter to test a diode that is connected to a circuit?

5. If a digital meter reads "OL" regardless of how the leads are connected, the diode under test is _____.

6. How much voltage must be applied to a germanium diode to cause conduction?

7. What is the purpose of making a resistance check between the emitter and the collector of a transistor?

8. What must you do before testing a transistor in the field?

9. When you use an analog ohmmeter to test transistors, what is an acceptable battery voltage?

10. An NPN transistor is similar in construction to two _____ that are connected by their _____.

11. What reading would you expect from a good NPN low-power transistor if you have the negative lead of the ohmmeter connected to the base of the transistor and the positive lead connected to the emitter?

12. A good transistor exhibits a resistance of _____ between the emitter and the collector, in either direction.

13. A silicon-controlled rectifier (SCR) does not conduct current until the gate is _____.

14. How can you cause a forward-biased SCR to conduct (and continue to conduct) while using an ohmmeter to check the resistance between the anode and the cathode?

15. A triac is constructed of two _____ connected in _____, with a common _____.

16. How does a triac differ from an SCR?

17. Which lead of a triac is designated "MT-2"?

18. Which components are most affected by electrostatic discharge (ESD)?

19. You should use a(n) _____ when working on specialized electronic equipment.

20. In general, what steps should you take before working on *any* electrical equipment?

21. What leads to unnecessary PC board replacements?

LESSON

Wiring Systems

The primary goal of this Lesson is to familiarize the student with acceptable wiring practices, and with the procedures used in the testing and troubleshooting of various wiring systems. The types of wiring systems discussed in this Lesson may be categorized as *power* wiring, *low-voltage* wiring, and *control* wiring. Figure 12-1 on the next page represents a simple power wiring system and its basic components.

Voltage drop in single-phase circuits

Measuring voltage drop in single-phase circuits like the one shown in Figure 12-1 can be done in two steps:

1. Start with the portion of the wiring system that extends from the power source to the controller (which may be a contactor, starter, relay, etc.). With the load operating under "normal" conditions, first measure the voltage across the conductors themselves—that is, measure the potential difference between L1 and the neutral line and between L2 and the

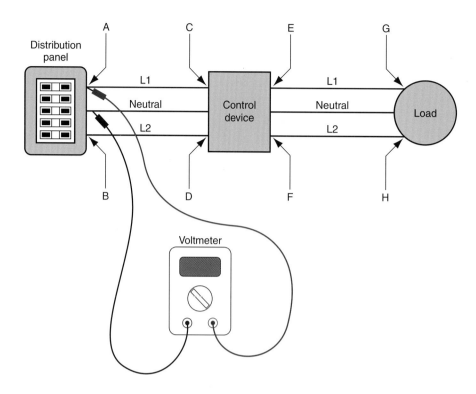

FIGURE 12-1. *Measuring voltage drop in a 230-V single-phase circuit*

neutral line. In Figure 12-1, take your voltmeter readings from point A to neutral, from point C to neutral, from point B to neutral, and from point D to neutral. Record your results.

2. Now continue with the portion of the wiring system that extends from the controller to the load (which may be a motor, compressor, transformer, etc.). With the load still operating under "normal" conditions, again measure the potential difference between L1 and the neutral line and between L2 and the neutral line. In Figure 12-1, take your voltmeter readings from point E to neutral, from point G to neutral, from point F to neutral, and from point H to neutral. Record your results.

For example, assume that you obtained the following data from the first step of your testing procedure (from panel to control):

A to neutral. . . . . 117 V		B to neutral. . . . . 117 V
C to neutral. . . . . 117 V		D to neutral. . . . . 117 V
Deviation. . . . . . . 0 V		Deviation. . . . . . . 0 V

The wire size is adequate for the load in this situation.

However, what if you obtained the following results from the second step of your testing procedure (from control to load)?

E to neutral.	117 V	F to neutral.	117 V
G to neutral.	115 V	H to neutral.	117 V
Deviation.	2 V	Deviation.	0 V

Now the data indicate that an improper wire size is in use between points E and G, or perhaps a terminal is loose. This situation can lead to more serious problems, and should be corrected immediately.

If the voltage drop across a wire that carries current to the control device or the load exceeds 2 V, repair or replace the wire. It may be too small for the application.

Voltage imbalance in single-phase circuits

Look at Figure 12-1 again. It is important to know that the correct voltage is being supplied to the control device from the distribution panel. It is also important to know that the correct voltage is being supplied to the load from the control device. Additional loads (new machinery and equipment) that have been added to existing circuits may cause excessive voltage drops and subsequent energy losses. To ensure that the proper voltage is being supplied to all electrical equipment on a circuit, you must be able to calculate voltage *imbalance*. The National Electrical Code (NEC) states that for reasonable efficiency of operation, voltage imbalance in single-phase circuits should be limited to 2% (between the power source and the farthest device).

The equation for determining voltage imbalance (expressed as a percentage) is as follows:

$$\% \text{ voltage imbalance} = \frac{V_{NL} - V_{FL}}{V_{NL}} \times 100$$

where

V_{NL} = no-load voltage

V_{FL} = full-load voltage.

In the example shown in Figure 12-2 on the next page, assume that you measure a no-load voltage from point A to point B of 230 V, and a full-load voltage from point G to point H of 220 V. Then:

$$\% \text{ voltage imbalance} = \frac{230 \text{ V} - 220 \text{ V}}{230 \text{ V}} \times 100$$

$$= \frac{10}{230} \times 100$$

$$= 0.0435 \times 100 = 4.35\%$$

The result, 4.35%, is well above the 2% allowable limit. There is a problem in this system.

If the voltage imbalance between the load and the supply exceeds 2%, look for an electrical terminal, contact, etc., that is loose or corroded and may be causing a high resistance in that leg. Examine the incoming power supply to the building and the distribution panels. Be aware, too, that a conductor may be damaged if a piece of heavy equipment falls or is dropped on the wire.

Current imbalance in single-phase circuits

Figure 12-3A shows an ammeter clamped around lines 1 and 2. Because the readings are the same (18 A), you can conclude that this system has no current imbalance problems. However, in Figure 12-3B, readings of 22 A for line 1 and

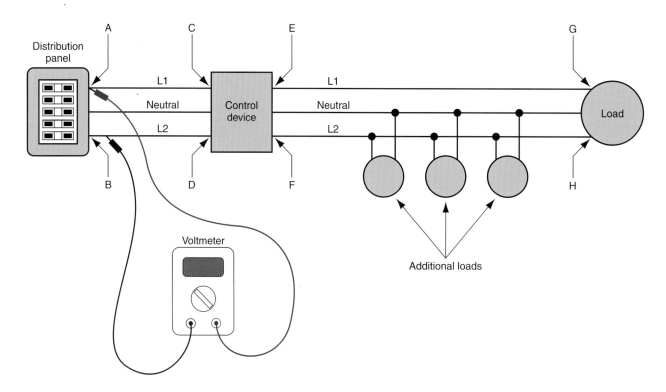

FIGURE 12-2. *Checking voltage imbalance in a single-phase circuit with multiple loads*

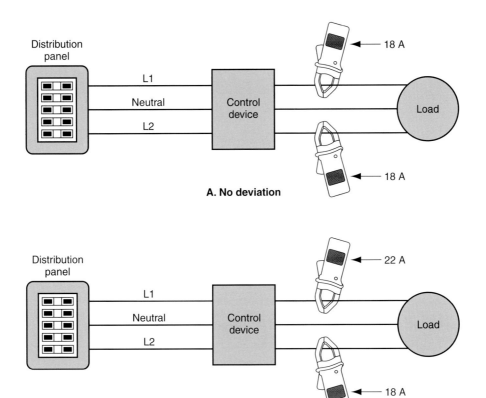

FIGURE 12-3. *Testing for current imbalance in a 230-V single-phase circuit*

18 A for line 2 indicate a 4-A deviation. You can use the following equation for calculating current imbalance (expressed as a percentage):

$$\% \text{ current imbalance} = \frac{\text{maximum deviation from average current}}{\text{average current}} \times 100$$

Find the *average* current by adding the two current readings together (22 A + 18 A = 40 A) and dividing by 2 (40 A ÷ 2 = 20 A). Then determine which reading represents the greatest deviation from this 20-A average. In this example, both the 18-A reading and the 22-A reading represent a 2-A deviation from the average. Therefore:

$$\% \text{ current imbalance} = \frac{2 \text{ A}}{20 \text{ A}} \times 100$$

$$= 0.1 \times 100 = 10\%$$

The current imbalance between any two legs of a single-phase system must not exceed 2%. The 10% imbalance found in this example means that the system has a problem that must be attended to. Recall that a voltage imbalance always produces a current imbalance, but a current imbalance may occur without a voltage imbalance. A current imbalance can occur when an electrical terminal, contactor, starter, etc. becomes loose or corroded, causing a high resistance in one leg. Since current follows the path of least resistance, the current in the other leg will increase, causing more heat to be generated.

Voltage drop in three-phase circuits

Figure 12-4 on the next two pages shows a basic 230-V three-phase wiring system for controlling a motor. To determine the voltage drop in a three-phase circuit, you must take and record several readings. As with single-phase circuits, any voltage imbalance of more than 2% will cause excessive heat, which can lead to wiring problems. With the controlled load operating under "normal" conditions, make and record the following voltage measurements:

1. **Interphase (between phases)—line side.** A reading taken between phases on the power supply side of the device is shown in Figure 12-4A. Examples of such measurements are given below.

   L1 to L2   A to B . . . . 230 V
   L1 to L3   A to C . . . . 230 V
   L2 to L3   B to C . . . . 230 V

2. **Between phase and neutral (or ground)—line side.** A reading taken between phase and neutral (or ground) on the power supply side of the device is shown in Figure 12-4B. Examples of such measurements are given below.

   L1 to neutral (or ground)   A to neutral . . . . 120 V
   L2 to neutral (or ground)   B to neutral. . . . . 120 V
   L3 to neutral (or ground)   C to neutral. . . . . 120 V

While the controlled load continues to operate under "normal" conditions, make and record the same voltage measurements on the load side of the current control device.

3. **Interphase (between phases)—load side.** A reading taken between phases on the load side of the device is shown in Figure 12-4C. Examples of such measurements are given below.

   L1 to L2   G to H . . . . 230 V
   L1 to L3   G to I . . . . 230 V
   L2 to L3   H to I . . . . 230 V

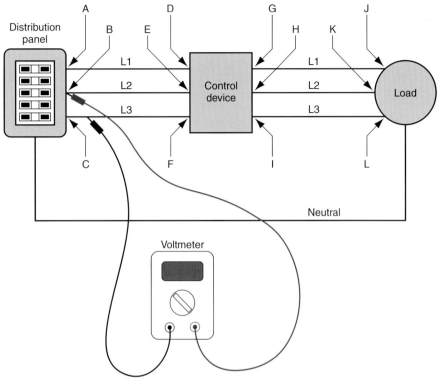

A. Measurements made between phases (line side)

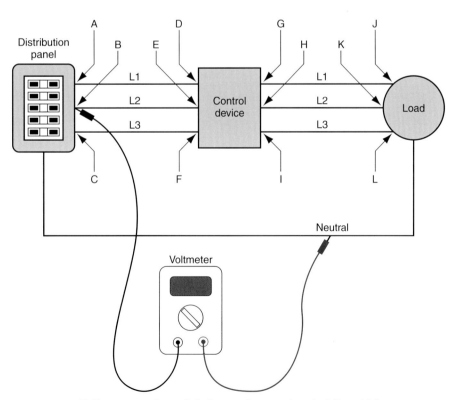

B. Measurements made between phase and neutral (line side)

FIGURE 12-4. *Measuring voltage drop in a 230-V three-phase circuit*

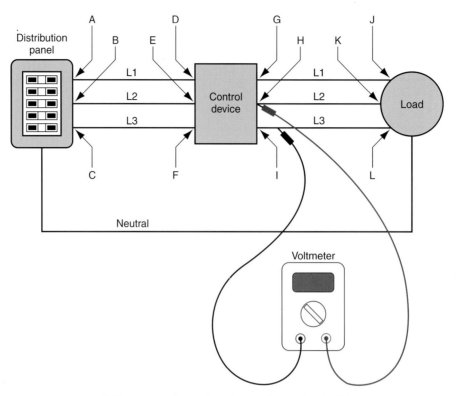

C. Measurements made between phases (load side)

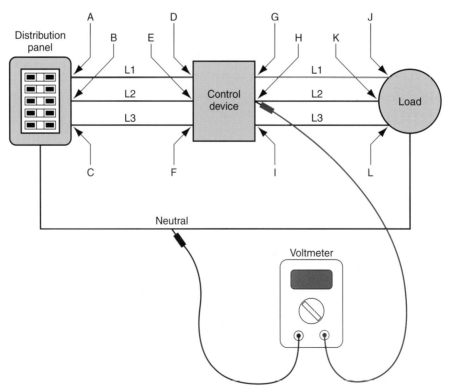

D. Measurements made between phase and neutral (load side)

FIGURE 12-4. *Measuring voltage drop in a 230-V three-phase circuit (continued)*

4. **Between phase and neutral (or ground)—load side.** A reading taken between phase and neutral (or ground) on the load side of the device is shown in Figure 12-4D. Examples of such measurements are given below.

L1 to neutral (or ground)   G to neutral . . . . 120 V
L2 to neutral (or ground)   H to neutral . . . . 120 V
L3 to neutral (or ground)   I to neutral . . . . 120 V

If the voltage drop across a wire or across the control device exceeds 0.5 V, replace the wire or the device, or repair the contacts as needed.

Voltage imbalance in three-phase circuits

Voltage imbalances in three-phase power supplies waste energy and increase equipment operating costs. Voltage imbalances result in unbalanced currents in the stator windings of motors, and can be caused by single-phase loads that have been tapped onto three-phase supply circuits (a commonplace practice). To determine the voltage imbalance in a three-phase wiring system, start by taking voltmeter readings between phases on the load side. First measure and record the voltage between line 1 and line 2, then between line 1 and line 3, and finally between line 2 and line 3. Assume that you obtain readings of 225 V, 230 V, and 230 V, respectively. Find the *average* voltage by adding these three figures together and dividing by 3:

Voltage measured between L1 and L2   225 V
Voltage measured between L1 and L3   230 V
Voltage measured between L2 and L3   + 230 V
                             Total   685 V

Average voltage = 685 V ÷ 3 = approximately 228 V

Next, determine which reading represents the greatest deviation from the average voltage. In this case it is the 225-V reading, which represents a deviation of 3 V from the 228-V average. Now you can use the following equation to calculate the voltage imbalance (expressed as a percentage):

$$\% \text{ voltage imbalance} = \frac{\text{maximum deviation from average voltage}}{\text{average voltage}} \times 100$$

$$= \frac{3 \text{ V}}{228 \text{ V}} \times 100$$

$$= 0.01316 \times 100 = \text{approximately } 1.32\%$$

Any voltage imbalance of more than 2% must be corrected. (The NEC allows for a voltage imbalance of not more than 1%.) Operating a motor or any other electrical device when the voltage imbalance is more than 2% is *not* recommended.

Current imbalance in three-phase circuits

To determine the current imbalance in a three-phase wiring system, first turn the power on and measure the current drawn by the L1 leg. Record your results. Then measure the current drawn by the remaining two legs, L2 and L3. Do this one at a time, and record your readings. For the example shown in Figure 12-5, the readings are 18 A, 20 A, and 18 A, respectively. Again, find the *average* current by adding these three figures together and dividing by 3:

Current measured in L1 leg	18 A
Current measured in L2 leg	20 A
Current measured in L3 leg	+ 18 A
Total	56 A

Average current = 56 A ÷ 3 = 18.67 A

The L2 reading represents a maximum 1.33-A deviation from the 18.67-A average. Now you can use the following equation to calculate the current imbalance (expressed as a percentage):

$$\% \text{ current imbalance} = \frac{\text{maximum deviation from average current}}{\text{average current}} \times 100$$

$$= \frac{1.33 \text{ A}}{18.67 \text{ A}} \times 100$$

$$= 0.07124 \times 100 = \text{approximately } 7\%$$

The current imbalance between any two legs of a three-phase system must not exceed 10%. Since the current imbalance in this example is slightly less than 10%, the situation may be considered borderline. If the current imbalance exceeds 10%, look for an electrical terminal, contact, etc., that is loose or corroded and may be causing a high resistance in that leg.

WIRE SELECTION

The term "ampacity" refers to the current-carrying capacity of a conductor. When current is conducted through a wire, some of the electrical energy is

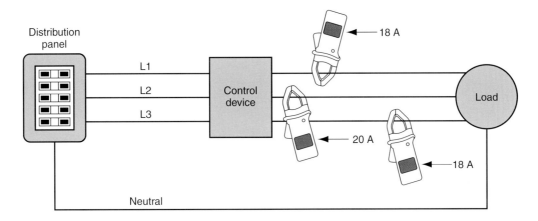

FIGURE 12-5. *Testing for current imbalance in a 230-V three-phase circuit*

converted into heat. The greater the current, the greater the amount of heat produced—in fact, doubling the current (without changing the size of the wire) increases the amount of heat *four* times. (That is, heat increases by the square of any increase in current.) This is why the size of the wire selected to furnish power to a load is so important. If the wire is not large enough to handle the current drawn by the load, the wire will overheat. Heat is wasted power. The NEC is not concerned with wasted power, but it is concerned with safety. If the current is greater than what the wire can accommodate, the wire may become hot enough to damage the insulation, or even cause a fire. *Ampacity*, then, is the maximum current (expressed in amperes) that a wire can *safely* carry.

The NEC has tested various sizes and types of wires, and specifies the ampacity of each. Table 12-1 lists the ampacities for several sizes and types of copper wire.

Another consequence of an undersized wire (in addition to overheating) is an increase in resistance. The result is a voltage drop. Since all electrical devices operate most efficiently at the voltage for which they are designed, the NEC specifies that the size of the conductor be selected to limit the voltage drop to an acceptable level. Tables 12-2 and 12-3 on the next page list the maximum allowable distances, in feet, over which wires of various sizes can carry specific currents while still limiting the voltage drop to 2%.

Note that in both tables, the figures represent *one-way* distances, not the total length for two-way distances. For all sizes marked with an asterisk (*), you must select a wire with sufficient ampacity, whether it is contained in a conduit or in free air. Comparison of these two tables will illustrate to you that a wire used in a 240-V application will carry the same current twice as

Wire size	Ampacity, amperes
14 AWG	15*
12 AWG	20*
10 AWG	30*
8 AWG	40
6 AWG	55
4 AWG	70
2 AWG	95

*In the NEC, the ampacities of these wires are shown as higher than this, but a footnote limits their overcurrent protection to the figures given here.

TABLE 12-1. *Ampacities for Types TW and THW copper wire at ambient temperatures of 70°F*

far as the same wire used in a 120-V application. If the percentage of voltage drop remains unchanged, it will carry twice the power (in watts).

Amperes	Watts at 120 V	Wire size (AWG)									
		14	12	10	8	6	4	2	1/0	2/0	3/0
		Distance, ft									
5	600	90	140	225	360	570	910				
10	1,200	45	70	115	180	285	455	725			
15	1,800	30	45	70	120	190	300	480	765	960	
20	2,400	20*	35	55	90	145	225	360	575	725	915
25	3,000	18*	28*	45	70	115	180	290	460	580	730
30	3,600	15*	24*	35	60	95	150	240	385	485	610
40	4,800			28*	45	70	115	180	290	360	455
50	6,000			23*	36*	55	90	145	230	290	365

TABLE 12-2. *Maximum one-way wire distances for 2% voltage drop in 120-V single-phase applications*

Amperes	Watts at 240 V	Wire size (AWG)									
		14	12	10	8	6	4	2	1/0	2/0	3/0
		Distance, ft									
5	1,200	180	285	455	720	1145					
10	2,400	90	140	225	360	570	910	1445			
15	3,600	60	95	150	240	380	610	970	1530		
20	4,800	45*	70	115	180	285	455	725	1150	1450	
25	6,000	35*	55*	90	140	230	365	580	920	1160	1460
30	7,200	30*	48*	75	120	190	300	480	770	970	1220
40	9,600		36*	56*	90	140	230	360	575	725	915
50	12,000			45*	70*	115	185	285	460	580	725
60	14,400				60*	95*	150	240	385	485	610
70	16,800				50*	80*	130	205	330	410	520
80	19,200					70*	115*	180	285	360	460
90	21,000					60*	100*	160	250	320	405
100	24,000					55*	90*	145*	230	290	365
125	30,000						75*	120*	190	240	300
150	36,000							95*	150*	195*	245
200	48,000							70*	115*	145*	185*

TABLE 12-3. *Maximum one-way wire distances for 2% voltage drop in 240-V single-phase applications*

LOW-VOLTAGE WIRING

The NEC classifies any equipment that operates at less than 50 V as *low-voltage* equipment. This includes most of the controls used in the HVACR industry. The testing and troubleshooting guidelines that follow will apply to a 24 to 30-V wiring system. Assume, for example, that you must check the wiring for a thermostat. The following five simple steps will quickly solve most of the problems that you might encounter:

1. Disconnect the wire from both ends of its circuit—that is, from the thermostat and from the equipment that it controls.

2. Test for voltage. With both ends disconnected from their respective connections, measure the voltage to ground to make sure that there are no ground loops causing feedback into the circuit. *Caution*: Remember that unless you are absolutely certain of the magnitude of the voltage or current to be measured, you should always start at the highest range setting of the instrument and work your way down. Figure 12-6 illustrates a typical method of testing a six-conductor wire to ground. Test each of the wires in sequence. (You will not test to ground for anything else, other than stray voltages in the thermostat wire.) If you find no measurable voltage from the conductor to ground, you may proceed to the next step. If you do read a measurable voltage, the source must be located before continuing. If the thermostat wire is running close to power wires, there may be mutual induction taking place. If so, you must correct the situation.

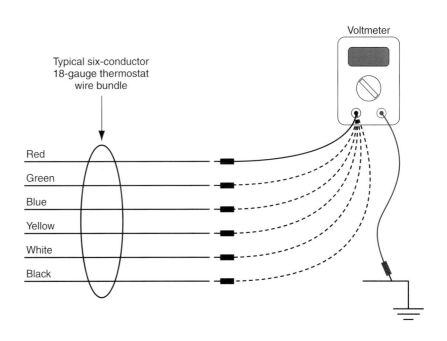

FIGURE 12-6. *Testing for voltage*

3. Test for resistance. This is similar to the previous procedure. With both ends disconnected from their respective connections, test each colored wire for any continuity to ground, as shown in Figure 12-7 on the next page. With the range switch set to R × 1, the ohmmeter should indicate

infinite resistance for each of the wires being tested to ground. Any reading of less than infinity indicates the presence of a short, and the thermostat wire should be replaced. If you find no short, proceed to the next step.

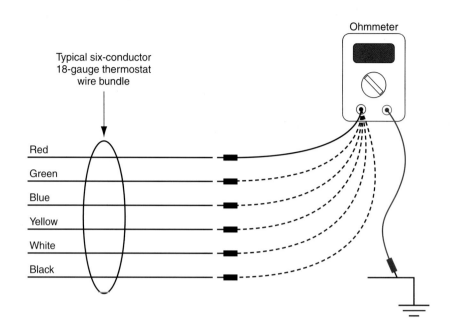

FIGURE 12-7. *Testing for resistance*

4. Test for continuity. Next, twist together all of the conductors at one end. From each of the other ends (the ones not twisted together) measure the "loop" resistance of the wiring as shown in Figure 12-8. Start with one color and record the resistance across that wire and each of the other colors in turn. The resistance should be the same for every pair. If the resistance is very high (greater than 100 Ω), the conductor is probably damaged and the wire should be replaced.

5. If the measured resistance is less than 100 Ω, check the manufacturer's published values for resistance per 1,000 ft. Remember that the actual

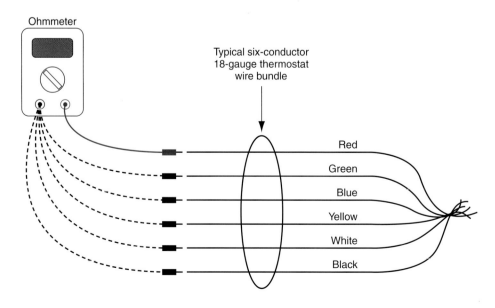

FIGURE 12-8. *Testing for continuity*

"electrical" distance is twice the run distance, because the ohmmeter current has to travel the entire closed loop of the wiring in order to complete the circuit. Record your actual ohmmeter reading for use in the following calculation.

For the purposes of demonstration, assume that the rooftop unit shown in Figure 12-9 is wired with 18-gauge copper wire. This wire has a resistance of 6.51 Ω per 1,000 ft, or 0.00651 Ω per ft, at 77°F. The resistance information is obtainable from the American Wire Gauge (AWG) data for solid copper wire (see Table 8-2 in Unit 2 of this Course).

If you measure the loop resistance with your ohmmeter and find that it is 11 Ω, what can you conclude? You know that the run is approximately 800 ft from the rooftop unit to the thermostat. Since 800 ft is 80% of 1,000 ft, you can calculate 80% of 6.51 Ω to form an estimate of the resistance (6.51 Ω × 0.8 = 5.2 Ω). But remember that you must double this figure, because you are working on a loop (5.2 Ω × 2 = 10.4 Ω). Now you have a working estimate of 10.4 Ω, and your reading of 11 Ω tells you that you have the correct continuity.

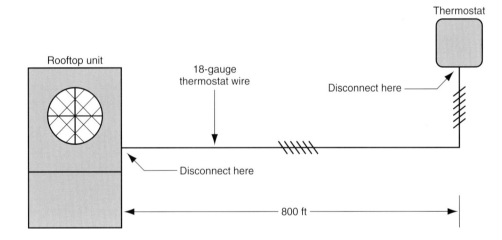

FIGURE 12-9. *Measuring resistance in an 800-ft run*

This test can be done with any number of conductors. It is a simple and effective way to "ring out" the wires (test for continuity).

CONTROL WIRING

High-voltage ac control wiring

Most high-voltage ac *control* wiring is done in "close-coupled" environments— that is, the runs are usually no longer than 50 to 100 ft. *High-voltage* control systems generally include 120-V, 220-V, and 460-V line-voltage applications. When you encounter problems in control wiring systems that use high voltages, look at the following items very carefully:

- First look for obvious problems, such as switches that may be set incorrectly, loose wires or connections, physical damage, and overheated terminals.

- Measure and record actual operating voltages. This procedure will help in locating faults.

- Measure the supply voltage at the controller and at the equipment being controlled.

- Check all circuit breakers and fuses. If circuit breakers or fuses are open or have been operated, they should *not* be closed until the cause of the fault has been located and cleared. Failure to follow this procedure may result in injury to personnel or damage to equipment.

- High temperatures are a major cause of electrical failure. Look for signs of discoloration and overheated wiring.

- Exercise extreme caution! Remember, you are working with very high voltages and currents.

DDC wiring

All electronic and DDC (direct digital control) wiring systems are considered proprietary. It is beyond the scope of this Lesson to cover every DDC system available today. The following paragraphs will, however, attempt to provide some basic troubleshooting techniques for generic DDC and electronic control wiring.

All DDC controller outputs use low dc voltages and currents. Start by checking the controller output with a digital multimeter (DMM), using the appropriate function and range switches. Output values generally exist in the following categories:

Voltages	Currents
0 to 16 V	4 to 20 mA
1 to 15 V	0 to 30 mA
2 to 10 V	50-mA "loop"
2 to 22 V	

In newer industrial markets, you may find electronic control systems operating in what are called "hostile" environments. These are environments in which intense magnetic fields, electrical noise, large voltage spikes, electromagnetic induction, and radio frequency interference (RFI) can interfere with DDC systems. Even a relatively small signal (digital or analog) can be altered by the action of any of the above phenomena.

If you encounter a problem in a DDC wiring system, or if the controller displays erratic operation, take the following steps:

- Look at all the wiring runs. They should be kept as short and as direct as possible.

- Make sure that the signal and control wiring is not in the same conduit as the power wiring.

- Make sure that all of the signal and control wiring is as far removed as possible from power wiring circuits. Whenever possible, do *not* run control wiring parallel to power wiring. If control wiring absolutely must cross power wiring, make sure that it does so at right angles.

- Make sure that none of the signal and control wiring is run over, on, or near fluorescent light fixtures.

Troubleshooting and servicing erratically operating circuits can be costly and time-consuming. The root cause is frequently electromagnetic interference (EMI) or electrical noise. The solution may be to use shielded cable (cable consisting of "twisted pairs" of wire completely surrounded by a Mylar® foil shield). When this type of wire is installed correctly and the shield is grounded properly, shielded cable can provide a reduction in EMI or electrical noise on the order of 30,000:1.

The procedures mentioned above for troubleshooting and locating faults in electronic control systems are general in nature. There are, in addition, some special cases that require occasional detective work, especially those that involve EMI/RFI and grounding problems. It is important to emphasize at this point, however, that before you decide on EMI/RFI as the culprit, all other "normal" diagnostic steps recommended by the manufacturer must be completed.

To identify an erratic operation problem, you will need to test the DDC loop, which may be either a 0 to 10-V dc loop or a 4 to 20-mA loop. First, see if there is an erratic voltage present in either the voltage or current loop. Use a DMM to test the line for voltage, as illustrated in Figure 12-10A at the top of the next page. The meter reading should be steady—that is, no sign of fluctuation should be visible.

To measure current, open one of the leads to the sensor from the controller, as shown in Figure 12-10B, and place the DMM in series across the open circuit. Again, the meter reading should show no sign of fluctuation.

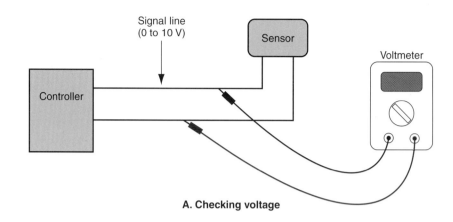

A. Checking voltage

If these steps fail to identify the cause of intermittent or erratic operation, something else may be interfering with the signals that are being sent to the controller from the sensors (or, in the case of a milliamp loop output, from the controller to the controlled device). Intermittent EMI/RFI problems are at best difficult to diagnose. However, some knowledge of proper grounding practices may help you to identify and correct the possible source of the problem. Shielded cable should be grounded to a *single-point ground* (SPG) bus only, located at the controller. Under normal conditions, there

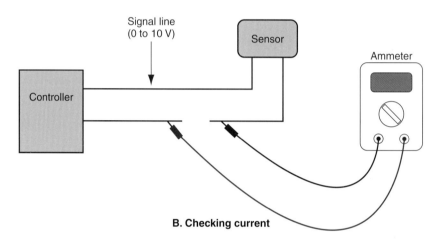

B. Checking current

FIGURE 12-10. *Testing a DDC circuit*

should be no current flowing in the grounding system or in the equipment grounding conductor. Observe the following grounding procedures:

1. Disconnect all external wiring from the controller, the sensor, and the controlled device. Leave only the ac power supply and equipment grounding conductor still connected to the controller. At the same time, disconnect the wiring from all sensors and controlled devices.

Note: The ground reference point used in the following diagnostic procedures is the single-point ground (also called the *isolated ground* or *grounding conductor*).

2. Next, set your DMM to the lowest possible range and measure the following:

    a. From each disconnected conductor, measure the ac voltage to ground. The purpose of this is to determine whether there is any

"stray" voltage being induced into the control system wiring.
If any voltage is found, record both the value and stability.
(*Stability* here refers to whether or not the reading is constant.
If the reading fluctuates, try to determine the range of fluctuation.)

b. Measure any ac current to ground, using the same procedure as in
the previous step (a).

3. If there is any conductor for which you obtained a measurable voltage
or current reading, twist the wires together at one end of the conductor
(in effect, forming a loop).

4. For each conductor loop formed, make and record the following
measurements:

a. ac voltage from one side of the loop to ground

b. ac voltage across the loop

c. ac current from one side of the loop to ground

d. ac current across the loop (place the DMM in series with the loop).

5. Any loop that shows either voltage or current in the previous step (b)
or (d) is highly suspect as the source of the EMI/RFI. Depending on
the frequency and magnitude of the induced voltages and currents, the
resulting problems could range from occasional operational problems
to serious damage to sensitive electronic equipment and circuits. When
you test any conductor, a meter display of more than 500 mV or 50 mA
makes it a candidate for replacement with shielded cable. When a cable
is replaced for EMI/RFI reasons, be careful not to rerun it in the same
manner as the original cable, if possible. Be sure to avoid all known or
suspected sources of EMI/RFI.

SUMMARY

Wires, switches, relay contactors, circuit breakers, and other device contacts,
when they are sized correctly and working properly, should present very little
or no resistance to the electric current that passes through them. Voltage drops
in excess of 0.5 V are an indication of a potential problem, as are deviations of
more than 2%. Such problems should be corrected at once. The wiring itself,
when properly sized, should pose no problems. Likewise, when a device is new,
it should present a resistance of 0 Ω, or perfect continuity. However, most

system devices do eventually develop some resistance. This may be due to several factors, including corrosion, wear and tear, arcing on make or break, and uneven mating of electrical contact surfaces.

Over a period of time, the contact surfaces of a control device may become pitted, thereby cutting down on the available surface area through which current can pass. Eventually, the contact surfaces may become burned, causing further resistance to the conduction of current. This, in turn, will cause even more heating and burning—and may also cause the associated wiring to overheat and possibly fail. Always look for loose and/or undersized wiring.

As part of your routine maintenance procedures, be sure to check for excessive voltage drops (greater than 0.5 V). You may wish to make up a chart similar to the one shown below to use for recording the voltage and current readings that you obtain. Remember, to calculate the voltage imbalance percentage, first find the maximum deviation from the average voltage. Divide this figure by the average voltage, and then multiply by 100.

Upstream from (before) the control:

L1 to L2	_____ V	L1 to neutral	_____ V
L1 to L3	_____ V	L2 to neutral	_____ V
L2 to L3	_____ V	L3 to neutral	_____ V

Downstream from (after) the control:

L1 to L2	_____ V	L1 to neutral	_____ V
L1 to L3	_____ V	L2 to neutral	_____ V
L2 to L3	_____ V	L3 to neutral	_____ V

Lastly, here are a few helpful general procedures to aid the technician in troubleshooting both electrical equipment and systems:

- Always begin by looking for the most obvious problems, such as incorrectly set switches, loose wires or connections, and visible physical damage (overheated terminals, corrosion, etc.).

- Actual operating voltages and currents should be measured and recorded at the time of installation, or when the equipment is operating normally. Keep this information on file—it can be a great help later on when you must locate the cause of a problem. Resistance measurements (of control loop resistance, thermostat loop resistance, etc.) should also be made and kept on record.

- Measure the supply voltage and current when you are engaged in fault location procedures, and compare your readings to previously measured values (as described in the previous step), or to the manufacturer's published data. Are these values within tolerance?

- Remember to check all circuit breakers and fuses. If circuit breakers or fuses are open or have been operated, they should *not* be closed until the cause of the fault has been located and cleared. Failure to follow this procedure may result in injury to personnel or damage to equipment.

- High temperatures are a major cause of electrical and electronic equipment failure. When equipment is originally installed, it should be located in an area that is dry and well-ventilated. Sources of excessive heat should be avoided (e.g., large current transformers, heating vents and radiators, electrical panel boards, etc.).

1. The maximum allowable voltage drop across the wire that carries current to the control device or the load is _____.

2. The voltage imbalance in single-phase circuits must not exceed _____%.

3. Explain how to calculate voltage imbalance (as a percentage).

4. If the current through one line of a single-phase system is 20 A and the current through the other line is 16 A, is the current imbalance acceptable?

5. In a 230-V three-phase system, the voltage measured between L1 and L2 is 230 V, the voltage measured between L1 and L3 is 228 V, and the voltage measured between L2 and L3 is 220 V. What is the percentage of voltage imbalance?

6. The current imbalance between any two legs of a three-phase system must not exceed _____%.

7. Define *ampacity*.

8. What is the ampacity of a 12-gauge copper wire?

9. In addition to overheating, what is another potential consequence of an undersized wire?

10. In a 120-V single-phase circuit intended to carry a maximum current of 20 A, what size wire should be selected for a *total* (two-way) run of 180 ft?

11. The NEC classifies any equipment that operates at less than _____ as "low-voltage" equipment.

12. When you test a low-voltage control circuit for resistance as shown in Figure 12-7, what ohmmeter reading indicates the presence of a short?

13. When you measure the loop resistance for any pair of low-voltage control wires, what ohmmeter reading indicates that the conductor should be replaced?

14. The wiring runs in high-voltage ac control circuits are usually no longer than _____.

15. If you find tripped circuit breakers or open fuses in the course of inspecting a high-voltage ac control system, should you reset them immediately?

16. What is meant by a "hostile" climate for electronic control systems?

17. If you must run DDC wiring close to power wiring, it is best to have the control wires cross the power wires at _____.

18. What is another way to minimize EMI?

19. Shielded cable should be grounded to a(n) _____.

20. What happens when the contact surfaces of electrical control devices become pitted?

Glossary of Terms

DEFINITIONS

Abort. To terminate a program prematurely (during execution).

Absolute pressure. Gauge pressure plus atmospheric pressure (14.7 psi).

Absolute zero. –459.57°F, or –273.15°C, the point at which all molecular and electron movement theoretically stops. (This temperature has never been attained.)

Acceleration, average. The rate of change of velocity—i.e., a change in velocity divided by the time it takes for that change to occur.

Access, direct. A method of retrieving information from memory in which the retrieval time is independent of the location in memory. Also called *random access*.

Access time. The time it takes a computer to retrieve a bit of information from its memory, also called *load time*. Or, the time it takes a computer to store information in its memory, also called *write time*. Typical access times for various storage media are:

TTL RAM . . . . 60 ms

MOS RAM . . . . 300 ms

Core . . . . 500 ms

Bubble . . . . 3 ms

Disk (fixed head) . . . . 8 ms

Disk (moving head) . . . . 50 ms

Floppy disk . . . . 100 ms

Cassette . . . . 10 s

Tape . . . . 10 s

Acoustic coupler. A device (or modem) that allows transmission of digital information over voice-grade telephone lines.

Adapter. A signal-conditioning device, inserted between any two of the hardware devices designed to accomplish certain applications, which include analog-to-digital interface, impedance matching, isolation sequencing, and reversing or selecting the highest or lowest signal.

Address. A location, area, or place where particular data or bits of information are stored, such as memory address or remote point address. This is usually an identification number or identification label.

Address selector. A switch on an I/O module used to create a module address.

Adjustable differential. A means of changing the difference between the "cut-in" and "cut-out" points on a control.

Air control damper. Used with central fan systems to control the mixture of outside air admitted to the system. It is installed in the fresh air intake leading into the return air ducts.

Air motion relay. Used to sense the air pressure differential across a coil or fan.

Air-over. A type of motor that must be mounted in the airstream for proper cooling.

Alarm printer. A printer utilized to log the time of day, point number, and the digital values of a variable that is in an alarm condition.

Algorithm. A set of rules or steps used for solving a problem. Frequently the problem is a mathematical one.

Alphanumeric. Characteristic of a display that combines alphabetic, numeric, and other characters, such as dollar signs, parentheses, etc.

Alternating current (ac). Electric current that reverses its direction at regular intervals.

Amber. Fossilized tree sap. (The ancient Greek word for amber was *elektron*. When rubbed with animal fur, amber became "electrified.")

Ambient. See *temperature, ambient*.

Ambient-compensated. A control whose setpoints are adjusted so that they are not affected by the surrounding environment.

American Standard Code for Information Interchange (ASCII). A standard eight-level code used to simplify and standardize communications between computers and other electronic equipment. It consists of seven code bits for information data, and one bit for parity.

American wire gauge (AWG). The standards adopted in the U.S. for the measurement of wire sizes. (As the diameter of the wire gets smaller, the number gets larger.)

A

Ammeter. A device used to measure the current in an electric circuit.

Ampacity. A combination of the words *ampere* and *capacity*. It is used to express the current-carrying capacity of conductors or wires, and refers to the maximum current that a wire can carry without overheating.

Ampere. A unit of measurement of current in an electric circuit. It is based on the number of electrons flowing past a given point per second.

Amplification. The amount of increase in voltage, current, or power.

Amplitude. The magnitude of variation in a quantity from its zero value, as measured in either the positive (above zero) or negative (below zero) direction. Generally applied to voltage, current, or power.

Analog. A term used to characterize a circuit or device in which the output signal varies as a continuous function of the input signal.

Analog inputs. Inputs that represent physical quantities or process variables, such as pressure, temperature, resistance, current, voltage, or humidity.

Analog-to-digital converter. A device or system that converts an analog signal to a digital signal or code. Abbreviated "A-D," "A/D," or "ADC."

Anemometer. An instrument used to measure the velocity of moving air or other fluid.

Annunciator light. A visual indicator of the status of a system—usually some form of light or panel of lights—that can be used for alarms or to let the operator know that the system is functioning correctly.

Anode. The positive terminal of an electronic device, or the "P" material in a semiconductor.

Anticipator. A small heater in two position controllers that deliberately causes a false temperature indication to minimize override.

Apparent power. The power apparently available for use in an ac circuit that contains a reactive element. It is the product of voltage times current, expressed in volt-amperes. It must be multiplied by the power factor to obtain the *true* or *actual* power available.

Arc. An unwanted flash or spark (a passage of electric current) caused by the ionizing of a gas or a vapor.

A

Armature. The rotating part of a motor or generator, or the movable part of a relay.

Assemble. To prepare an object language program from a symbolic language program. This is accomplished by inserting machine operation codes for symbolic operation codes.

Assembler. A computer program that converts mnemonic language to numeric machine language. The usual ratio is 1:1.

Asynchronous. Having no regular time relationships. Asynchronous program executions are unpredictable in relationship to time or instruction progression. The opposite of *synchronous*.

Asynchronous communication. A method of electronic communication in which the data transmission time frame varies between characters.

Asynchronous computer. A computer whose operations are not controlled by a master clock.

Atom. The smallest particle of an element that still maintains its identity—that is, has the same number of protons as any other atom of that element.

Attenuation. A systemized reduction or lowering of an energy level or signal level.

Automatic changeover. Usually pertains to a thermostat, referring to a system that changes from cooling to heating, and vice versa, without a manual control.

Automatic control. A system that reacts to a change in one of its variables by adjusting one of the other variables in order to maintain the balance of the system.

Automatic reset. A control that will automatically return to its original position or setting.

Automation. Refers to an automatically controlled operation or system, either electronic or mechanical, that takes the place of human observation, effort, and decision.

Autotransformer. A transformer in which the primary and secondary are connected together to form one winding.

Auxiliary contacts. A set of contacts mechanically attached to and operating in conjunction with a relay, contactor, or actuator motor. They are usually pilot-duty contacts.

Auxiliary device. Any component added to a system that is controlled or actuated by the output signal of one or more controllers.

Auxiliary potentiometer. A potentiometer that is attached to an actuator and controls another actuator in proportion to the first motor's action.

Auxiliary switch. A switch connected to a valve, motor, or relay that controls a separate circuit.

Averaging element. A thermostat sensing element that will react to the average temperature in a duct, or to some other controllable variable.

Averaging relay. A relay used in applications that operate a final control device or set a controller by the average signal of two controllers.

Back up. To copy electronic information from one storage device to another.

Balancing relay. A pivoted armature that swings between two electromagnetic coils. As the coils change magnetic strength, the relay moves toward the stronger of the two. Also called a "mousetrap relay."

Ballast. An auxiliary device used to control voltage and current in gas discharge lamps (such as fluorescent and mercury vapor bulbs).

Band. In communications, the range of frequencies that lies between two defined limits.

Bandwidth. The difference between the highest usable frequency of a device (upper frequency limit) and the lowest usable frequency of the device (lower frequency limit), measured at the half-power points.

Barometer. An instrument for measuring atmospheric pressure.

Barrier. An insulator that separates electrical terminals on a relay, compressor, or other electrical device.

Base. The center semiconductor layer of a junction transistor.

Base (number). The number of distinct symbols used in a number system. For example, since the decimal number system uses ten symbols (0, 1, 2, 3, 4, 5, 6, 7, 8, 9), the base is 10. In the binary number system, the base is 2, because only two symbols (0, 1) are used. Also called *radix*.

Battery. Two or more cells connected together. The term does not apply to a single cell.

Baud rate. A unit of signalling speed, usually equal to the number of bits or elements per second. Named for Baudot (1845-1903), a French engineer and the inventor of the five-channel teletype code. Sometimes used interchangeably with *bit rate*.

Bel. A unit of measure for expressing the ratio between two amounts of power (generally used to refer to the intensity of sound energy). One bel = 10 decibels.

Bimetal. A strip or coil made of two metals that have different thermal expansion rates, laminated together so that changes in temperature bend the strip or twist the coil.

Bimetallic element. A coil or strip of two dissimilar metals used in temperature-sensing devices.

B

Binary. a) Having two elements, parts, or divisions. b) Having only two possible conditions or values, usually opposed pairs (ON/OFF, open/closed, etc.). c) A number system that uses only two numerals—one and zero. Also called *base 2*. Computers utilize a binary code in which the value of each digit's position is based on the powers of 2, as follows:

128	64	32	16	8	4	2	1
—	—	—	—	—	—	—	—

0000	0000	=	0
0000	0001	=	1
0000	0010	=	2
0000	0011	=	3
0000	0100	=	4
0000	1000	=	8
0001	0000	=	16
0010	0000	=	32
0100	0000	=	64
1000	0000	=	128
1111	1111	=	255

Binary-coded decimal (BCD). A mathematical representation of a digit in a decimal number by a four-bit binary number, as follows:

80	40	20	10	8	4	2	1
—	—	—	—	—	—	—	—

0000	0000	=	0
0000	0001	=	1
0000	0010	=	2
0000	0011	=	3
0000	0100	=	4
0001	0000	=	10
0010	0000	=	20
0011	0001	=	30
0110	0100	=	64
1001	0110	=	96
1001	1001	=	99

Binary digit. One of the two states in the binary system—either 1 or 0.

Binary number. A number in the base 2 number system. For example, the number "9" in base 10 (or decimal) notation is "1001" in base 2.

Binary synchronous communications. A data protocol system developed by IBM whereby information is transmitted twice in order to eliminate errors. Its name is derived from the fact that data are transmitted twice.

Bit. The single smallest portion of information that a computer can read. It is the abbreviation for *bi*nary digi*t*.

Bit rate. The speed at which bits travel over a communications channel, expressed in bits per second (bps). Compare with *baud rate*.

Black light. See *ultraviolet*.

Bleeder resistor. A resistor that is placed in parallel with a capacitor in order to discharge it.

Block diagram. A simplified schematic that uses blocks or symbols to represent the various functions in a system.

Boolean algebra. A discipline of mathematics that uses alphabetic symbols to represent variables, and "1" and "0" to represent states. There are three basic logic operations—AND, OR, and NOT. Named for George Boole (1815-1886), an English mathematician.

Brake winding. The winding in an actuator motor that holds the armature against the brake shoe. This holds the motor in its open position after the limit switch opens. When both brake and motor windings are energized, the motor winding overcomes the brake winding.

Branch circuit. Any circuit that extends from the main power lines.

Bridge. Generally refers to techniques and/or equipment used to match circuits to each other.

Bridge circuit. A type of circuit intended to "bridge" or "bypass" another circuit, causing a "null" or no current to be measured.

British thermal unit (Btu). The amount of heat required to raise one pound of water one degree Fahrenheit at sea level.

Brush. The device that carries the current to the armature or commutator of a motor. Usually made of carbon.

Buck-boost transformer. See *autotransformer*.

Buffer. A circuit or system located between two pieces of equipment or between two data storage units. Information can be held in the buffer until the computer is ready to use it.

B

Bug. A program or hardware malfunction.

Bulb. The name given to the sensing element of a controller. Also applied to a device that emits light.

Burn. A permanent set of instructions entered into a PROM or EPROM.

Burn-in. A procedure for testing equipment or components to verify their stability and to detect early failures.

Bus. A set of parallel conductors that connects pieces of hardware in any computer system.

Bus bar. A primary power distribution point. Sometimes used to denote small copper or aluminum conductors. See also *strap*.

Bus, bidirectional. A set of parallel conductors that allows for the transmission of data in either direction between pieces of hardware in any computer system.

Bypass. A pipe or duct controlled by a valve or damper, used to carry air or some other fluid around a device in the system.

Byte. Usually, eight bits of information. Memory is normally measured in the number of bytes of information that it can store.

Cad cell. A cadmium sulfide cell changes resistance with light. As light falls on the cell, the resistance decreases. Used in conjunction with primary oil controls.

Calibration. A correction or adjustment to the scale of a control or a device in order to bring it into compliance with certain standards—for example, adjusting a controller's setpoint to match the ambient temperature that it is controlling.

Calorie. The amount of heat required to raise the temperature of one gram of water one degree Celsius.

Capacitive reactance. Opposition by a capacitor to the flow of current in an ac circuit, measured in ohms. Its symbol is X_c.

Capacitor. A device used for storing an electric charge.

Capacitor-start, capacitor-run (CSCR). A type or motor that uses both a start capacitor and a run capacitor to increase starting torque and running efficiency.

Capacitor-start, induction-run (CSIR). A type or motor that uses a start winding and start capacitor *only* during starting.

Capacity index (Cv factor). The quantity of water, measured in gallons per minute at 60°F, that will flow through a given valve with a pressure drop of 1 psig. See also *flow coefficient*.

Capillary tube. A small-diameter tube used as a metering device in a refrigeration or air conditioning system. Also, the small tubing that transmits the temperature to a controller from a sensing element.

Card cage. An enclosure designed with slots for holding printed circuit boards.

Carrier. An analog signal at a fixed amplitude and frequency that combines with an information signal in a modulation process to produce a transmittable signal.

Cascade control. A control system in which the controls are linked in a chain-like fashion, with the output of one stage feeding the input of the next stage. Sometimes called "piggy-back" control.

Cathode. The negative terminal of a device, or the "N" material in a semiconductor.

Cathode ray tube (CRT). A display terminal, similar to a television set's picture tube.

Cavitation. The formation and collapse of vapor pockets (bubbles) in a liquid, due to the increase and decrease of pressure as the liquid flows through a restriction.

Celsius. Formerly *Centigrade*, a thermometric scale in which 0° is the freezing point and 100° is the boiling point of water at sea level.

Central control unit (CCU). In an automated control system, the central site at which all of the master controls and peripheral equipment are located.

Central processing unit (CPU). The part of a computer that performs arithmetic operations, controls instruction processing, and provides timing signals.

Centrifugal starting switch. A switch mounted on the shaft of a motor that switches the start winding in and out of the circuit, depending on the rotor speed.

Changeover. The process of changing from a heating to an air conditioning system, or vice versa.

Channel. A frequency band wide enough for one-way communication from a radio or television station, or from a microwave source. An electrical transmission path between two or more stations in communications. Also, a termination furnished by wire or radio or both.

Character. A numeral from 0 to 9, a letter from A to Z, a mathematical symbol, a punctuation mark, or any other symbol that a CRT or printer can process as output or input. Usually a numerical representation in a computer.

Chatter. See *relay contact bounce*.

Chip. See *integrated circuit*.

Choke coil. A coil of wire of low resistance and high impedance, used with some shaded-pole motors for speed control.

Circuit. The complete path necessary for an electric current to flow. It must consist of a source, a path, and a load.

Circuit breaker. An electromagnetic or thermal device that interrupts current flowing a circuit.

Circular mil. An area equal to that of a circle with a diameter of 0.001 in. It is used in measuring the cross section of a wire.

Clear. Usually a state denoting zero or blank.

Clock. Any device that controls a circuit by using time—e.g., the oscillator in a computer.

Close-off rating. The maximum allowable pressure drop (inlet to outlet) that a valve will tolerate when fully closed. The power available from the actuator usually determines this value.

Closed loop. An automatic control system that incorporate a feedback signal to correct any errors between the actual value and the desired value.

Coaxial cable. A cable or transmission line that consists of two or more conductors, each separated by a dielectric material from the others, with a common axis.

Code. A system of symbols used for communication, or a system of symbols that represents data.

Code, binary. A computer language that uses only ones and zeros (base 2).

Code, hexadecimal. A computer language that incorporates the numerals 0 through 9 and the letters A through F to represent a group or groups of four binary digits (base 8).

Collector. The end portion of a junction transistor that is reverse-biased with respect to the base.

Command. A signal or pulse to start, stop, or continue an operation in a computer. A synonym for "instruction."

Common. A terminal, connection, or wire that is shared by other parts of an electrical network.

Commutator. The copper segments on a motor's rotor that, through brushes, connect the armature coils to the power source.

Compandor. A device used on some telephone channels to "compress" or "expand" the speed, range, and volume of incoming and outgoing signals.

Compensated control. Refers to a controller whose setpoints are not affected by ambient temperature.

Compiler. A program that a computer uses to translate user-level language into machine-level instructions.

Complementary metal-oxide semiconductor (CMOS). An integrated circuit with low power requirements and very high noise immunity.

Compressor. A machine used for increasing the pressure of gases. The device that provides the pressure difference in a refrigeration or air conditioning system.

Computer. A machine designed to receive data (input), process the data by performing certain operations at high speeds, and then produce the results (output).

Computer, analog. A computer that designates variables by physical analogies. An analog computer translates conditions such as flow, pressure, temperature, voltage, or current quantities into proportional electrical data.

Computer, digital. A computer that processes data by using discrete number systems—e.g., binary, hexadecimal, etc.

Condenser. A device that reduces a vapor to a liquid. Also, an older electrical term for *capacitor*.

Conductance. The ability of a conductor to carry current. The inverse of resistance, conductance is measured in mhos (the reciprocal of resistance in ohms) or siemens.

Conductivity, electrical. The property of a material the permits an electric current to pass through it.

Conductivity, thermal. The rate of heat flow through a material under stable conditions—that is, when the temperature difference between the two ends of a heat conductor remains constant.

Conductor. Any material suitable for carrying an electric current.

Constant cut-in. A control whose "cut-out" setting can be adjusted, but whose "cut-in" remains the same. Also called an *off-cycle defrost* control.

Constant cut-out. A control whose "cut-in" setting can be adjusted, but whose "cut-out" remains the same. Used in two-temperature refrigerators and defrost systems.

Contact rating. The electric power or current-handling capability of switch or relay contacts. Usually measured in amperes, volts, or horsepower, either resistive or inductive.

Control. A device used for the regulation of a system. This can be accomplished by sensing changes in temperature, pressure, or other variables in any substance whose condition can be regulated.

Control agent. The medium manipulated by a control system to cause a change in the controlled medium—for example, the steam in a heating system or the refrigerant in a cooling system.

Control, direct digital (DDC). A control loop in which data are updated periodically through a set of given control algorithms.

Control, distributed. Distribution of data and operational control, usually through computers, by networking. Each individual controller must be able to

295

maintain independent operation, even if the communication with the rest of the network is lost.

Control, floating. A type of system in which a change in a controlled variable causes a control to make a contact, which in turn causes an operator to run. The operator will not stop until the variable returns to the control setpoint on the controller.

Control, hunt. A condition of instability in a control system in which the controller overreacts in either direction. See also *hunting*.

Control, integral. A control method (or algorithm) in which the final control element is moved in a corrective direction at a rate proportional to the error (deviation) of the controlled variable, until the controller is satisfied.

Control loop. A series of components that make up a control system. If feedback is incorporated, it is called a "closed-loop" system. If not, it is called an "open-loop" system.

Control point. The middle of the range of values that a control tries to maintain under given conditions.

Control, proportional/integral/derivative (PID). A control algorithm that enhances the PI control algorithm by adding a component that is proportional to the rate of change (derivative) of the deviation (error) of the controlled variable. This serves to anticipate future errors under current conditions. Also called *three-mode control*.

Control range. The actual operating range of a control.

Control unit. Part of the CPU. It directs the sequence of operations, initiates commands to the computer circuits, and executes instructions.

Controlled device. A device that receives the converted signal from the controller and makes an appropriate action. Usually the final element in the control chain—e.g., a damper, relay, or actuator.

Controlled medium. The substance (usually air, water, steam, or refrigerant) whose characteristics (such as temperature, pressure, flow rate, volume, concentration, etc.) are being controlled.

Controlled space. The volume of the controlled medium, such as a room to be heated or cooled.

Controlled variable. The quantity, characteristic, or condition of the controlled medium that is to be measured—for example, temperature, pressure, etc.

Controller. An instrument that receives a signal from a sensing device, converts it to a signal that can measured, and initiates the needed action.

Conversational. A method of communication in which a human communicates directly with the CPU of a computer, by issuing commands and obtaining responses in return.

Converter. A device or circuit that changes the information or voltage in a system—e.g., ac to dc voltage, analog to digital, etc.

Copy. To duplicate a program or data without changing the original information.

Core. A shape formed from a magnetic material that affords a path for magnetic flux.

Core-resident. A program that is located permanently in the main memory of a computer.

Corona. A luminous discharge around the surface of a conductor caused by the ionization of the surrounding air by high voltages.

Corrective action. Action that is initiated in response to a deviation of a signal from the desired value, and results in a change in the manipulated variable.

Coulomb. A measure of the quantity of electricity. One coulomb is equal to the charge of 6.28×10^{18} electrons. See *joule*.

Counter. A device for storing a number and increasing or decreasing it. Also, a register or storage location for recording the number of occurrences of an event.

Counter electromotive force (CEMF). A voltage impressed on a coil that opposes the applied voltage, usually found in inductive circuits.

Crash. An unplanned system shutdown caused by a software, hardware, or power failure.

Critical pressure drop. Fluid flow through a valve increases with increased pressure drop until a critical point is reached. Any pressure drop in excess of this value will cause noise and wear.

Cross ambient fill. A vapor pressure element sufficiently large to ensure that there is liquid in the bulb, regardless of whether the bulb is warmer or cooler than the ambient temperature.

Crosstalk. The unwanted transfer of a signal from one path to another—e.g., between data and/or communication transmission lines.

Current. The movement of electrons past a reference point. The passage of electrons through a conductor, measured in amperes. The symbol for current is "I."

Current limiter. A protective device for a circuit, usually a fuse or circuit breaker.

Cursor. An indicator on the face of a CRT or visual display to show where the next character will be placed.

Cut-in setting. The point at which the contacts on a control will close.

Cut-out setting. The point at which the contacts on a control will open.

Cycle. One complete alternation of electric current, consisting of one positive half-cycle and one negative half-cycle. See also *frequency*. Also, a repeated sequence of events or operations, or the complete course of operation of a system.

Cycle time. The least amount of time allowed between subsequent accesses to the same memory.

Cycling. See *hunting*.

Damper. A device that controls the flow of air by the use of pivoted vanes or blades.

Damper, opposed-blade. Alternate blades rotate in opposite directions, which provides an equal flow characteristic.

Damper, parallel-blade. All blades rotate in the same direction, which provides a fairly linear air flow.

Data. A general term used to denote all numbers, letters, symbols, and other information that can be stored, altered, or transmitted. Generally pertains to the information stored and processed by a computer.

Data base. A sizable amount of electronic information, stored in a computer, that can be retrieved with special instructions pertaining to organizing, sorting, deleting, etc.

Data file. A raw file of data in a format that can be used and understood by a computer program.

Data link. An information channel that connects any input, output, or other peripheral device to the data-processing apparatus.

Day clock. A type of computer clock that keeps track of both the time of day and the date.

Day-night thermostat. A device that consists of two thermostats operating at different times or temperatures. Now done with micro-electronics.

dBm. A unit of measurement used in the telephone industry to represent power levels. The abbreviation stands for decibels above (or below) a one-milliwatt reference.

Deadband. In a control system, the range of values through which the controlled variable can be altered without initiating a corrective response.

D

Dead man timer. A method used to detect a computer malfunction that requires a corrective action.

Debug. To identify, locate, and remove faults from a computer program or routine. Synonymous with *troubleshoot*.

Debug program. A utility program that provides an on-line capability to inspect, control, and debug other programs during executive command.

Decibel (dB). A unit of measure for expressing sound intensity levels. The smallest change in sound intensity that the normal human ear can detect. See also *bel*.

Decimal. A number system in which the numerals 0 through 9 are used (base 10). Each number is called a *digit*. The system has a *radix* of 10.

Decimal number. A figure written in the base-10 number system. When a number is read from left to right, each digit is perceived to be multiplied by a progressively higher power of 10. The positions of the digits are referred to as the *ones*, the *tens*, the *hundreds* positions, and so on.

Decision. In computer terminology, decisions are "yes" or "no" answers to simple questions that have been refined until they can have only one of two possible answers. Computers can make these decisions so rapidly that a complex logic routine appears to be done instantly, giving the appearance—and forming the mistaken notion in some people's minds—that computers can "think."

Dedicated line carrier. A form of two-way communications between input and output devices and controllers that requires only a two-wire communications link.

De-energize. To terminate the current flow to a device.

Default value. The value assumed by a program, unless another value is stipulated by the user.

Degradation. Refers to a reduced level of service at which a system is operated.

Delta. Prefix meaning "three." Derived from the Greek letter *delta* (Δ), which looks like a triangle. It refers to "the change in" or "the difference between" in such terms as "delta T," applied to temperature (ΔT = final temperature minus initial temperature).

Delta transformer. A three-phase transformer whose windings are wired in the "delta" (triangular) pattern.

Demand. The power (measured in kVA) drawn from an electrical utility averaged over a suitable period of time—usually 15 or 30 minutes.

Demodulate. To remove a radio frequency (RF) signal from its carrier.

Design conditions. Space temperature conditions that require the full heating or cooling capacity of a system.

Desired value. The point at which the value of the controlled medium is to be maintained.

Deviation. The difference between the controlled condition and the setpoint, or between a maximum (or minimum) and an average value. See *droop*.

Device. An item designed to serve a specific purpose—e.g., a computer peripheral or an electronic component.

D

Dew point. The temperature at which water vapor (at 100% humidity) condenses.

Diagnostic. A special routine designed to locate a malfunction (and identify its cause) in a computer or other device.

Dielectric. A nonconductive material used to separate and insulate the electrodes of a capacitor from one another.

Differential. In a temperature or pressure control application, the difference in temperature or pressure between the opening and closing of the contacts.

Differential pressure control. A controller that measures the difference between two separate pressures.

Digit. A character used to represent an integer smaller than the base radix— e.g., 0 to 9 in decimal notation, 0 or 1 in binary notation.

Digital. Pertains to having two states, such as ON and OFF, open and closed, 0 and 1. See *binary*.

Digital device. Any piece of equipment that employs digital methods in its operation.

D

Digital-to-analog converter. A device that accepts a digital input signal and converts it to an analog output, usually voltage or current. Abbreviated "D-A," "D/A," or "DAC."

Digitize. To change an analog signal or measurement into digital form.

Diode. A two-element device that allows current to flow in one direction only. It can be either a vacuum tube or a solid-state device.

Direct-acting. An instrument in which the output signal changes in the same direction as the controlled variable changes—i.e., the response increases as the change in the variable increases.

Direct current (dc). An electric current that flows in one direction only, such as a battery delivers (the current flows from the negative to the positive terminal).

Direct digital control (DDC). A control loop in which data are updated periodically through a set of given control algorithms.

Direct reset. In multiple-input (usually two-input) applications, a control technique in which an increase at the second (open-loop) sensor causes the controller setpoint to be increased.

Distributed input/output (DIO). An I/O technique used by Computer Automation, Inc. that multiplexes the primary computer bus.

Distributed processing. A concept whereby decision-making is shared by multiple computers and peripherals.

Double-pole. A switching arrangement in which two separate contacts open and close simultaneously.

Double-seated valve. Fluid pressure is introduced between two seats, enabling the valve to close off against high pressure.

Double-throw. A switching arrangement in which contacts make in one position and simultaneously break in the other.

Downline load. The transfer of electronic information from a central processing unit to ancillary devices, such as floppy disks.

D

Downtime. The period of time during which equipment is malfunctioning or otherwise off-line. Also, production time lost while faulty equipment is being repaired.

Drift. In a control system, a change (over a period of time) in the input-output relationship unrelated to input, environment, or load.

Droop. In a control system, the difference between the setpoint and the control point. See also *offset*.

Dropout. The value of current or voltage at which an energized relay will be de-energized.

Dry-bulb temperature. The temperature indicated by an ordinary thermometer, it indicates the sensible heat of air and water vapor mixture.

Dual in-line package (DIP). A packaging technique for integrated circuits that incorporates two parallel rows of connecting pins.

Dual thermostat. A two-temperature thermostat (usually two separate thermostats in one case).

Dump. To read out the entire contents of a data base or a computer's memory into another computer or a printer.

Duty cycle. An energy management program that lowers the consumption of electric power by cycling the equipment so that minimum operating time is used for comfort conditions.

Duty cycle (motor). The relationship between the time during which a motor is operating and the time during which it is at rest. There are two terms used in the HVACR industry—*continuous* cycle, which refers to a motor that operates for periods of more than one hour at a time, and *intermittent* cycle, which refers to a motor that operates for periods of 15 to 30 minutes at a time.

EAROM. Electrically alterable read only memory, a type of memory that combines the characteristics of RAM and ROM. It is non-volatile (like ROM), but can be written into the processor (like RAM). EAROM has a substantially longer writing time than RAM (currently about 2 microseconds versus about 400 nanoseconds), as well as a limited number of writes (about 1,000,000) before the chip can no longer be programmed.

Economizer control. A system of ventilation control used to ensure the proper mixed-air temperature, and to achieve "free cooling."

Eddy currents. Induced circulating currents in a conducting material that are caused by varying the magnetic field.

Edit. To add, rearrange, or delete information from computer programs, files, or data bases.

Editor. A utility program that permits editing procedures on computer programs and data.

Electric demand limiting. The controlling of the instantaneous draw of power from a utility's circuits.

Electrical degree. $\frac{1}{360}$ of a cycle in a sine wave. One complete cycle equals 360 electrical degrees.

Electrical rating. The designated electrical power-handling capacity of a switch or relay.

Electro-luminescence. The direct transformation of electrical energy into light energy in a semiconductor (such as an LED).

Electrolyte. The chemical paste used in some batteries that dissociates into negative and positive ions, thus forming a conducting medium for an electric current.

Electromagnet. A magnet formed by wrapping a current-carrying wire around an iron core.

Electromotive force (EMF). The difference of potential that forces electrons through a resistance, measured in volts.

Electron. One of the fundamental particles of an atom. Electrons are negatively charged.

Electronic data processing (EDP). The manipulation of raw data by electronic means to produce useful data.

Electro-pneumatic (EP) switch. A switch that opens or closes an air valve with an electrical impulse.

Element. Any device in a system, such as a resistor, capacitor, or transformer. Also, any of a class of substances (composed of atoms) that have the same number of protons. Elements cannot be broken down into simpler substances.

Emitter. The end portion of a junction transistor that is normally forward-biased with respect to the base.

Encode. To place into a coded format.

Energize. The application of some form of energy to a device   e.g., to apply a voltage.

Energy. The ability to do work—i.e., to move something through a distance against a resistance.

Enthalpy. The thermodynamic property of a substance, sometimes called the "heat content" or "total heat" of the substance. Both latent heat and sensible heat are included.

Entropy. The amount of energy that is unavailable for work during a natural process—i.e., energy not practically usable for a given application.

EPROM. Erasable, programmable read only memory, a type of memory capable of being electrically programmed by external means to the computer.

It then functions as a read only memory when used by the computer. It can be erased by ultraviolet light, and then re-programmed.

Execute. To run a program or perform an instruction in a computer.

Executive. In computer terminology, a set of commands, instructions, or routines that controls the computer's resources. Also called the *operating system*.

Face-and-bypass damper system. A heating system in which the air is bypassed around a heating or cooling coil (face) by the use of opposed operating dampers.

Fail-safe. Capable of compensating automatically for a failure by returning to a default position—e.g., a damper will close if there is a loss of power.

Farad. The basic unit of capacitance. A capacitor has a capacitance of one farad when a potential difference of one volt across it produces a charge of one coulomb.

Feedback. The return of a portion of the output of a circuit or device to its input. In a "closed-loop" control system, it is the signal from the controlled process to the controller.

Field (electric). The region around (or within) a current-carrying conductor in which an electric force can act on a charge.

Field (magnetic). The region in which the magnetic forces created by a permanent magnet can act on another magnet.

Field (motor). The stationary part of a motor that furnishes the magnetic field surrounding the armature.

Filter. In electronic circuits, a device that blocks an unwanted signal—e.g., a power supply filter removes excess noise.

Fire stat. A high-temperature safety control, designed to shut down a system when it detects a high temperature in the ductwork.

Firmware. Any computer program that resides in a ROM, PROM, or EPROM.

Fixed differential. The difference between the "cut-in" and the "cut-out." It is factory-set and cannot be adjusted.

Fixed duty cycle. A fixed number of "ON" minutes for which a system will operate each hour.

Fixed setting. A factory-set variable for which no user adjustment is available.

Flame safeguard control. A control that proves that there is a flame established before allowing the burner control to operate.

Floating action. In a control system, continuous action in which the rate of change of the output is a predetermined function of the input. The movement of a controller toward its open or closed position.

Flow chart. A diagram that depicts all of the steps of a process, program, or system in a logical sequence.

Flow coefficient. A measurement of valve capacity expressed as the number of gpm of water (at 60°F) that will flow through a fully opened valve with a pressure drop of 1 psi. Its symbol is C_v. See also *capacity index*.

Flow rate. The amount of fluid flowing past a given point per unit of time. Typical units are gpm for water, lb/hr for steam, and cfm for air.

Flux. See *magnetic flux*.

F

Footcandle. A unit of measure of the intensity of light falling uniformly on a surface, equal to one lumen per square foot (originally referred to the light produced by a standard candle at a distance of one foot from a given surface).

Force. The push or pull on a body that tends to change its state of motion.

FORTRAN. *FOR*mula *TRAN*slator, a type of high-level language used in computers to solve scientific and engineering problems.

Fractional horsepower. A horsepower value of less than one.

Frame. Refers to a system developed by NEMA for standardizing the mounting of electric motors according to various dimensions.

Free electrons. Electrons once loosely held in orbit around an atom that have become dislodged and are free to move elsewhere.

Freeze stat. A type of control used to prevent the freeze-up of coils and other devices.

Frequency. The number of vibrations or cycles in a given period of time— e.g., cycles per second (Hertz), revolutions per minutes (rpm), etc.

Full-load amperes (FLA). The term used to indicate the current drawn by a motor running at its full rated horsepower and voltage.

Full-wave rectifier. A device with circuitry that utilizes both the positive and negative cycles of an alternating current to produce a direct current.

Function key. A button or key on a computer that gives the machine a specific command to perform a specialized job.

Fuse. A non-reusable device that breaks a circuit when the current exceeds a certain level.

Gain. Any increase in the strength of a signal, calculated as the ratio of the output signal to the input signal.

Galvanometer. An instrument that measures very small direct currents.

Gas, inert. A gas that causes no chemical reactions and undergoes no change of state. Krypton, argon, boron, helium, xenon, and neon are some of the inert gases (also called "noble" gases).

Gate. A circuit that may have one or many inputs with just one output. The output usually remains unchanged until certain conditions of the input are met. These circuits will perform Boolean logic operations.

Generator. A device that converts mechanical energy into electrical energy.

Germanium. A crystalline semiconductor material, used to make transistors and diodes.

Gradual switches. Manual switches that proportion the controlled condition in reference to the position of the switch. In pneumatics, a device for adjusting the air pressure from zero to full line pressure.

Ground. Any conductor that connects to the earth (earth ground). Also may refer to a cabinet or chassis ground that serves as a common conductor.

Ground loop. The current that flows between two or more ground connections. This is a very prevalent condition when one or more of the connections has a higher resistance than the others. This causes a difference of potential.

Ground wire. Any wire that is connected to the chassis or to an earth ground, commonly identified by its green insulation. In electrical conduit, the ground wire is usually the bare wire.

Hard copy. Any printout on a permanent material, such as paper, of electronically stored information.

Hardware. The physical components of a computer system—e.g., disk drives, power supplies, printers, modems, etc. See also *software*.

Hard-wired. A system that uses fixed wires for connecting remote devices to the central processing equipment (as opposed to cordless).

Harmonic. A frequency that is a whole-number multiple of a smaller fundamental frequency. The chart below shows a few harmonics of 60-Hz power (the "F" stands for *fundamental*).

Harmonic	F	2nd	3rd	4th	5th	6th	7th	8th	9th
Frequency, Hz	60	120	180	240	300	360	420	480	540

Heat. A form of energy that acts on a substance to cause a rise in its temperature.

Heat gain, latent. Heat gain that takes place during a change of state (melting, vaporization, etc.), and is *not* accompanied by a change in temperature.

Heat gain, sensible. Heat gain that is caused by convection, conduction, or radiation, and *is* evidenced by an increase in temperature.

Heat gain, total. The sum of both heat gains, sensible and latent.

Heat sink. A device used to draw off (conduct away) heat. Usually pertains to a semiconductor device.

Henry. The unit of inductance. Its symbol is "H." One henry of inductance is present in a circuit when a change in current of one ampere per second induces an EMF of one volt.

Hermetic. Completely sealed.

Hertz (Hz). A unit of frequency equal to one cycle per second.

Hexadecimal number. A number written in the base 16 number system. The first ten numbers are the integers 0 through 9, the last six "numbers" are the letters A through F. Also called a "hex" number.

G
H

High-level language. A program language that is more English-like than hex or binary code, and thus not as restricted by the limitations of the computer. High-level languages include ALGOL, COBOL, FORTRAN, etc.

High limit. The point at which a system is shut down to prevent damage to the equipment, or to personnel.

High-limit control. The control that prevents a system from reaching a dangerous level.

Holding current. The minimum current necessary to keep an SCR or triac turned on.

Horsepower. A measure of the rate of doing work. One horsepower is equal to 746 watts.

Hot. Designates any point in an electrical system that has a potential other than ground.

Hot wire. The conductor that is not at ground potential, usually identified by black or red insulation.

Humidity control. A device that measures and controls the amount of moisture in the air.

Hunting. Cycling above and below the setpoint. This behavior occurs when a controller cannot maintain the controlled variable at the desired preset level.

Hydrometer. An instrument used for measuring the specific gravity of a liquid.

Hygrometer. An instrument used for measuring humidity.

Hysteresis. The lagging of a magnetic field behind the magnetic force that causes it. Hysteresis results because the atoms of a magnetic material resist a change in their magnetic alignment.

I/O (input/output). A term used to describe communication with a computer, and the data and physical components involved in that communication.

I/O, parallel. The simultaneous transfer of all the bits in a byte of information over parallel conductors.

I/O, serial. The transfer of data one bit at a time over a single wire.

Impedance. The total opposition to an alternating current in an electric circuit. It is the joint effect of resistance, inductive reactance, and capacitive reactance. The symbol for impedance is "Z."

Impedance relay. A relay that has a high-impedance coil and is used to "lock out" a circuit.

Inch of mercury. A unit of pressure equal to the pressure exerted by a column of mercury one inch high at a temperature of 32°F.

Inch of water. A unit of pressure equal to the pressure exerted by a column of water one inch high at a temperature of 39.2°F.

"In" contacts. This term applies to a relay when the coil is energized and the contacts are pulled "in"—i.e., when the contacts are closed.

Indicator. Any device used to indicate the condition of a variable—e.g., a thermometer, pressure gauge, etc.

Inductance. The property of an electric circuit that tends to oppose any change in the existing current flow. The symbol for inductance is "L."

Induction. The act or process of producing voltage and current by the relative motion of a magnetic field across a conductor.

Inductive load. Any load that exhibits inductive reactance, such as a coil, motor, or transformer.

Inductive reactance. The opposition to the flow of an alternating current caused by the inductance of a circuit, expressed in ohms. Its symbol is X_L.

Infrared. A form of radiant energy not visible to the eye. Its frequency range is less than that of visible light, and its wavelengths are longer. With specialized equipment, it can be used for transmitting wireless signals.

Initialize. To start or open, to initiate the start-up procedures in a computer.

In phase. Applied to the condition that exists when two sine waves of the same frequency pass through their maximum and minimum values of like polarity at the same time.

Input. Any data or instructions sent to a computer or controller for processing. Also, any signal sent to a controller that may cause a change in its output.

Input module. A transducer that converts the medium variable (temperature, pressure, humidity, power) into a digital format for a microprocessor-based controller.

Instruction. A command that tells a computer what to do.

Insulation (electrical). The non-conductive material that covers electrical wires.

Insulator. Any material that will not allow electrons to pass freely through it.

Integral horsepower. Refers to motors rated at one horsepower or more.

Integrated circuit (IC). A complete electronic circuit manufactured as a single unit or "package." Also called a "chip."

Intelligent device. Any device that contains a microprocessor.

Interface. A system that links, in an organized manner, such entities as hardware, software, and a human operator.

Interlock switch. A device that prevents a machine from being operated while the cabinet door is open.

Ion. An electrically charged atom or group of atoms. Negative ions have an excess of electrons. Positive ions have a deficiency of electrons.

IPLV. Integrated part load value, a term that pertains to the flow of water in a chiller system.

IR drop. The voltage drop across a load, either resistive or inductive.

Jog. In motor starter terminology, to force a motor into motion by delivering power in small increments (pulses). In load shedding terminology, to prevent the power level from staying inside the deadband for an extended period of time.

Joule. A unit of energy or work. One joule of work is equal to one watt times one second (power × time).

K. Generally lower-case, the abbreviation for *kilo* (1,000).

Keyboard (keypad). A device that sends an encoded signal to a computer when a key is pressed.

Kilo. Prefix meaning *one thousand* (1,000).

Kilobyte. Roughly one thousand bytes of information.

Kilohertz (kHz). One thousand cycles per second.

Kilohm (kΩ). One thousand ohms.

Kilovar. One thousand volt-amperes reactive.

Kilovolt (kV). One thousand volts.

Kilowatt (kW). One thousand watts (equal to 1.34 horsepower).

Kirchhoff's Laws. A series of laws that pertain to current and voltage in parallel circuits. More specifically: (1) The algebraic sum of the current flowing toward any point in a circuit and the current flowing away from it is equal to zero. (2) The algebraic sum of the products of current and resistance in any closed path in a circuit is equal to the algebraic sum of the electromotive forces in the path.

Lag. In a control system, the delay in response to a change in the variable being controlled, or a condition in which the sensing element of a control reacts too slowly.

Laminated core. An iron core of a transformer that is made up of many thin, flat pieces of iron.

Lamp. Any device that produces visible light when a current is passed through it (incandescent, fluorescent, or mercury vapor).

Large-scale integration (LSI). Generally considered to have more than one hundred elements in a single integrated circuit or chip.

Laser. A mechanical device that produces intense, coherent light (*l*ight *a*mplification by *s*timulated *e*lectromagnetic *r*adiation).

Latent heat. The amount of heat required to change the state of a substance—e.g., changing water to ice requires the removal of 144 Btu per pound of water at sea level. Also called "hidden" heat.

Leakage current. A small amount of unwanted current that travels through insulation whenever there is voltage present.

K
L

Light-emitting diode (LED). A semiconductor device that emits light when a current is passed through it.

Limit control. A controller that keeps pressure, temperature, or humidity within certain limits, usually to protect the equipment or to prevent the development of unsafe conditions.

Line of force. Imaginary "lines" used to depict properties (e.g., direction, intensity, polarity) of a magnetic or electric field. Also called *flux* lines.

Line printer. A printer that prints a complete line of information at a very high speed.

Line voltage. The normal supply voltage for equipment (as distinguished from control voltage). In the U.S. and Canada, line voltages can be 120 V, 220 V, or 460 V, either single-phase or three-phase.

Linear. Any output that varies in direct proportion to the input.

Linear sequence. In load shedding, it is first OFF, last ON.

Liquid fill. Refers to a temperature-sensitive element that is completely filled with liquid. Any increase in temperature causes the liquid to expand. Any decrease in temperature causes the liquid to contract.

Liquid-line solenoid valve. An electrically operated valve that shuts off the refrigerant liquid line. See *pump down*.

Load. a) Any device that converts electrical energy into heat or mechanical energy. Any device that consumes electric power. b) An HVACR component that can be turned ON and OFF to conserve energy. c) In computer terminology, the ability to place a word into a register, or to place a program into the memory.

Locked-rotor amperes (LRA). The excessive current that a motor draws when its rotor is "locked" (cannot rotate).

Logging. The recording of data onto a "hard copy."

Logic. A system of mathematical computation used in digital circuit design to produce signal responses in a predetermined, orderly fashion. It applies to "truth tables," "switching," and "gating." The logic symbols are: AND, OR, NOT, NAND, and NOR.

Loop. In electronics, a complete electric circuit. In computer terminology, a series of instructions that repeats itself until a specific condition exists to terminate its operation.

Low-limit control. A device that prevents a variable in a control system from going below a specified limit.

Low-pressure control. Any device that opens an electric circuit when the pressure falls below a given point.

Low voltage. According to the National Electrical Code (NEC), any voltage below 50 V. Normally, 24 V is considered to be "low voltage."

Lumen. A unit of measure relating to the amount of light produced by a light source. One lumen is equal to the flux (illumination) produced by a uniform point source of one standard candle to each square meter of the inside surface of a sphere that has a radius of one meter. Two of these candles, if identical, would produce twice the illumination, or two lumens per square meter.

Machine language. A series of binary codes that instructs a computer to perform a specific function.

Magnet. Any object or material that attracts iron and common steel. See also *electromagnet*.

Magnetic circuit. The complete path of a magnet's lines of force.

Magnetic disk. A magnetically coated disk on which data are stored electromagnetically.

Magnetic field. The region (extending from a north polarity to a south polarity) in which the magnetic forces created by a permanent magnet or by a current-carrying conductor or coil can be detected.

Magnetic flux. Similar to "lines of force," imaginary lines used for convenience to designate the direction in which magnetic forces are acting.

Magnetic poles. Those sections of a magnet (called the *north* pole and the *south* pole) where the flux lines are concentrated and toward which they converge.

Magnetic tape. Plastic tape that has a magnetic coating on which data can be stored.

Manipulated variable. A condition or quantity controlled or regulated by an automatic control system.

Manometer. An instrument used for measuring pressure, usually a "U" tube filled with a liquid. The liquid may be water, oil, or mercury.

Manual reset. Any control (usually a protection device) that has to be physically reset after it "opens."

Mass. The quantity of matter in a body, measured by its resistance to acceleration and proportional to its weight.

Measured variable. The condition of a medium being measured by the sensing element in a control system. The measured variable may be temperature, humidity, pressure, or velocity of air, water, steam, etc.

Medium-scale integration (MSI). A micro-circuit that contains more than 12 and fewer than 100 elements.

Meg. Prefix meaning *one million* (1,000,000). When measuring computer memory, 1,048,576 units or bytes of information. Abbreviated "M."

Megabyte. Roughly one million (1,000,000) bytes of information. See *meg* above.

Megahertz. One million (1,000,000) cycles per second.

Megger. See *megohmmeter*.

Megohm. One million (1,000,000) ohms.

Megohmmeter. An instrument that measures very high insulation resistance. Sometimes referred to as a "megger."

Memory. The circuit or system that stores information, either in a computer or in a peripheral device such as a printer or disk drive.

Memory, bubble. Magnetic materials called "garnets" make up bubble memory. By applying a magnetic field, very small (2 to 5 microns) magnetized regions are formed. When viewed through a microscope by polarized light, they look like bubbles. Bubble access time is rather slow compared to semiconductor memory, but offers the advantages of non-volatility, low power dissipation, and no moving parts.

M

Memory capacity. The maximum amount of information that a storage device can retain.

Memory, dedicated. A special reserved location in the main memory of a computer—e.g., real-time programs and program interrupts.

Memory, dynamic. A special semiconductor memory that must be refreshed or recharged on a periodic basis to inhibit the loss of data.

Memory, main. The memory that the central processing unit accesses directly. Also called the "core" or "main" storage.

Memory, non-volatile. A memory system that will not lose its information if power is lost to the system.

Memory, off-line. A memory that is *not* under the control of the CPU.

Memory, on-line. A memory that *is* under the control of the CPU.

Memory, programmable. Any memory that can be written to or read from a processor. Synonymous with *RAM*.

Memory, volatile. Any form of computer memory that loses its information when power is lost.

Mercury bulb. A type of switch that uses a small quantity of mercury in a sealed glass tube to make or break an electric circuit.

Mho. The unit of conductance (the reciprocal of the ohm).

Micro. Prefix meaning *one one-millionth* (0.000001).

Microammeter. A meter that is sensitive enough to measure currents in the microampere range.

Microampere (μA). One one-millionth (0.000001) of an ampere.

Microbar. A unit of pressure equal to one one-millionth (0.000001) of the pressure of the atmosphere.

Microcomputer. A computer designed around a single chip or integrated circuit. It usually contains some ROM, some RAM, and some I/O interfaces. Most have 8-, 16-, or 32-bit word lengths.

Microfarad (μF). One one-millionth (0.000001) of a farad (a common rating for capacitors).

Micron. A unit of measurement equal to one one-millionth (0.000001) of a meter, or one one-thousandth (0.001) of a millimeter.

Microprocessor. A miniaturized computer CPU located on a single chip.

Microsecond. One one-millionth (0.000001) of a second.

Microvolt (μV). One one-millionth (0.000001) of a volt.

Milli. Prefix meaning *one one-thousandth* (0.001).

Milliammeter. An instrument that can measure currents in the milliampere range.

Milliampere (mA). One one-thousandth (0.001) of an ampere.

Millisecond. One one-thousandth (0.001) of a second.

Millivolt (mV). One one-thousandth (0.001) of a volt.

Milliwatt (mW). One one-thousandth (0.001) of a watt.

Mixed air. Supply air that is composed of outside air and return air.

Mixing box. A device used to mix outside and return air.

Mixing valves. Three-way valves that mix fluids in different proportions.

Modem. A device that connects a computer to telephone lines. It is a contraction of the words "*mo*dulator-*dem*odulator."

Modulating. The process of adjusting by increments and decrements.

Modulating controllers. Devices that are constantly repositioning themselves in proportion to system requirements.

Modulation. The act of changing the shape of a carrier sine wave by combining it with a signal of changing frequency, phase, or amplitude.

Moisture content. The amount of moisture or water vapor in a given amount of air, expressed in grains.

M

MOS. Abbreviation for "metal-oxide semiconductors," a form of transistor technology in which low costs and high densities are achieved.

Motor. A device that converts electrical energy into mechanical (usually rotational) motion.

Motorized valve. An automatic control valve consisting of a motor, an actuator, and a linkage.

MTBF. Mean time between failures, the average length of time between equipment or device failures.

MTTR. Mean time to repair, the average time required to diagnose and repair faulty equipment.

Mush coil. A coil made with round wire.

Mutual inductance. A circuit property that exists when the relative position of two current-carrying conductors causes the magnetic lines of force from one to link with those of the other.

Nano. Prefix meaning *one one-billionth* (0.000000001).

Nanosecond. One one-billionth of a second.

Negative charge. The electrical charge of a body that has an excess of electrons.

Negative ion. An atomic particle that has a negative charge because it contains more electrons than protons.

Negative temperature coefficient. Pertains to the relationship of resistance to temperature in a thermistor—specifically, as the temperature increases, the resistance decreases.

Negative terminal. The terminal of a battery or power supply that has an excess of electrons, and thus is said to be negatively charged.

Neutral bus. The bus bar in an electrical panel to which all the bare wires are connected. The neutral bus is at ground potential.

Neutral wire. The conductor (commonly identified by its white insulation) that is grounded at the distribution panel.

M
N

Neutron. A particle in the nucleus of an atom that has no electrical charge.

Nibble. A group of four bits, or one half of a byte.

Night setback. The adjustment of a temperature control during unoccupied hours to reduce operating costs.

NMOS. N-channel MOS, a MOS circuit in which electrons are the charge carriers. This system is faster than PMOS.

Noise. Electrical or electronic interference with a signal. Any undesired sound or frequency encountered in a signal system.

Nonvolatile RAM (NVRAM). A random access memory that does not lose its information when its power supply is turned off.

Nonvolatile storage. A storage system that retains its information even when there is a loss of power. Contrast with *volatile* storage.

Normally closed (NC). Describes a switch, relay, valve, or damper that automatically assumes a closed position when power is *not* being applied.

Normally open (NO). Describes a switch, relay, valve, or damper that automatically assumes an open position when power is *not* being applied.

Nucleus. The core of an atom.

Null. The zero level of potential in an electric circuit.

ODP. Abbreviation for *open drip-proof*, a type of motor that has an open frame, but drops of liquid falling at a 15° angle will not affect its operation.

Off-line. The status of a piece of equipment that is effectively turned off, either by a CPU or by human means.

Offset. A term used to describe the difference between the setpoint and the control point. Also called *droop* or *deviation*.

Ohm. The unit of electrical resistance. One ohm is equal to the resistance of a circuit in which a potential difference of one volt produces a current of one ampere. Its symbol is Ω.

Ohmmeter. An instrument that measures electrical resistance.

Ohm's Law. A law that describes the relationship among current, voltage, and resistance in an electric circuit. More specifically: The current in an electric circuit is directly proportional to the electromotive force (voltage) applied to the circuit, and inversely proportional to the resistance of the circuit. The most common form of Ohm's Law is $E = I \times R$.

On-line. The status of a piece of equipment that is effectively turned on, either by a CPU or by human means.

ON/OFF control. Any two-position controller that allows operation only in one of the two extreme positions.

Open circuit. Any electric circuit that does not provide a complete path for the flow of electrons.

Open circuit voltage (OCV). The voltage read at the output of a transformer or power supply without a load.

Open loop. A system in which there is no self-correcting action for errors, as there is in a closed-loop system.

Operating system. A set of programs that manages the overall operation of a computer.

O

Optical isolation. A method of protecting sensitive electronic circuits by using light emitters and receptors for the purpose of connecting with input and/or output devices.

Orifice. An opening in a tube designed to regulate the flow of a fluid.

"Out" contacts. This term applies to a relay when the coil is de-energized and the contacts are "out"—i.e., when the contacts are open.

Output. In computer terminology, processed information that is delivered by a computer. In electronics, the signal or power delivered by a system.

Output module. Any device used to interface a microprocessor-based controller with the user's devices. The module contains circuitry that will convert the digital output signals to voltages, currents, or ON/OFF levels compatible with the user's devices.

Overcurrent device. A fuse or circuit breaker type of device that opens a circuit when its current capabilities are exceeded.

Overload. A condition that occurs when the allowable current level of a device is exceeded.

Overshoot. The amount of deviation from the setpoint that occurs before a controlled variable stabilizes, after a change of input. When a control system has a tendency to fluctuate above and below setpoints, the system requires longer response times to adjust for changes.

Parallel circuit. A circuit in which two or more electrical devices are connected across two common points, so that separate current-conducting paths are provided for each device.

Parameters. The specific characteristics of a system or device that describe its operational limits or the acceptable range of values for best performance.

Parity check. An error detection system used in computers.

Part wind start (PWS). A type of motor that has two separate starting devices, such as contactors or starters. When starting is required, one contactor energizes the first winding. Then, after a specific period of time (usually one to two seconds), a second contactor energizes the second winding.

PASCAL. A high-level computer language, named for Blaise Pascal (1623-1662), a French mathematician.

PCB. a) Polychlorinated biphenyl, an industrial chemical compound once used extensively as a dielectric in run capacitors and transformers. It was found to cause cancer and is no longer used. b) Printed circuit board, a board made of plastic or similar material on which flat copper foils are used in place of wires.

Peak power. The maximum value of power output or demand.

Peak-to-peak. The maximum voltage or current values represented by a sine wave, equal to 1.414 times the RMS level.

Peripheral. Any device that is connected to a CPU, such as a monitor or printer.

Permalloy. An alloy of nickel and iron that has very high magnetic field retention properties.

Permanent magnet. A piece of material that is magnetized to such an extent that it retains its magnetism indefinitely.

Permanent split-capacitor (PSC). A type of electric motor that, by the use of one capacitor in the circuit at all times, achieves good running efficiency and moderate starting torque.

Permeability. The measure of the ability of a material to act as a path for magnetic lines of force, compared to that of air. (Air has a permeability of 1.)

Phase. The relationship, expressed as an angle, between two alternating currents or voltages when the current or voltage is plotted as a function of time.

Phase angle. The number of electrical degrees by which one current or voltage waveform in an ac circuit either leads or lags another. Also called *phase difference.*

Photodiode. A semiconductor device that will either allow or restrict the flow of current in response to the application of light.

Photon. A theoretical "packet" of light energy used to describe the particle-like characteristics of light.

Pickup current. The amount of current needed to cause a relay to energize.

Pickup voltage. The amount of voltage needed to cause a relay's coil to energize and pull in its armature or solenoid.

Picofarad (pF). One micro-microfarad (a millionth of a millionth of a farad).

Piezoelectric. The characteristic of some minerals, primarily quartz crystals, to exhibit generated current when pressure is applied to them. Conversely, they will vibrate when a voltage is applied to them.

Pilot duty. Refers to a relay in which a low voltage (e.g., 24 V) at a low current (usually around 1 or 2 A) controls a larger voltage and current.

PMOS. P-channel MOS, a MOS circuit in which holes are the charge carriers. This is the oldest type of MOS circuitry.

Pneumatic-electric (PE) switch. A switch that opens or closes in response to changes in air pressure.

Polarity. The property or characteristic of having two opposite magnetic poles, one north and the other south. The term also applies to the directions (north or south) of an electric field.

P

Pole. Either of the ends of a magnet where the flux lines are concentrated. Also, either of the connections to a battery, or the number of points at which current can enter a switch (single-pole, double-pole, etc.).

Poll. A signal sent from a central processing unit to tell a remote device to transmit data.

Polling. A routine that invites another device or remote station to transmit data. Contrast with *selecting*.

Polyphase. A circuit that uses more than one phase of alternating current. Also called *multiphase*.

Port. The opening in the seat of a valve. Also, the I/O connection on a computer.

Positive charge. The electrical charge of a body that has a deficiency of electrons.

Positive ion. An atomic particle that has a positive charge because it has lost one or more electrons and thus contains an excess of protons.

Positive temperature coefficient. Pertains to the relationship of resistance to temperature in a thermistor—specifically, as the temperature increases, the resistance increases.

Potential. The difference in electrical energy between one body and another body, measured in volts. The difference in voltage between two points of a circuit.

Potential relay. A relay that operates on the counter-electromotive force (CEMF) of a motor to take the start capacitor out of the circuit.

Potentiometer. A type of variable resistor, used for positioning proportional controls in accordance with deliberate changes in its resistance. See also *rheostat*.

Pounds per square inch (psi). A unit of measurement for pressure. Frequently used to express atmospheric pressure, or the pressure exerted by a liquid or a confined gas on a given area.

Pounds per square inch, absolute (psia). The sum of gauge pressure plus 14.7 psi (atmospheric pressure at sea level at 32°F).

Pounds per square inch, gauge (psig). The pressure read on a gauge that has been adjusted to read zero for atmospheric pressure at sea level.

Power. The rate of doing work or expending energy.

Power factor. In an alternating current circuit, the ratio of the *true* or actual power (in watts) as measured by a wattmeter to the *apparent* power (in volt-amperes) as determined from voltmeter and ammeter readings.

Power fail/restart. A system that allows a computer to restart after a power failure.

Pressure. The normal (perpendicular) force exerted by a gas or liquid on the walls of its container.

Pressure, absolute. The sum of gauge pressure and atmospheric pressure.

Pressure, atmospheric. The pressure exerted by the atmosphere, as indicated by a barometer. Standard pressure at sea level is 14.696 psi or 29.921 inches of mercury at 32°F.

Pressure, back. The pressure in the low side of a refrigeration system. Also called *suction* pressure or *low-side* pressure.

Pressure control. Any device, either electrical or pneumatic, that uses pressure to open or close a circuit.

Pressure drop. The difference between the inlet pressure and the outlet pressure of a fluid passing a restriction in its path.

Pressure, gauge. Pressure above atmospheric pressure.

Primary control. A device that directly or indirectly controls the control agent in response to the needs of the controller. Usually a motor, valve, or relay.

Primary element. The "sensor" part of a controller—e.g., the bimetal element in a thermostat—that senses a change in the controlled variable and initiates the necessary corrective action.

Printer. Any device that prints characters on a hard-copy medium, such as paper.

Progressive sequence. In load shedding, it is first OFF, first ON.

PROM. Programmable read only memory, a type of memory that can be programmed by the user. However, it can only be programmed once.

Proportional action. A type of control in which the output of a device is moved or controlled in direct proportion to the input.

Proportional band. The fraction of the controller span required to cause an actuator to be driven through its complete stroke.

Proportional control. A control system that corrects the output by adding feedback to the input. It is always proportional to any variations in the input of the controller.

Proton. A positively charged particle in the nucleus of an atom.

Psychrometer. A device for measuring the humidity or hygrometric state of the atmosphere.

Pull-out torque. The maximum torque that a motor can deliver without stalling. Also called *breakdown* torque.

Pump down. A system in which the compressor pumps most of the refrigerant into the receiver and shuts off on a low-pressure control. This decreases the pressure on the low side of the system and increases it on the high side.

Push-button switch. A switch that is operated manually by pressing on it.

Pyrometer. An instrument for measuring extremely high temperatures.

Raceway. An enclosure, channel, or conduit for holding conductors, cables, or optical fiber bundles.

Radix. The base of a number system. For example, in the decimal system the radix is 10, because there are 10 symbols used (0, 1, 2, 3, 4, 5, 6, 7, 8, 9).

Ramp. A current or voltage that varies at a uniform or constant rate.

Random access memory (RAM). A temporary memory for storing data in a computer.

Range. The span of values from one point of reference to another—e.g., a thermostat's range may be from 50 to 90°F. The difference between the minimum and maximum points of operation of a properly functioning control.

Rangeability. The ratio of maximum to minimum flow of a fluid.

Rated load amperes (RLA). The maximum current that a motor can draw under any operating condition. Rated load current is a function of the motor and the motor protector.

Ratio. The comparison of one set of values to another set of values. Mathematically, the relation between two quantities expressed as the quotient of one divided by the other.

Reactance. The opposition offered to the flow of an alternating current in an electric circuit, measured in ohms.

Read only memory (ROM). A type of permanent memory used in computers that allows commands to be stored and accessed at any time. It is a memory that can only be read *from*—nothing can be written *to* it.

Real time. Refers to the actual time in which an event occurs.

Rectifier. A device for converting alternating current to direct current. See also *diode*.

R

Register. A short-term storage circuit in a computer where a certain amount of data can be stored.

Reheat. The process of adding heat to already cooled air to maintain humidity levels.

Relative humidity. The ratio, expressed as a percentage, of the water vapor actually contained in the air to the vapor contained in saturated air at the same temperature.

Relay. An electrical switch that uses a small amount of current or voltage to control a larger amount of current or voltage.

Relay contact bounce (chatter). The unwanted rapid opening and closing of a set of relay contacts, usually caused by a low-voltage condition on the relay's coil.

Reluctance. A measure of the opposition that a material offers to magnetic lines of force.

Remote-bulb thermostat. A thermostat that has its sensing element located separately from the mechanism it controls.

Reset. To change the setpoint of a controller automatically by the use of a second sensor. Not to be confused with *automatic reset*. Also, to close an opened circuit breaker.

Reset controller. Two controllers operating together, one sensing a condition other than the controlled space, and changing the setpoint of the second controller.

Reset ratio. The change in the outdoor temperature to the change in the indoor temperature control point. For example, if the reset ratio is 2:1, then for every two-degree outdoor change, the indoor temperature would change one degree.

Resident. A program located in a computer's memory (usually in the main memory).

Resistance. The opposition to the flow of an electric current caused by certain physical characteristics of a conductor, measured in ohms.

Resistance temperature detector (RTD). A resistor, usually made of platinum wire, that is affected by changes in temperature. Used for measuring temperature with a special resistance thermometer.

Resistive load. A load that contains only resistance. (It does not contain any capacitive or inductive reactance.)

Resistive rating. The resistance rating of a control that does not use an inductive load.

Resistor. A component that acts to oppose the flow of current in an electric circuit.

Response time. The time required for a computer to respond to an input from one of its peripherals.

Reverberation. The persistence of reflected sound in an enclosed space after the source of the sound has stopped vibrating.

Reverse-acting. An instrument in which the output signal changes in the opposite direction of that in which the controlled variable changes—i.e., the response decreases as the change in the variable increases.

Reversing relay. A relay that will operate in a manner opposite that of its normal operation.

R

Rheostat. A type of variable resistor used for adjusting the current in a circuit.

RMS value. The *root-mean-square* value of an alternating current sine wave, calculated as the square root of the average of the squares of all the instantaneous current values throughout one complete cycle.

Routine. A set of special coded instructions that tells a computer what to do and when to do it.

RS-232, RS-422, RS-484. A series of configurations developed by the EIA, each of which establishes an interface of connections between a CPU and its peripherals.

Run time. The amount of time required for a computer to run a program. Also, the amount of time required for a refrigeration of air conditioning system to maintain the load for given conditions.

Scaling. The conversion of a standard signal into an appropriate unit of measurement—e.g., 4 to 20 mA into –40 to 260°F.

Schematic. A wiring diagram that shows by the use of symbols and lines the functional components and connections of an electric circuit.

Scrolling. The next new line of information following the last line on a CRT screen. As the last line fills up the screen, the first line is replaced.

Sealed VA. The volt-amperes after a controlled device, such as a relay or a contactor, has been operated.

Seat. The stationary portion of a valve.

Secondary winding. The coil of wire on a transformer that receives its voltage and current by mutual inductance.

Selecting. The process of inviting another device to receive data. Contrast with *polling*.

Self-induction. The production of a counter-electromotive force in a conductor when its own magnetic field collapses or expands with a change in current in the conductor.

Semiconductor. A material that is neither a conductor nor an insulator. Silicon and germanium are the two most common semiconductor materials.

R
S

Sensible heat. The heat that can be measured with a thermometer. Heat energy that changes the temperature of a substance without changing its state.

Sensing device. A device that monitors a measurable condition and responds to changes in the controlled variable by signalling a controller to initiate an action. A bulb on a thermostat is a sensing device.

Sensitivity. The capability of a controller to measure and act upon variations in a controlled condition.

Sensor. A device used to detect and measure changes in a variable, and transmit the information as an analog signal to a central processor.

Series circuit. A circuit in which the components are connected one after another, and the current is the same throughout the circuit.

Service factor. The reserve margin built into a motor—e.g., a service factor of 1.25 means that the motor can deliver 25% more that its rated horsepower without dangerously overheating.

Setpoint. The point at which the desired value of the controlled variable is set.

Shaded-pole. A type of small induction motor that has no start winding, no brushes, and no commutator. It uses a copper shading coil to provide the necessary phase shift for starting.

Short circuit. An unintentional current path between two components in a circuit, or between a component and ground.

Signal. Any electrical information that can be transmitted either through wires or by means of electromagnetic waves.

Significant digit (SD). A digit that contributes to the accuracy of a number. SDs are counted beginning with the first digit on the left that is *not* a zero and ending with the last digit on the right that is known or assumed to be precise. For example, the number "2,300.0" has five SDs, but "2,300" (without the decimal point) probably has only two (it is not known whether the last two digits are precise). The number "2,301" has four SDs, "0.0023" has two, and "23.045" may have either four or five, depending on whether or not the "4" is uncertain—if the "4" is uncertain, then so is the "5."

Silicon. A semiconductor material that is often used to make transistors and integrated circuits. It can withstand higher temperatures than germanium.

Silicon-controlled rectifier (SCR). A semiconductor device that functions as an electrically controlled switch by conducting current when the gate is triggered.

Single phasing. The condition that occurs when one phase of a three-phase system opens.

Single-pole, single-throw switch. A two-terminal switch or relay contact that either "breaks" or "makes" (opens or closes) one circuit.

Skip day. A designated day on which a particular program schedule will not function.

Slip. The difference between the synchronous speed and the actual speed of the rotor in a motor.

Small-scale integration (SSI). Integration of less complexity than medium-scale integration.

Snap-action controllers. Controllers that "snap" open or closed when operated (usually due to the interaction between a magnet and a bimetal strip).

Soft copy. Output presented on a CRT screen.

Soft start. See *part wind start*.

Software. Any written program or routine to be used with digital equipment. See also *hardware*.

Solenoid. A magnetic coil that contains a movable plunger.

Solid-state devices. Electronic devices that use semiconductor materials and have no moving parts. They require less power than vacuum tubes.

Sone. One sone is defined as the loudness of a 1,000-Hz signal with the pressure of 40 decibels.

Space thermostat. A thermostat whose sensor is in the controlled space.

Span (actuator). The change in the controller's output needed to drive the actuator through its complete stroke.

Span (controller). The difference between the highest and lowest value of the setpoint adjustment.

Specific gravity. The ratio of the density of a substance to the density of water at a given temperature. See *hydrometer*.

Specific humidity. The weight of water vapor in the air, expressed in pounds of water vapor per pound of dry air. Also called "humidity ratio."

Spike. See *transient*.

Split-phase. A type of motor that has two separate windings, and is controlled by a switch or relay.

Start point. In pneumatic actuators, the pressure necessary to overcome the opposing force of the spring.

Start relay. A relay that controls the start winding of a motor through the use of applied voltage or current.

Starter. A heavy current relay or contactor that has some form of overload protection built into it.

Starting torque. The amount of torque produced when power is applied to a motor at rest.

Static electricity. Electricity in the form of a stationary (unmoving) charge. Usually produced by friction between two surfaces in close contact with each other.

Static pressure rating. The maximum pressure (from inside the body to outside the body) that a valve will tolerate.

Stator. The stationary (non-rotating) part of an induction motor, on which the coils are wound.

Stem. The shaft that moves the plug from or onto the valve seat.

Stepper motor. A type of dc motor that provides precise control by operating in a series of discrete steps of uniform magnitude.

Storage. A general term given to any device that can retain or hold electronic information for an extended period of time.

Storage capacity. The maximum amount of data that can be retained in a computer's hard drive or other storage device.

Strap. A wire or switch used for making electrical connections.

Stroke. The distance the valve stem moves.

Sub-master controller. A controller that is set by the conditions of the master controller.

Subroutine. A portion of a computer program that is stored only once in the memory, but can be used repeatedly when called by the running "master" routine.

Summer-winter switch. Usually a fan switch on a furnace used to provide air conditioning in the summer.

Switch. Any device used to open (interrupt the current) or close (complete a path for the conduction of current) an electric circuit.

Synchronous. Occurring concurrently and with regular time periods (frequency). The opposite of *asynchronous*.

Synchronous communication. Data transmitted at a fixed rate or frequency. The receiver and transmitter use the same clock signals for synchronization.

Tachometer. An instrument for measuring the speed of a rotating device, such as a motor.

Temperature, ambient. Generally speaking, the temperature of the air surrounding an object.

Terminal, computer. A peripheral device that communicates with a computer—e.g., a keyboard, video display, printer, etc.

Terminal, electrical. A point or junction at which conductors can be connected.

Thermal relay. A relay that is opened or closed in response to changes in temperature.

Thermistor. A semiconductor device that changes resistance in response to a change in temperature.

Thermocouple. A device made of two dissimilar metals that produces a voltage when heat is applied to it.

Thermopile. A series of individual thermocouples connected in series, used to generate a sufficiently high voltage to operate a gas valve without the aid of outside power. (Also called "self-generating.")

Thermostat. A device that opens or closes a circuit in response to changes in temperature, thereby causing a signal to be sent to some form of actuator.

Three-phase. A term applied to alternating current in which each phase differs from the next by one-third of a cycle, or 120 degrees.

Three-way valve. A valve that has three connections, with one common to the other two.

Throttling range. The amount of change in a variable that will cause the controlled device to go through its full range.

Time-delay relay. A relay in which there is an interval of time between the energizing or de-energizing of the coil and the opening or closing of the contacts.

Torque. The twisting or turning force that a rotating shaft produces when it is transmitting power.

T

Total heat. The sum of the sensible and latent heats. Any change in the wet-bulb temperature is indicative of changes in total heat.

Totally enclosed. A term used to describe a type of motor designed to be used in dirty or damp places. The term is *not* used to mean "waterproof" or "explosion-proof."

Transducer. Any device that converts one form of energy to another form of energy.

Transformer. A device consisting of two coils of wire, a primary and a secondary, electrically insulated from each other and wound on the same ferromagnetic core. Energy is transferred from the primary to the secondary by means of electromagnetic induction.

Transient. An unwanted, instantaneous surge of electrical energy that occurs because of a sudden change of current or voltage. Also called a *spike*.

Transistor. A semiconductor device that can transfer a signal from one low resistance to a higher resistance, thereby producing amplification.

Transmission. The act of conveying energy from one point to another.

Transmission line. Any conductor that carries energy from the source to its load.

Transmitter. A device that converts a signal (in proportion to changes in the variable being measured) to some form of energy that can be sent over wires, through fibers, through tubing, or through the air.

Triac. A solid-state switching device used to control current during both alternations of an ac cycle. Similar in construction to two SCRs back-to-back, with a common gate and common terminals.

Troubleshoot. To locate and diagnose faults in equipment by means of systematic checking or analysis.

True power. The power actually consumed by an electric circuit, as measured directly with a wattmeter.

Twisted pair. A cable composed of two small insulated conductors twisted together in a common covering.

Two-position control. Any controller that has only "ON" and "OFF" positions. Compare to *proportional control*.

Two-stage controller. A controller that operates in two separate stages, one following the other in sequence—e.g., a two-stage thermostat, in which the switches are separated by a certain temperature range, so that the first stage may be made at 68°F and the second stage at 70°F.

Two-way valve. A valve that has only two connections (one inlet and one outlet) and operates only in the fully open or fully closed position.

Ultraviolet. The invisible, high-frequency portion of the light spectrum. Used with certain chemicals for detecting leaks in refrigeration systems. Also called "black light."

Universal motor. A motor that can be operated either on alternating current or direct current. It normally runs at 5,000 rpm and has brushes.

Unload (compressor). To disengage certain cylinders in a compressor by bypassing some of the discharge gas back into the suction section. (This, in turn, lowers the capacity of the compressor.)

Upstream. Closer to the power source—e.g., the fuses are upstream from the disconnect box.

U-tube manometer. A low-pressure measuring device that contains a liquid in a "U"-shaped tube. The level of the liquid on one side of the tube becomes lower as the pressure applied to it increases, while the level of the liquid on the other side of the tube becomes higher. The difference in the two levels is in proportion to the applied pressure. Differences in the liquid levels can be calibrated to give direct pressure readings.

Vacuum. The absence of matter, including air, in either an open or confined space.

Valve. A device used for controlling or regulating the pressure or flow of a liquid or gas.

Valve, solenoid. Usually an electrically actuated valve (consisting of a coil with a plunger), used to control the flow of a fluid.

Variable. A condition or a factor that can be monitored, measured, and/or altered by a control—e.g., temperature, current, voltage, humidity, liquid level, pressure, etc.

Variac. A term used to describe a variable transformer (actually a trade name of the General Electric Company). See *autotransformer*.

Varistor. A semiconductor device with voltage-sensitive resistance, commonly used as a lightning arrester. Overvoltages can be passed quickly, but operating voltages have no effect.

VARs. Abbreviation for *volt-amperes reactive*, the power consumed by an inductive or capacitive circuit. It is derived by multiplying the voltage times the reactance times the power factor.

Vector. A line used to represent both direction and magnitude. Used in calculating capacitive reactance, inductive reactance, and impedance in alternating current circuits.

Very large-scale integration (VLSI). A microcircuit generally considered to have more than a thousand elements.

Voice-grade line. A telephone communication channel that has a bandwidth wide enough for voice broadcast.

335

Volatile memory. A memory that will lose its information or data when power is removed.

Volatile storage. A storage system that will lose all of its data when power is lost. Contrast with *nonvolatile* storage.

Volt. The unit of electromotive force.

Voltage. The amount of potential difference across two points in a circuit. See *electromotive force*.

Voltage drop. The difference in voltage between two points. The result of the loss of electrical energy as a current flows through a resistance.

Volt-ampere (VA). The unit of apparent power in an ac circuit in which the voltage and current are out of phase. One volt-ampere is one volt times one ampere.

Voltmeter. An instrument used to measure voltage.

Watt. The unit of electric power. One horsepower equals 746 watts.

Wattmeter. An instrument used to measure the actual or true power in an alternating current circuit.

Wave. A progressive, energy-bearing disturbance propagated from point to point in a medium. A physical activity (like ripples in a pond) that rises or falls periodically as it travels through a medium—e.g., sound, light, heat, radio and TV signals, etc.

Wavelength. The distance between the corresponding valleys or peaks of adjacent electrical or electromagnetic waves.

Wet-bulb temperature. The air temperature indicated by a thermometer with a wetted wick on the bulb.

Wire. A conductor, either bare or insulated, through which electrons can flow.

Word. In computer terminology, a unit of information composed of a certain number of bits in one location.

Write. To copy from one form of storage to another—for example, to copy information from a hard disk drive to a floppy disk.

V
W

Wye transformer. A transformer that has its windings connected together in the shape of a "Y." In a three-phase alternating current circuit, this produces a balanced load.

Zener diode. A semiconductor device that controls or regulates the voltage in a circuit. Also called an *avalanche diode*.

Zone control. A heating/cooling control method in which a building or large space is divided into two or more smaller areas, each of which is controlled by its own thermostat.

COMMON ABBREVIATIONS AND ACRONYMS

A	ampere
ac	alternating current
ACCA	Air Conditioning Contractors of America
ACR	air conditioning and refrigeration
A-D, A/D, ADC	analog-to-digital converter
AFUE	annual fuel utilization efficiency
Ag	silver
AGA	American Gas Association
AHA	adjustable heat anticipator
AIEE	American Institute of Electrical Engineers
Al	aluminum
AMCA	Air Movement and Control Association
ANSI	American National Standards Institute
ANT	anticipator
ARI	Air Conditioning and Refrigeration Institute
ASA	American Standards Association
ASCII	American Standard Code for Information Interchange
ASHRAE	American Society of Heating, Refrigerating, and Air Conditioning Engineers
ASI	American Standards Institute
ASME	American Society of Mechanical Engineers
ASTM	American Society for Testing and Materials
ATC	automatic temperature control
atm	atmosphere
AUX	auxiliary
AWG	American wire gauge
BCD	binary-coded decimal
Bhp	brake horsepower
BPM	brushless permanent magnet

Btu	British thermal unit
Btuh, Btu/hr	Btu per hour
C	carbon; Celsius; Centigrade; thermal conductance
CAP	capacitor
CC	compressor contactor; closing coil
CCU	central control unit
CCW	counterclockwise
CEMF	counter electromotive force
cfm	cubic feet per minute
CMOS	complementary metal-oxide semiconductor
COM	common
COP	coefficient of performance
COS	change of state
CPU	central processing unit
CR	control relay; cooling relay
CRT	cathode ray tube
CSA	Canadian Standards Association
CSCR	capacitor-start, capacitor-run
CSIR	capacitor-start, induction-run
Cu	copper
CW	clockwise
DA	direct-acting
D-Λ, D/Λ, DAC	digital-to-analog converter
DAT	discharge air thermostat
dB	decibel
dc	direct current
DDC	direct digital control
DGT	discharge gas thermostat
DIA	diameter
DIO	distributed input/output.
DIP	dual in-line package
DMM	digital multimeter
DOE	Department of Energy
DOT	Department of Transportation
DPDT	double-pole, double-throw
DPST	double-pole, single-throw
E	symbol for voltage
EAROM	electrically alterable read only memory
EC	enthalpy control
ECM	electronic commutated motor

ECON	economizer
EDP	electronic data processing
EER	energy efficiency ratio
EIA	Electronic Industries Association
EIP	event-initiated program
EMF	electromotive force
EMI	electromagnetic interference
ENCL	enclosure
EP	electro-pneumatic
EPA	Environmental Protection Agency
EPROM	erasable programmable read only memory
ESD	electrostatic discharge
F	farad; frequency; Fahrenheit
FC	fan contactor
FL	fusible link
FLA	full-load amperes
FM	fan motor
FPC	freeze protection control
ft-lb	foot-pound
ft/min	foot per minute
FU	fuse
g	gram
GEN	generator
GFCI	ground fault circuit interrupter
GND	ground
gpm	gallons per minute
GRI	Gas Research Institute
H	henry
Hg	mercury
HP	horsepower; high pressure
HVACR	heating, ventilation, air conditioning, and refrigeration
Hz	hertz
I	symbol for current
IC	integrated circuit
ICM	integrated controlled motor
ID	inside diameter
IEEE	Institute of Electrical and Electronics Engineers
IFM	inducer fan motor
IMP	impedance

IMR	inducer motor relay
I/O	input/output
IPLV	integrated part load value
IR	infrared radiation
ISA	Instrument Society of America
ISO	International Organization for Standardization
K	Kelvin
kA	kiloampere
kHz	kilohertz
kΩ	kilohm
kV	kilovolt
kVA	kilovolt-ampere
kVAR	kilovolt-ampere reactive
kW	kilowatt
kWh	kilowatt-hour
L	symbol for inductance
LCD	liquid crystal display
LED	light-emitting diode
LPC	low-pressure control
LPPDC	low-pressure pump down control
LRA	locked-rotor amperes
LS	limit switch
LSI	large-scale integration
LWS	low water switch
LWTS	low water temperature switch
m	meter
mA	milliampere
MAX	maximum
MCA	minimum current amperes
MF, MFD, μF	microfarad
mH	millihenry
MHz	megahertz
MIN	minimum
MMI	man-machine interface
MOCP	maximum overcurrent protection
MΩ	megohm
MOS	metal-oxide semiconductor
MOT	motor
ms	millisecond
MSD	most significant digit

MSDS	Material Safety Data Sheet
MSI	medium-scale integration
MTBF	mean time between failures
MTTR	mean time to repair
mV	millivolt
MV	megavolt
mW	milliwatt
MW	megawatt
NAIMA	North American Insulation Manufacturers Association
NAPHCC	National Association of Plumbing Heating Cooling Contractors
NC	normally closed
NEC	National Electrical Code
NEG	negative
NEMA	National Electrical Manufacturers Association.
NEUT	neutral
NFPA	National Fire Protection Association
NIOSH	National Institute of Occupational Safety and Health
NMOS	N-channel metal-oxide semiconductor
NO	normally open
NOM	nominal
NTC	negative temperature coefficient
NVRAM	nonvolatile random access memory
OCV	open circuit voltage
OD	outside diameter
ODP	open drip-proof
ODT	outdoor thermostat
OEM	original equipment manufacturer
OFC	oil failure control; outdoor fan control
OFM	outdoor fan motor
OFS	oil failure switch; overflow switch
OPEI	Outdoor Power Equipment Institute
OSHA	Occupational Safety and Health Administration
P	power
PB	push button
PCB	polychlorinated biphenyl; printed circuit board
PE	pneumatic-electric
PEL	permissible exposure limit
pF	picofarad
PF	power factor

PID	proportional/integral/derivative
PMOS	P-channel metal-oxide semiconductor
POS	positive
POT	potential; potentiometer
ppb	parts per billion
ppm	parts per million
PROM	programmable read only memory
PSC	permanent split-capacitor
psi	pounds per square inch
psia	pounds per square inch, absolute
psig	pounds per square inch, gauge
PTC	positive temperature coefficient
PVC	polyvinyl chloride
PWS	part wind start
R	resistance
RA	reverse-acting
RAM	random access memory
RC	run capacitor
RETA	Refrigeration Engineers and Technicians Association
REV	reversible
RF	radio frequency
RFI	radio frequency interference
RH	relative humidity
RLA	rated load amperes
RMS	root-mean-square
ROM	read only memory
rpm	revolutions per minute
RSES	Refrigeration Service Engineers Society
RTD	resistance temperature detector
RTL	resistor-transistor logic
RTS	refrigerant temperature switch
RV	reversing valve
s	second
SC	start capacitor
SCR	silicon-controlled rectifier
SD	significant digit
SEER	seasonal energy efficiency ratio
SF	service factor
SHC	sensible heat capacity
SMACNA	Sheet Metal and Air Conditioning Contractors National Association

SP	static pressure
SPDT	single-pole, double-throw
SPST	single-pole, single-throw
SSI	small-scale integration
SSU	Saybolt seconds universal
SW	switch
TC	thermostat, cooling
TD	temperature difference
TE	totally enclosed (motor)
TEAO	totally enclosed, air-over
TEFC	totally enclosed, fan-cooled
TENV	totally enclosed, non-ventilated
TH	thermostat, heating
TLV	threshold limit value
TR	transformer
TTL	transistor-transistor logic
TXV	thermostatic expansion valve
UART	universal asynchronous receiver-transmitter
UEL	upper explosive limit
UL	Underwriters Laboratories
USDA	United States Department of Agriculture
UV	ultraviolet
UVEPROM	ultraviolet erasable programmable read only memory
V	volt
VA	volt-ampere
VAV	variable air volume
VFD	variable-frequency drive
VLSI	very large-scale integration
VOM	volt-ohm-milliammeter
VVHC	variable-volume heating/cooling
VVT	variable-volume temperature
W	watt
WR	inertia
WT	water temperature
X	symbol for reactance
Z	symbol for impedance

1666 Rand Road   Des Plaines, IL 60016   800-297-5660   www.rses.org